ISBN 978-1-330-70758-6
PIBN 10095083

This book is a reproduction of an important historical work. Forgotten Books uses
state-of-the-art technology to digitally reconstruct the work, preserving the original format
whilst repairing imperfections present in the aged copy. In rare cases, an imperfection in
the original, such as a blemish or missing page, may be replicated in our edition. We do,
however, repair the vast majority of imperfections successfully; any imperfections that
remain are intentionally left to preserve the state of such historical works.

English
Français
Deutsche
Italiano
Español
Português

www.forgottenbooks.com

Mythology Photography **Fiction**
Fishing Christianity **Art** Cooking
Essays Buddhism Freemasonry
Medicine **Biology** Music **Ancient
Egypt** Evolution Carpentry Physics
Dance Geology **Mathematics** Fitness
Shakespeare **Folklore** Yoga Marketing
Confidence Immortality Biographies
Poetry **Psychology** Witchcraft
Electronics Chemistry History **Law**
Accounting **Philosophy** Anthropology
Alchemy Drama Quantum Mechanics
Atheism Sexual Health **Ancient History**
Entrepreneurship Languages Sport
Paleontology Needlework Islam
Metaphysics Investment Archaeology
Parenting Statistics Criminology
Motivational

JACOB
WRESTLING WITH THE ANGEL.

SERMONS

ON GENESIS CHAPTER XXXII.

JACOB WRESTLING WITH THE ANGEL.

Now, by that touch, Mysterious man! I know
Thy nature's more than human!—Let *thee* go!
Not till thou bless me. If, through all the night,
My daring, struggling limbs increas'd in might;
If thou thy strength attempered e'en to mine,
If thus resisting I o'ermastered thine;
Then wilt thou too, my daring speech approve,
For all thy wrestling was but tender love!
My name is JACOB—thou hast made me bold,
Thine arms that have repell'd me, *must* enfold!
Thou shalt, Oh Wondrous Stranger! e'er we part—
Stamp thine eternal blessing on my heart!

Thy name no more is JACOB! Thou hast seen
By faith's keen vision, what thy trials mean!
Thy name is ISRAEL! Knighted Prince of God!
For thou with him the wrestling ring hast trod!
Nay—cease! Ask not for my peculiar name,
Enough to know 'twill put thy foes to shame:
Take this white stone—'tis deeply graven there,
With thine, a token of prevailing prayer!
Forth to **thy** work—thy darkest dangers brave,
My name goes with thee, and 'tis strong to save!

AMERICAN EDITOR.

JACOB

WRESTLING WITH THE ANGEL.

SERMON I.

GENESIS XXXII. 24.

*And Jacob was left alone : and there wrestled a man with him
until the breaking of the day.*

THE verse we have just read, forms a part of one of
the most wonderful narratives contained in the Holy
Scriptures ; and upon which we intend to meditate on
this and some future occasions.

Strengthened and refreshed by the promise, ' I will
do thee good,' the Patriarch Jacob, at the express
command of his God, had removed from Haran, where
for a long period he had served his uncle Laban, in
order to return to his native land. This displeased
Laban so much, that he went in pursuit of his son-in-
law, and overtook him on Mount Gilead. His anger
was inflamed against him to such a degree, that he
would certainly have done the Patriarch a serious injury : since he boasted that, with the help of God, he
had power enough for that purpose, if God had not
forbidden this Syrian, in a dream, to take heed not to

2

speak otherwise than in a friendly manner to him : although Rachel was, nevertheless, in peril of her life. At length every thing was amicably settled, and they parted in a peaceful and friendly manner.   Laban turned back ; and whilst Jacob was proceeding on his journey, he was met, to his great comfort, by the angels of God.   Thus pleasingly was he extricated from this trying situation.

Scarcely, however, had he been rescued from this danger, then he fell into another of a much more serious nature.   The fury of his brother Esau, and his threat, ' The days of mourning for my father are at hand, then will I slay my brother Jacob,' had compelled the latter to seek his safety in flight.   When he returned into Esau's neighborhood, his first concern was to gain his favor.   He attempted to accomplish this by sending messengers to him ; who, in the humblest terms, were to endeavor to secure his good will.   But they soon returned with the intelligence, that his brother Esau was coming to meet him, with four hundred men.   ' Then Jacob was greatly afraid and distressed ;' and that with reason : for what other intentions could Esau have than such as were hostile ? And what had Jacob to oppose to such a host ? Nothing ; not even flight.   What a distressing and helpless situation !   O God, into what painful circumstances dost thou sometimes suffer thy favorites to fall ; and yet it is only for the attainment of the most blessed ends.

Jacob's anxiety, however, is not so great as to deprive him of all reflection ; although his confidence in God is not lively enough to render him as courageous as a young lion. He makes such prudent arrangements that the possibility of escape it afforded to one part should the other be destroyed by Esau. Nor did he neglect any thing which seemed likely to reconcile Esau and win his heart : to which several considerable presents, which he prepared for that purpose, were intended to contribute.

But the pious Patriarch did not let the matter rest there ; he did not ground his confidence upon these arrangements, but upon God. In the midst of his anxious preparations, he applied to Him by earnest prayer, which emanated from the depth of his distress. He appears openly before his covenant God ; he frankly confesses his fears, and does not conceal his wretchedness ; he thanks Him for all his former undeserved benefits ; he bows himself in deep humility ; he cleaves by faith to the command and gracious promise of the Lord ' Thou, saidst, I will surely do thee good ;' he cleaves to the power and goodness of God, and beseeches Him to deliver him. He passed a sleepless night in making the arrangements he thought necessary ; and conducted his flocks, his family, and his people over the brook Jabbok.

He was then left entirely alone : which he preferred, as being the best suited for his state of mind at the time. He was desirous of pouring out his heart still more fully before the Lord ; of praying still more fervently ; of pressing to the throne of Grace, unhindered by external things, at a time when he required help. The good hand of God which was extended over him, drew him into this retirement, because it had something great and particular in view with him.

It was night : a season calculated in itself to excite a
feeling of awe. The heavens above him, with their
countless stars, reminded him of the promise given to
his holy forefather, and sealed it to him also, that thus
numerous should his descendants be. The gloomy earth
was full of terrors to him, and Esau not far off; perhaps
even very near. His help was solely in the name of
the Lord, who made heaven and earth. What a blessed night he had already once enjoyed, when sleeping in
a desert with a stone beneath his head, and when heav-
en opened itself above him! But this was a night of
anxious fear. It was not only night around the holy Patriarch, but it had also become dark in his soul. He was
greatly afraid. This fear seemed to be justified by the
circumstances in which he was placed : yet still it had
its root in his want of faith ; and if Christ blamed his
disciples on account of the unbelieving fear which
they manifested in the most imminent danger of death,
Jacob was also deserving of a similar reproof on account
of similar misconduct ; although that must be an uncommon confidence, which can preserve us from fear under
such appalling circumstances.

Jacob was manifestly, according to the expression
of the Apostle, ' not perfect in love ;' for the latter
expels fear. Fear, however, proceeds more especially
from an evil and defiled conscience. No sooner had
Adam incurred the latter by his disobedience, than he
was afraid, and fled from the face of God. A guilty
conscience is like a dangerous and poisonous impost-
hume in the individual, which finally prepares him for
the flames of hell, unless healed by the blood of

Christ, the only remedy. This alone, appropriated by the power of the Holy Spirit, brings peace. Who does not know that Jacob was an object of God's love, and therefore also a partaker of this peace. But as the renovation of the children of God here upon earth is progressive, so this part of it is particularly so, and is more obvious when trying occasions and circumstances occur, than at other times. Besides which, God, as Moses says in Psalm xc., places, in the times of visitation, our trangressions before him, and our secret sins in the light of his countenance. He begins, at some after-period, to reckon with his servants, and to set before their eyes what they have done ; and then is fulfilled what is written in Psalm xcix. 8, ' Thou answeredst them, thou forgavest them, though thou tookest vengeance of their inventions.' They are perhaps not sufficiently aware of the greatness of the guilt ; its abominable and culpable nature, and the aggravating circumstances which attend it. They have not been rendered sufficiently contrite, humble, and heart-broken on account of it ; they have not sufficiently accused themselves before God because of it ; they have been desirous of excusing, if not of justifying themselves in some measure ; their hatred to sin is perhaps not sufficiently powerful ; their desire for deliverance, and their gratitude on account of it, not sufficiently ardent. They must be made to ascend higher, and to descend deeper. Their self-knowledge is to receive an addition, and their view of the real nature, extent, necessity, and preciousness of Divine grace, to become brighter. Their conscience is to be rendered more tender,

2*

their walk more circumspect, their looking unto the
Lord more fixed, their abiding in Him and his abiding
in them more intimate ; and themselves, generally
speaking, more fit for every good work, by faith in
Christ Jesus. The potter takes the clay into his form-
ing hand, and purifies and ennobles it from one
degree to another. The path of the child of God is
from faith to faith, from strength to strength. The
fruitfulness which was at first but thirty-fold, becomes
sixty-fold, and the latter an hundred-fold. In the blade
the ear is formed ; the latter shoots pleasingly forth
from its envelopement, and fills itself with corn, which
ripens in the sunshine and the storm. The child becomes a youth, the youth a man and a father in Christ ;
in whom, as the Head, they all grow together in all
things. Such is the conduct of the Father with his
elect, whom he has chosen in Christ, before the foundation of the world, that they might be holy and without blame before him in love ; and such was the path
by which he led Jacob whom he loved.

Something had occured in the life of this Patriarch,
which was out of order, and this was the blessing of his
father. Isaac intended to have bestowed it upon Esau ;
but with the assistance of his mother, who gave the
preference to Jacob, even as Isaac strangely did to Esau,
he deprived Esau of the blessing intended for him, and
procured its bestowment upon himself. We know the
artful manner in which this was accomplished, and
how the old blind patriarch was deceived, who took
Jacob for Esau, and blessed him instead of the latter.
It is true that the blessing descended upon him for

whom God had intended it. For before the children were born, and had done neither good nor evil, it was said to Rebecca, the elder shall serve the younger, in order ' that the purpose of God according to election might stand, not of works but of Him that calleth, as it is written, Jacob have I loved, but Esau have I hated.' It is true also, that Isaac, on afterwards learning the real state of the case, instead of retracting his blessing, confirmed it, and did not suffer a single word of disapprobation to fall, respecting the manner in which he had been deceived and imposed upon. But deception continues to be deception, and consequently sinful and not to be excused but reproved, in whatever cause it may be employed. Some, indeed, with the venerable Luther at their head, have not only excused the mode of acting of Rebecca and her son, but have even justified and defended it as the consequence of a noble faith. Jacob, however, did not regard it in this light, but was apprehensive, lest by such conduct he should have inherited a curse instead of a blessing from his father ; and when his mother endeavored to pacify him by saying, ' Upon me be thy curse, my son !' it is evident she means nothing by it, and is a proof that she was unable to make a proper reply. To defend such a transaction, is in reality only to maintain the abominable position, that the end sanctifies the means. But this is certain, that God never fails of attaining his aim, and that even the improper conduct of individuals must promote the accomplishment of his purposes. Yet these improprieties are not thereby justified ; otherwise the curse on account of the crucifixion of Christ, would have unjustly adhered to the Jews to the present day. 'Shall we do evil, that good may come ?   God forbid !'   The condemnation of those who act from such a motive is just.

Those words in Psalm I. are often verified, 'These things hast thou done and I kept silence : but I will reprove thee, and set them in order before thine eyes.' Jacob's conduct in that affair now seemed ready to avenge itself upon him, and he might be apprehensive of the curse, respecting which he had previously so easily satisfied himself with the unmeaning words of his mother.   How easily might such thoughts as the following occur to him : " Thy father did not in reality bless thee, but Esau, his first born, for whom thou didst give thyself out.   The blessing has no reference to thee.   Thou art a deceiver, and that of the basest kind.   Although thou hast imposed upon thy venerable father, and abused his lamentable blindness, which ought to have induced thee to act with the greatest sincerity; yet the eye of God has only been the more acutely fixed upon thee ; thou hast been unable to deceive Him.   Thou art a deceiver ; thou art worthy of death !   And lo ! Esau, who was blessed in thy person, is now coming against thee with four hundred men, to execute, as a servant of Divine justice, the sentence of death upon thee !   Thou oughtest to have acknowledged, confessed, and made reparation for thy fault.   The long-restrained wrath of God is awaking over thee.   It is now too late.   How couldst thou dare, how could such a man as thou venture to suppose that God had said to thee, ' I will do thee good.'

Wilt thou make God the minister of sin, by supposing that he will be gracious to such a wretch as thou art ? The Devil must have been justly permitted to suggest such pleasing thoughts to thee, in order the more infallibly to destroy thee. Instead of making the commencement with repentance, thou hast imagined thyself, to thy own injury, in a state of grace. It will now be proved. Esau—what a noble character he is compared with thee ! He has threatened thee with death ; and what else dost thou deserve at his hands ? Hast thou not most basely endeavored to rob and murder him, by cunningly stealing the blessing intended for, and in reality pronounced upon him ? ' Be Lord over thy brother !' it was said in the blessing which thou didst so unjustly seek to appropriate to thyself. Dost thou not now evidently see who has experienced the fulfilment of it ? Thou, a poor servant ; he, a lord with four hundred men ; and thou entirely in his hand, O thou poor deceived Jacob ! Where is there a poorer man than thou ?" And he lifted up his voice and wept bitterly.

And are you, my friends, entirely unacquainted with trials of this kind ? I can scarcely suppose it, unless you are novices in the Christian course. You have put on the armor. Until you are at liberty to put it off, many things may occur, of which it is unnecessary now to speak in detail. Let this suffice ; if you are children, call upon the Father, who without respect of persons, judgeth according to every man's work. Therefore pass

children, you will not be without chastisement ; and the

dearer the child the sharper the discipline. David once said when it went well with him, ' I shall never be moved ;' for the Lord, in his mercy, had made his mountain to stand strong. But no sooner did he hide his face than he was troubled. Therefore be not high-minded, but humble. Be not self-confident, but take heed lest thou fall, whilst thinking thou art standing. Boast not thyself of to-morrow, for thou knowest not what a day may bring forth. Build thy house upon the rock, and take heed lest thou regard that as a rock, which is not so in reality. And though it be the rock, yet remember how easily thou mayest build wood and stubble upon it, which the fire will destroy. If it be genuine gold, it must still pass through the fire. For the fire shall try every man's work of what sort it is. ' Thy filthiness is so abominable,' it is said in Ezekiel xxiv. 13, ' that although I have purged thee, yet thou wast not cleansed, therefore thou shalt not be purged from thy filthiness any more, till I have caused my fury to rest upon thee.'

The holy Patriarch wrestled in faith with the temptations above-mentioned, and prayed, or at least wished to do so, and to hold converse with the Lord. The following was probably his train of thought and anxious inquiry : " Art thou then really my God and Father, or art thou so no longer ? Have I deceived myself in firmly believing, that notwithstanding all my unworthiness, thou lovest me, that I might be so much the more to the praise of the glory of thy grace, after seeing and tasting it, and when I loved and praised thee on account of it ? Certainly it can never be. But the feeling of it is now so much obscured, and so doubtful, that I can no longer rejoice in it ; especially now, in this my time of trouble, when I so particularly need it. O look upon me therefore in mercy, and cause thy face to shine ! Cast a friendly ray into my darkness."

In this manner probably he prayed. ' And there wrestled a man with him.' Wonderful occurrence. What terror must it have inspired ! Jacob justly thought himself quite alone. All at once he suddenly feels himself laid hold of by some one. Who it is he knows not ; he is only conscious that it is not a wild beast seeking to devour him, but a man. This man does not appear to be his friend, but his foe—perhaps one of Esau's four hundred men. Whoever it is, he struggles with him. He lays hold of the terrified patriarch in such a manner as if he would either push him away from his place, or throw him upon the ground. Jacob defends himself; he grasps his antagonist, whom he does not yet know, and refuses either to move from the spot, or to let himself be thrown down. He exerts all his strength, and the conflict lasts ' until the breaking of the day.'

Who was this man ? Jacob did not know at first: but by degrees it became apparent to him who he was.ʳ If we form an opinion of him from the circumstance of his seeing that ' he prevailed not against Jacob,' we shall think very differently of him on reading what immediately follows :—' he touched the hollow of his thigh, and the hollow of Jacob's thigh was out of joint,' for to this, a more than human power is requisite. When he says, ' Let me go,' he appears inferior to Jacob, and dependent upon him. But when Jacob entreats his blessing—he exalts him far above him, and even above his father Isaac, who had already blessed him in the name of God. When the man gives him the name of Israel, and explains to him the meaning of that appellation, by telling him with whom he had been wrestling, and over whom he has prevailed— ' with God and with men '—every veil falls away, and the man presents himself to us in his true form. Although he declines mentioning his name, in reply to Jacob's simple question, yet he reveals it the more clearly by the act of ' his blessing him there.' But when the sun arose in Jacob's comprehension, upon the whole affair, he called the place Peniel; ' for,' said he, ' I have seen God face to face, and my life is preserved.'

" Extraordinary occurrence ! Who can fathom it ?" What ! does this appear so strange to you, although you have seen the Son of man under such entirely different circumstances ? Remember that it was predicted of old, that His name should be called ' Wonderful.'

This man wrestled with him until the breaking of the day. This man had for a time, assumed a human body, in order to wrestle with Jacob bodily. He seized him with his hands, and held him fast with his arms, in order to expel him from the place, or else throw him upon the ground. Can we suppose that complete silence was observed during the conflict; and that nothing more was spoken than what we find recorded ? We can scarcely imagine it. But may we venture to fill up the gap which Moses has left here, by our own suppositions, if they are religious, founded on the word

of God, and conformable to faith and experience?
Why should we not? It is at least certain, that if any
thing was spoken during the struggle, it was nothing
consolatory and encouraging on the part of the angel
of God; but in character with the act of wrestling,
which was no token of friendship. But what is it that
the Spirit discovers to the individual, and with which he
upbraids him? Is it not his sin? And had Jacob no
sin? Might it not have been said to him, ' Away with
thee from this holy place where angels linger!' Might
not the whole catalogue of his guilt have been unfolded
to him in all its particulars; and might it not have been
most clearly proved to him, that in himself there did
not seem the slightest ground for that love which God
had toward him; but that it must be sought and found
in quite a different place? In this way, in a spiritual
manner also, his hip might have been disjointed, and
the last idea of his own worthiness, &c. destroyed.
If Satan upbraids a soul with sins; if he appears at the
right hand of a Joshua in unclean garments, to accuse
him; we are well aware what his intentions are—to
distress, to plunge into immoderate grief, to cast into
despair, and entirely to destroy. But the Son of God
does not act thus. He does it only to humble us, and
to allure us to himself, in order afterwards to comfort
us the more. How did he act towards Saul? Did he
not call out to him, ' Thou persecutest *me?*' How
towards Peter? Did he not thrice inquire if he loved
him? How did he conduct himself towards the Syrophenician woman? Did he not almost call her a dog?
And did not the angels of the seven churches receive

3

almost all of them a particular and emphatic reproof?
We know for what purpose.   As soon as Paul perceived that Satan had his hand in the matter, he advised the
Corinthians to comfort and forgive the sinners amongst
them so much the more, that they might not sink into
excessive sorrow, and be over-reached by Satan.

If the angel of God wrestled with Jacob, the latter
struggled also with all his might with God, or acted as
a prince towards him.   He would by no means let himself be moved away from his place, but resisted with all
his strength, both bodily and spiritual.   Tears and
prayers were the most powerful and victorious weapons
with which he wrestled and overcame the Son of
God.   " Upbraid me,"—will have been his prayerful
language, amidst a flood of tears,—" upbraid me with
all my sins ; unfold and develope them in all their
odiousness ; reveal to me each aggravating circumstance ; shew me my whole desert.   I grant it all, I do
not excuse, cloke, or palliate any thing.   But this I tell
thee also, I do not stand here on my own righteousness,
for I have none ; but rely upon thy mercy.   Art thou,
yea, art thou not thyself, however hostile may be thy
position towards me—art not thou thyself JEHOVAH ZID-
KENU, the Lord my righteousness ? Is there the slightest
spot, wrinkle, or blemish in it ?   Was my forefather
Abraham justified by his works—was he not by thy
grace ?   No ; thóu wilt never reject the poor sinner
who takes refuge with thee.   Hast thou not given thy
word upon it, that thou art not come to call the righteous but sinners to repentance ?   Wilt thou begin with
met o invalidate thine own word ?   Thy truth and faith-

fulness will not suffer this. Thy great mercy itself presents me with weapons against thy justice."

In this, or a similar manner, the fight of faith is carried on. Secretly and imperceptibly all kinds of suitable weapons are handed to the warrior, even as to the Canaanitish woman the suitable reply, ' Yea, Lord, but the dogs eat of the crumbs that fall from their masters' table,' by which she set Jesus fast—so to speak—and obliged him to yield the victory to her.

The conflict was violent and lasted long, even ' until the breaking of the day.' The longer it lasted the more profound were the views which the struggling patriarch received of his corruption, and the grounds of his faith. The longer it lasted, the humbler and weaker he became, the more compelled to build every thing on mere mercy, and entirely despair of himself : to which a circumstance—the dislocating of his hip, which we shall afterwards consider—greatly contributed. For the present, we will break off, with the intention of taking an early opportunity of considering the result.

My hearers will doubtless have already been able to make their observations and useful application of the subject. The chiefest of these is, See to it, that you build the house of your hope upon the rock, that it may stand firm when assaulted. So much is certain, that Jacob hazarded too much, when at his mother's words, ' the curse be upon me,' he exposed himself to the danger. He ought to have had very different reasons for so doing. Rebecca, indeed, was certain of her cause ; but this was not sufficient for her son : Do

not mimic others, nor rejoice in the light of another.
It is in ourselves that we must be regenerated, experience Divine influence, and be sealed with the Spirit of
promise, for godliness does not consist in words, but in
power.

May those that are inwardly assaulted, also learn from
Jacob's conflict, an appropriate demeanor in the attacks
upon their confidence and their hope.   Expect them,
but do not flee from them ; at least no where but to
Jesus ! Ask boldly, even when it seems as if he would
drive you from the place.   Lay hold of the promises ;
strive with them against the threatenings ; weep and
supplicate, even though he seem to be himself opposed
to you.   May he strengthen us for this purpose ! Amen.

SERMON II.

GENESIS XXXII. 25.

And when he saw that he prevailed not against him, he touched the hollow of his thigh; and the hollow of Jacob's thigh was out of joint as he wrestled with him.

'I KNOW, O Lord, that thy judgments are right, and that thou in faithfulness hast afflicted me.' This confession is made by the writer of the cxixth Psalm, in the seventy-fifth verse. In the sixty-seventh, he had said, 'Before I was afflicted I went astray; but now have I kept thy word.' The word afflicted implies being distressed, agonized, rendered poor and wretched, in consequence of which the individual is deprived of all presumption and boldness, and feels humble and abased. That which produced this effect upon the Psalmist, he calls the judgments of the Lord—that is, siftings and trials, which, though painful to the feelings, are salutary in their results, and he ascribes these afflictive events to the Lord; since, without his will, not a hair can fall from our heads. He calls them right or just, and is therefore far from believing any wrong has been done him; on the contrary he thinks there is sufficient reason existing for his being thus afflicted. He acknowledges, that it is *in faithfulness* that the Lord has afflicted him, in order that he might fulfil his promises

3*

in him—not in. wrath for the purpose of destroying him, which he probably apprehended when under the pressure; *in faithfulness*, that thus he might bestow upon him the most glorious blessings; although it seemed to him at the time that he was being led to destruction; *in faithfulness*, in order to heal him of his many infirmities; whilst his iniquities pressed hard upon him, and unrighteousness seemed to have increasingly the upper hand of him; *in faithfulness*, since he secretly held him fast and supported him; for though the Lord lays a burthen upon us, he also helps us to bear it; whilst he at one time thought the Lord was no longer his help; but then again perceived the hand of the Most High; *in faithfulness*, as long as it was needful to abase him, however much he might pray, cry, sigh, and complain against it, and say, ' Is thy mercy clean gone for ever.?' but not a moment longer did the time of suffering last, and then appeared his powerful aid. The Lord afflicted him *in faithfulness* to the degree which was requisite, so that he went bowed down, and bent beneath it, and the burden continued to increase until it became too heavy to be borne; but that very moment it was changed in such a wonderful manner, that it might be said, ' Who redeemeth thy life from destruction, who crowneth thee with loving-kindness and tender mercy;' whilst even under his burden he also thought he should yet praise him; *faithful* in attacking him just on that side where it certainly pained him the most, but where it was also the most necessary; although he might probably think, Ah, if it were only any thing else but that; and yet

just that was requisite for him, whilst something different was required for other patients.   In short, it is *in
faithfulness* that God afflicts and humbles his children.
Formerly they went astray, and with the best will and
intention, began the work improperly; but their conduct is now conformable to the rule of the word.   Certainly, he that has already passed through the furnace,
may boast and declare the judgments of the Lord to be
right.   Let us be satisfied that we have an unspeakably
faithful Lord and Master; and may this also become
more apparent to us from the meditation we are at
present about to resume on the subject.

We proceed with the consideration of Jacob's con-
fliet, and its results; after having, on a former occasion,
made ourselves somewhat more acquainted with the
two combatants.

'When the Son of God saw that he could not prevail over him'—such is the continuation of the wonderful narrative—victory declared itself for Jacob, and
the Son of God is obliged to yield!   Nor is this any
wonder, since he had bound his own hands by the promise, 'I will do thee good;' and thereby pointed out
to his Omnipotence the direction it ought to take.   It
was able to clear away those things which were a hindrance to Jacob; but not to accelerate his destruction;
it was able to pour out benefits upon him, but not to
divest him of them.   Omnipotence is the minister of
Divine truth, and could do nothing against, but every
thing for the truth.   It could have rent heaven and
earth asunder; but it was under the necessity of preserving Jacob unconsumed.   Omnipotence is a Divine

attribute, the exercise of which depends upon the will of God, who can therefore exert or restrain it at his pleasure. But with his truth the case is different; for it is a constituent part of his being, and it is impossible for him to act contrary to it, or he would cease to be Jehovah—that is, to be what he is. He has often entirely renounced his Omnipotence; so that nothing but weakness was visible in him. Where was his Omnipotence, when he fled into Egypt before the face of Herod? What—is this the man who intends to save his people? Is this he who is to overcome the strong man armed, and bind him? Is this the child who is the mighty God? Where was his Omnipotence, when he was bound, and nailed hand and foot to the cross, and when he was laid in the sepulchre? He still indeed possessed it; but he restrained it for the truth's sake, as he himself says, that the Scriptures might be fulfilled. There was a necessity for it; for Omnipotence cannot be exercised against the truth, since God is willing to employ it only in favor of the truth. He had said of his sheep, ' No man shall pluck them out of my hands;' the power of God was therefore obliged to be immediately exerted, when it seemed as if Jesus's assertion was about to be put to shame in the case of Peter, who denied his Master even with oaths and curses; the Lord then turned and looked at Peter, and regarded Satan, who was sifting him, with an omnipotent look: Omnipotence then became the servant of truth.

No one comprehended better than Abraham, Jacob's grandfather, what he possessed in Divine truth, and

what he might risk and expect, when he had the word
of God on his side.   A posterity had been promised to
him in Isaac, which should be blessed and made a blessing.   Yet him he was commanded to sacrifice.   He
boldly seized the knife, most firmly convinced, that
God must keep his word, because he was able to do so;
and thus he expected that his Omnipotence would minister to his truth, and that Isaac, though slain and burnt
to ashes, would be raised from the dead, sooner than
that God would suffer himself to be made a liar, for that
was impossible; but otherwise every thing was possible with God, and through him, to him that believeth.

Jacob understood this also.   The Lord had promised
him, saying, ' I will do thee good.'   Hence his Omnipotence could only be exercised towards him in so far
as it was in accordance with this promise; and because
ne adhered to it, the Almighty was unable to expel
him from the place, but succumbed in the conflict.

Where is there a God like unto him, and how does
Eternal Wisdom sport with his children!   We may
well pray with David (Psalm cxix. 38), ' Stablish thy
word unto thy servant.'   We should then see the glory
of God, and find in it a consolation which does not suffer us to perish in our misery.   Has he not promised
us every thing requisite for our salvation, joy, and prosperity?   And is it not made doubly sure to us by letter
and seal, by Baptism and the Lord's Supper?   What
more can we desire?   Will he not forgive transgression
and sin?   Why do we therefore suffer anxious fears to
perplex us?   The devil, and our own deceitful hearts,
may murmur against it as much as they please.   Will

he not give us a new heart, and make such people of us, as shall walk in his commandments, keep his statutes, and do according to them? And yet we are foolish enough to fear that we shall be obliged to retain our depraved hearts, because we cannot change them ourselves. Christ himself has engaged to be made unto us wisdom; can it be possible, therefore, that we should always continue foolish? He has undertaken our sanctification, and can we continue impure? In reality, we ought justly to feel much astonished at not being perfect saints: for what is the reason that we are not so? I think the chief cause of it lies in this, that we are too proud and self-righteous to expect every thing from pure grace, and for the sake of the word and promise of God; and are still desirous of accomplishing too much of ourselves, and of becoming too much in ourselves. Does not the true and faithful Word tell us that the Lord careth for us, and enjoin us to cast all our care upon him? But who believes this cheering truth? He that does so, finds rest and peace and refreshment when he is weary. But almost all refuse to listen to it, and care for themselves instead of believing. Hence they experience so little of the glory of God, and torment themselves in vain with a burden which they have not strength to bear. We think it rational to trust to the creature, but absurd to hope in the living Creator. O what fools we are to act thus, seeing that we cannot change a single hair white or black! How happy we might be did we believe the words, 'He careth for you;' therefore cast all your care upon him, both externally and internally. Were

we at the same time humble, docile, and sufficiently re-
signed to his will, Jesus would not then put us to the
blush by the example of the birds; but, like the lark in
the storm, we should sing hymns of praise in the midst
of difficulties; in short, in quietness and confidence
would be our strength, and by returning and rest we
should be saved. And is not his written word, whose
minister and performer is Omnipotence, entirely of such
a nature as to render us perfectly tranquil and easy?
'For though the mountains may depart, and the hills
be removed: yet my kindness shall not depart from
thee, neither shall the covenant of my peace be removed, saith the Lord, that hath mercy on thee.'

But are not the justice and holiness of God, such attributes as ought reasonably to render us timid in ap-
plying his promises to us; and will not the consideration that we are sinners, make a great alteration in the
matter? If Jacob had thought thus, and acted accordingly, he would soon have fled from the scene of conflict; for what else was he but a sinner; and if he were
otherwise, how did he become so—of himself or by the
favor of him that called him? 'Even before the
twins were born,' says Paul, ' or had done either good
or evil,' in order that the purpose of God according to
election might stand, not of works, but of him that
calleth, it was said to Rebecca ' The elder shall serve
the younger.' It is true we are sinners, but Jesus is
come to save sinners; hence our right to the Savior
increases—if I may so speak—in the degree in which
we become conscious of our sinfulness. We ought also
to know, that God did not give Canaan to the people

of Israel for the sake of their righteousness—for I know, says he, that thou art a stiff-necked and rebellious people—and likewise that his promises are founded on free grace, and on the blood of Jesus Christ. If any one were to imagine that he had claims upon the Divine promises because of his good qualities and his good conduct, he would greatly deceive himself, and obtain little or nothing, because he did not understand how to buy without money. God knows what miserable sinners we are, much better than we do; and has so marked and designated us in his book, that it is difficult to think more highly of ourselves than we ought, according to the description there given. But notwithstanding this, he has, to the praise of the glory of his grace, vouchsafed the greatest and most precious promises to these very characters; and Christ, by his obedience, sufferings, and death, has sufficiently provided for the manifestation of Divine grace towards us, without any opposition from Divine justice and holiness. Grace, so to speak, is older than justice. The tree of life also is mentioned before the tree of the knowledge of good and evil, with the threatening attached to it. The promise, according to the doctrine of Paul (Gal. iii. 17), is at least four hundred and thirty years older than the law, which revealed the righteousness and holiness of God, but which detracts as little from his promised grace, as a legal testament among men, which is in force on the death of the testator, can afterwards be set aside: and ' this testament,' says the Apostle, ' that was confirmed before of God in Christ, cannot disannul, that it should make the promise of none effect.' We have therefore not to do with the law, which says, ' Do this!' but with the Gospel, which says, ' Ask of me; I will give thee.' If the Ethiopian nobleman could say, ' What doth hinder me to be baptized ?'—we ought reasonably to say, " What hinders my mind from the free exercise of faith and confidence, and from regarding itself in no other light, than as if every thing were already overcome, as if we were already in heaven, seeing that when we have once entered into the conflict of faith, and persevere in it, there is nothing to hinder us from obtaining the crown of life. For believers are kept by the power of God through faith unto salvation. Oh, if we only understood aright what belonged to our peace, we would rejoice from gladness of heart, and the wicked one be unable to touch us !" Jacob understood it excellently—so excellently that he prevailed, even when the Almighty himself entered into conflict with him, but not before he had bound his own hands with the strong cords of love, and the firm bands of his faithful promises; for his omnipotence took the part of his antagonist, in order to bring him successfully through every trial. O certainly, all things are possible to him that believeth! and assuredly if thou believest, thou shalt see the glory of God. If thou hast but one promise on thy side, thy glorious victory is rendered quite certain; even if it should seem as impossible as the restoring of Lazarus to his sisters, after being dead four days, and having become a prey to corruption.

Thus did Jacob act like a prince, even as God boasts of him by the prophet Hosea: just as it becomes a spiritual king, who does not cease to fight till the victory is decided. But what occurs? ' When he saw that he prevailed not against him,' it is said, '.he touched the hollow of his thigh, and the hollow of Jacob's thigh was out of joint as he wrestled with him.' This was a new wonder; and was a remarkable one, for it is mentioned twice. The cause of the dislocation is stated in the words, ' He touched the hollow of his thigh,' and whilst depriving Jacob of all power to continue the combat, he proved his entire superiority, but at the same time added that which was incomprehensible, to that which was wonderful, by declaring himself, notwithstanding, to be vanquished, when he said to the Patriarch, ' Let me go.'

The hip, is, so to speak, the foundation of the edifice of our body. If dislocated, the body falls down. A dislocation of the hip is an extremely rare case, only practicable to astonishing strength ; and almost inconceivable in the position which a person must assume in wrestling with another, who is seeking to drive him from his place, as was the case with Jacob. But if it occurs, and takes place by means of a mere touch, as in the present instance, it is a singular wonder. Such a dislocation is naturally attended with very violent pain. Whether the Son of God caused Jacob to experience the latter also, we know not ; it depended upon his will, and the effect was in every case the same. The good man could wrestle no longer ; nothing therefore was left him but to hold fast to his opponent by his arms, to cleave to him with all his might ; and this he did likewise in such a manner, that his opponent could not remove from the place without dragging him along with him; hence it was that he said, ' Let me go.' But Jacob could no longer either stand or go; much less continue to wrestle; he was compelled to let himself be carried; and to this he was forced by the Son of God himself, who deprived him of all his strength, and left him no alternative but to hang upon his neck if he wished to be preserved from falling. But what is the meaning of this? Why did the Son of God put his hip out of joint, and perhaps cause him violent pain by so doing? What was the object, the intention, the reason?

First of all, we must know that God, by the prophet Isaiah, has replied to Jacob's inquiry of his antagonist, ' What is thy name?' when he says, ' His name shall be called Wonderful.' There is doubtless as much humility as wisdom, whilst inquiring why God acts in this or that particular manner, if we can perfectly satisfy ourselves with the reply, Because it pleases him to act thus; for in the sequel, we shall probably receive satisfactory light upon the subject. In his method of government, much that is incomprehensible occurs, and we must learn to humble ourselves under his mighty hand; he will then exalt us in due time. So long as Job continued to say, ' The Lord gave, and the Lord hath taken away; blessed be the name of the Lord!' it is said, ' In all, this Job sinned not.' But when he afterwards disputed with his friends upon the cause and intent of what had befallen him, they fell into a degree of confusion, from which they were unable to extricate themselves. Job wished to accuse God of injustice; his friends, to charge him with ungodliness; and both

were in the wrong. At length God himself interfered,
and said, ' If thou art so wise as to be able to fathom
everything, gird up now thy loins like a man, for I will
demand of thee, and answer thou me.'   On which Job
however reversed the matter, and said, ' I have uttered
that I understood not; things too wonderful for me,
which I knew not.   Hear, I beseech thee, and I will
speak; I will demand of thee, and declare thou unto
me.'   It was then said, ' My servant Job hath spoken
right concerning me.'

If Abraham had been desirous of ascertaining first of
all the object and intention of offering up his son Isaac,
he would have frustrated them; but he believed that
God could do nothing but what was in accordance with
his word, and thus he ascended Mount Moriah, and
obtained the high commendation expressed in the
words, ' Now I know that thou fearest God.'

When Christ began to wash the feet of his disciples,
Peter wished first of all to know the intention of this
act, before he would consent to give up his feet for that
purpose; but he was told, ' What I do thou knowest
not now, but thou shalt know hereafter;' and when
this proved unavailing, the Lord said, ' If I wash thee
not, thou hast no part in me.'

' My sheep follow me,' says Christ; but he not
unfrequently leads them in such a manner, as if he
were not a shepherd, but was only conducting them to
the butchery.   Are these the people of God, it might
be asked, who appear only to exist in order to be per-
secuted, slain, torn by dogs and wild beasts, and covered with pitch to illuminate the streets of Rome with the

slow flame? But they counted not their lives too dear
to them, and are destined to shine in heaven as the stars
for ever and ever. The Lord of his people wears, instead of a golden coronet, a crown of thorns; instead
of a sceptre, a weak reed; and hangs on a cross, instead of sitting upon a throne. What a Lord! what a
people!

True it is, that the preaching of such things seems
foolishness, and that the natural man becomes quite
foolish in consequence of it. But do thou only believe;
wait for the Lord in the way of his judgments; the
end of it all will be glorious—a glory which no eye
hath seen, no ear heard, and which has never entered
into the heart of man. His name is 'Wonderful;'
and he is so in his works and guidance. Even if we
were unable to discover any wisdom in his conduct towards Jacob, yet we ought still to believe, that he acted
thus towards him for very wise and salutary reasons,
although it may not have pleased him to reveal any
thing to us respecting them.

It is, however, not difficult to discover some of the
salutary intentions of such a procedure. The chief of
them is this: that when God suffers us to become conscious, by inward experience, that we have no righteousness of our own, and that we are unable to acquire
any: that by our own wisdom we cannot accomplish
any thing: and that when he thus humbles us, it is a
a path by which he conducts all his children, although
the means are various by which he attains this end.
These paths are painful to the old man, even as the

dislocation of his hip was to Jacob; but the pain is richly compensated by the fruits which follow.

At first we form to ourselves strange and unfounded ideas of religion. We imagine such a growth in it as we perceive in children, who have gradually less need of their mother's care and attention, until they can at length entirely do without it. But Christ prefers comparing his people to the branches of the vine, which never bring forth fruit of themselves, but solely by their abiding in the vine. In like manner, says he, 'Ye cannot bring forth fruit of yourselves, except ye abide in me; for without me ye can do nothing.' The ideas we form of religion at the commencement, correspond little with this figure. We think of aged Christians, that they are far advanced; and they may have really advanced as far as Jacob, who could no longer stand nor go of himself, much less wrestle, and who had no alternative but to cling to the Son of God, that he might be sustained by him, or according to the expression of the Apostle, To live in the faith of the Son of God, who loved us, and gave himself for us. When they are weak he is their strength: they have nothing, and yet possess all things; are unable of themselves, even to think any thing good, and yet are able to do all things; and many more such singular descriptions of the inward life, which may justly be called a continual riddle, which cannot be solved without personal experience.

Real growth, which must certainly take place in every real Christian, does not consist in an increasing facility in the performance of religious duties in and by ourselves; but it is rather an increase in grace and in the knowledge of Jesus Christ; an increasing facility in making use of Christ in the manner in which he is made and given unto us of God, and this can naturally be learnt in no other manner than by the destruction of our own wisdom, righteousness, sanctification, and redemption, by which *we* decrease, but Christ increases.

The hip, if I may so speak, on which the whole body of a natural godliness rests, the foundation that supports it, is nothing else than confidence in ourselves. Hence the upright are proud of their uprightness, and have reason to be so, because it is a consequence of their diligence; they are indebted for it to their discernment, their own reflection, or to the understanding which they possess, and their commendable conduct is the result of the good resolutions they formed, and which they were strong enough to carry into effect. The noise which is made about human inability, they regard as idle talk, by which nothing else is demonstrated than the individual's own slothfulness; or else they look upon it as an artifice, designed to cover his worthlessness, and to enable him to reject, in a hypocritical manner, a strictly moral deportment; and the appealing to grace is, in their eyes, little more than blaming God because we are not better than we are. Both, in their opinion, are equally abominable; and they thank God that they are not enthusiasts and nominal Christians, like these people. These are the strong who need not a Physician.

Natural men, who lead an ungodly life, and therefore cannot appeal to their virtues, always excuse themselves, because they have not committed this or that particular sin, or else deceive themselves with the idea that when once they find it necessary to amend, they shall soon be able to accomplish it ; but that there is still time enough for such a purpose. With that real religion, to which they will not concede the appellation, both of these classes refuse to have any thing to do, but are opposed to it, since the greatest part of it appears to them extremely irrational and absurd, so that a sensible man has reason to be ashamed of it. They rely upon their own understanding and their own strength, and do not comprehend upon what a person can otherwise depend. But let them go; for they are blind!

When the Lord, however, begins to wrestle with a soul—by which we mean, when he begins his work of grace in a man—he struggles with him in such a manner, that to a certainty, either earlier or later, the hip will be dislocated, and so put out of joint, that no other choice will be left him than that which was left Jacob —that of embracing with the arms of faith the Son of God ; there will be no alternative but to let himself be borne and carried by him. By degrees he is entirely brought off from from his previous method of existing and acting, and conducted into a path, of which he must himself confess that flesh and blood have not revealed it to him ; that he has not learned it from books, from sermons, from other men, or from his own wisdom ; but that wondrous grace first reduced him to the state of a little child, and then began to reveal to him the mystery of the kingdom of God. He now learns to believe from the heart those passages of Scripture, where it is said, ' Not of him that willeth, nor of him that runneth, but of God that sheweth mercy;' and others of a similar nature, which had secretly given him offence before, but which now become wisdom itself to him. He now experiences how much reason Peter had to call the light, to which the chosen generation is called out of darkness, ' a marvellous light.'

We could still say much in pointing out how the Lord, in repentance, commences the destruction of the false ground of self-confidence, and then carries it on and completes it by a variety of trials, and in a very strange manner, until the sinner, stripped of everything, casts himself into the arms of his blessed Lord and Savior. But we break off, and leave the subject to a future opportunity.

We only ask, in conclusion, What becomes of our wisdom according to the wisdom of the Christian religion, which, as the way to wisdom, directs that we should become fools according to the maxims of the world, and affirms, that he who thinks he knows any thing, knows yet nothing as he ought? What becomes of our strength, when Christ is only mighty in the weak, and we without him can do nothing? What becomes of our righteousness, since we are all declared to be unrighteous, and that there is no difference amongst us, except what is made by the grace of God? What becomes of our labor and efforts, since we are saved by grace? Lord, open our eyes, that we may behold wondrous things out of thy law!

SERMON III.

IT is evident, especially from Matt. xiv. 36, what a salutary and healing power Jesus must have possessed. He came into the land of Gennesaret. Scarcely had he left the vessel and stepped on shore, than he was immediately recognized. The people of that place sent out into all the country round about, in order to make it every where known. A number of sick persons from far and near, who labored under a variety of diseases, were brought to him, and they besought him that they might only touch the hem of his garment : and as many as touched it were made whole, whatever might have been their complaint.

" How much it is to be regretted," might some one think, " that Jesus is no longer upon earth !" But wherefore ? If he could heal the sick, even at a distance from them, he must still be able to do so now that he is ascended up on high. And it would be highly derogatory to him to pretend, that Jesus is now so shut up in heaven, that it is impossible for us to experience, or become conscious of anything more of him ; since he has said, ' Lo, I am with you always, even to the end of the world !' But it would also be a matter of regret, if we had such an abundance of temporal things as to render Jesus indifferent to us, because he no longer heals our bodily diseases, except through a medium. We all require his medical aid, his healing power, in a more important sense than the people of Gennesaret experienced it—I mean with respect to our souls, whose disease is called *sin ;* the natural consequence of which. is death, eternal death. Of this we must necessarily be healed ; and may be so, although we cannot, and ought not, to accomplish it as of ourselves. Jesus is also our physician, and so full of healing power, that he is at the same time the medicine. If we wish to be healed, we must at least touch the hem of his garment. ' Thou art clothed with light,' says David, ' and art very glorious.' The glory of Jesus Christ is a perfect glory. The skirt of his garment is his meekness and humility, which fit him to be the physician of such diseased creatures as we. His invitations and promises are the hem which we ought to touch. It is not permitted to every one to approach the great and the mighty upon earth ; but the contrary is the case with the monarch of the skies. We may touch him, if we entreat him to let us do so. And we really touch him by the feeling of our wretchedness, and by our sincere longing and desire for the sanctification of our souls, by prayer, and particularly by believing confidence. But what benefit was derived from thus touching Jesus ? All who did so were made whole. And such is still the case. Jesus retains the reputation of being a perfect, and at the same time the only, physician of souls. Deeply feel thy need of him, and then thou wilt also say with Jacob, ' I will not let thee go, except thou bless me.'

GENESIS XXXII. 26.

And he said, Let me go, for the day breaketh. And he said, I will not let thee go, except thou bless me.

In the remarkable event recorded in this and the two preceding verses, one wonder succeeds another. The Son of God puts Jacob's thigh out of joint; but Jacob, so far from losing courage, throws himself upon the neck of him who had deprived him of all his strength, that he may be borne by him, since he is no longer able to stand of himself. A new wonder now occurs; the Son of God entreats Jacob—the victor the vanquished—the strong the weak—to let him go. But Jacob wisely takes advantage of the opportunity, and replies, ' I will not let thee go except thou bless me.'

' Let me go,' says the Son of God to Jacob; and these words belong to those wondrous expressions, of which there are many in the Scriptures—to those expressions which, at first sight, seem to intimate something absurd, and yet bear upon them the impress of Divine wisdom. If we were desirous of producing a whole series of such paradoxes, of such seeming contradictions, they would be such as the following: ' When I am weak,' as Paul says, ' then am I .strong.' ' As sorrowful, yet always rejoicing; as poor, yet making many rich; as having nothing, yet possessing all things.'

' Let me go.' Was he in earnest, or did he merely dissemble? Dissemble? Who can think that of him who is faithful and true. If he had been in earnest, it would have been an easy thing to extricate himself from the arms of Jacob. It was therefore a new temptation, into which he led the patriarch. It would have been ill for the latter, if he had let him go; he would have miserably sunk upon the ground, the Son of God would have vanished, and with him the blessing which he obtained by holding him fast.

'Let me go.' Could he not have dislocated his arms; which is an easier matter than putting a hip out of joint? No, his power did not extend so far, because it necessarily remained within the limits assigned to it by the Divine promise, ' I will do thee good.' But the dislocation of Jacob's arms, the extricating himself from them; the hasting away without conferring a blessing, would not have been a benefit, but an injury; and this he certainly could not inflict for his word's sake.

'Let me go.' Did he need for this purpose the consent of his friend? Assuredly he did. He had established the covenant of grace with him, and with all the spiritual descendants of Abraham, according to which he engaged to be their shield and their defence. He has bound himself to bless them and to do them good, and cannot free himself from this obligation, which he has confirmed with an oath, without the consent of those in alliance with him; and he himself has, in their regeneration, imparted such a feeling to them, that they never can nor will consent to it. ' When thou saidst, Seek ye my face; my heart said unto thee, Thy face, Lord, will I seek.' ' If we deny him, he will

5

also deny us ; if we believe not, yet he remaineth faithful, he cannot deny himself. (2 Tim. ii. 12, 13)   Our unbelief cannot render the faith of God without effect.' (Rom. iii. 3)   But did he really desire that Jacob should exonerate him from the obligation to do him good ?   Certainly not : but he wished to have the pleasure of seeing how firm, by his grace, are the hearts of his allies, even when many waters of affliction go over them ; and how the seed of God remains in his children.   It was therefore uncommonly pleasing to him, when Job exclaimed, 'Though he slay me, yet will I trust in him ;' and equally so when his disciples said, ' Lord, to whom shall we go ?   Thou hast the words of eternal life ;' and in the same manner when his church continues to cleave firmly to him in the extremity of tribulation and temptation.   He himself is the author of this constancy ; and hence it is, that it is so pleasing in his sight ; for he takes pleasure in all his works.   What joy it will have caused him at being unable to shake off Jacob ; when the latter held firmly by his word, and did not suffer himself to be moved away from the spot, whatever the Lord might say or do to him, after he had once engaged to do him good ; that he even threw himself upon his neck, after he had deprived him of the ability to stand alone, and continued immutably firm, when it was said to him. ' Let me go !'   And what pleasure it still causes him, when the Christian does not suffer himself to be dismayed by afflictions and temptations, but even then cleaves to his word and his grace, when every thing seems against him ; when he continues faithful unto death !

' Let me go.' The Lord said this to the Patriarch, to try him whether he really loved him who attacked him so severely, and caused him such sensible. pain. That which the Lord here says to Jacob, was said to Job by his wife, ' Dost thou still retain thine integrity, although God visits thee with such unheard of afflictions?' Take leave of him and let him go. It is in reality no small attainment, not only to act patiently in tribulation, but even to glory in it, and not to doubt for a moment of the goodness, compassion, and merciful kindness of the Lord. And when induced to complain with the church, in Isaiah lxiii. 15, ' Where is the sounding of thy bowels and thy mercies towards me ? are they restrained?' still to say, "Doubtless thou art our Father;' to confess with David, ' Thy way is in the sanctuary;' and with Jeremiah, in his Lamentations, ' Thy goodness is every morning new !' This is no easy matter.

In the present season of distress, God has certainly given many of his children an opportunity of refusing to learn this lesson ; and the Tempter may have said to many, what the enemies of Jesus called out to him, when he hung upon the cross : ' He trusted in God, let him deliver him now.'

' Let me go.' The Lord spoke thus to the Patriarch to put his faith to the test, and ascertain whether he would still cleave to the promise, ' I will do thee good,' although the hostile conduct of the Son of God seemed to prove just the contrary.

Faith has various gradations: at one time, it is a faith which arises from seeing, feeling, tasting, and from the Lord's drawing near in loving kindness and tender mercy to the pardoned soul, in such a manner that the individual is able to say, " I believe, not merely because of thy word, but because I experience in myself that Jesus Christ is the Savior of the soul." This is valuable experience, sweet in the sensation, and precious in the fruit. But faith, which seems in these circumstances to be uncommonly strong, is in reality very weak. It supports its steps with the staff of sensation. Sensible joy in the Lord is its strength. It has its foundation more in itself than in the Lord; and often sinks down to the extreme of despondency, when the transports it previously felt diminish. A higher degree is, not to see, and yet believe; pray according to the word, and believe that the prayer will be answered, although there is no tangible proof of it; believe that the Lord's ways are goodness and truth, although reason does not see them to be so.

But it is a step further still, where we believe in hope, where nothing is to be hoped for—nay, even against hope, and against feeling. Thus the Captain of our salvation believed, in defiance of every thing to the contrary, when, forsaken of God, assaulted by the visible and invisible world, he hung upon the cross for three hours together, full of pain in body and soul. God laid him in the dust of death, and yet he called him, in faith, his God.

This is the highest degree of faith. He who is desirous of exercising it, must be established in the knowledge of the mystery of God, and far advanced in the denial of himself; the joint of confidence in his own strength and wisdom, must be considerably dislocated; he must be able to look pretty deep into the heart of Jesus, and yet say with Paul, 'We are perplexed, but not in despair.' (2 Cor. iv. 8) 'I believed, therefore have I spoken.' (Psalm cxvi. 10.)

'Let me go.' Jacob's courage was also put to the test. "Let him go," he might have thought. "Thy tears, thy prayers, have been altogether fruitless. He has put thy thigh out of joint, and what else does the pain of it tell thee, than that he cherishes no favorable sentiments towards thee. Who knows what injury he may still occasion thee? Although he sees that thou must miserably sink to the ground, and thus, without even being able to escape from Esau, must fall into his cruel hands, yet he desires thee to let him go." But Jesus had already taken care that he should not be able to let him go, by leaving him no choice, but placing him under the necessity of cleaving to him. No, Jesus must himself repulse him, and let go. his hold of him; but this he did not do, and rejecting is what Jesus cannot do; for he has said, 'Him that cometh to me I will in no wise cast out.' Hence we must exercise courage, or else give up all for lost. Jacob was constrained to act thus.

O happy souls, whom Jesus has wounded in such a manner that he alone can heal them, and whom he binds to himself by the feeling of their misery; to whom he leaves only the choice between life and death; and who are compelled to say with Hosea, 'Come and let us return unto the Lord; for he hath torn, and he will heal us; he hath smitten, and he will

5*

bind us up. He will raise us up, and we shall live in his sight.' (ch. vi. 1, 2) Happy is he who feels compelled to continue cleaving, though he may be under the necessity of persevering in doing so, even to the end of his life, without receiving consolation; because, unless he does so, he sees nothing but death and destruction before him! O wait on the Lord; though he tarry, be of good courage and undismayed, and wait, I say, on the Lord!

'Let me go.' What courage must this have imparted to Jacob! For what did the words imply? That the Son of God was in his power, and that he would not depart, unless Jacob gave his consent to it; and this he had himself rendered impossible. What a futile reason was that which he adduced, 'For the day breaketh.' " Let it break," might Jacob have replied, " what is that to me? I have a thousand reasons why I will not let thee go, and even the breaking of the day is one of them. A painful day is approaching. I am afraid of my brother Esau. I stand in especial need of thy blessing. Thou dost well to remind me of it, that I may cleave to thee still more closely."

O how pleasing must it have been to Jesus, that his pupil stood the test so well, and that his good work shone forth in such a lovely manner in him! In consequence of the promises which are given us, Jesus is also in our power in like manner; and however wonderfully he may deal with us, as his name imports, yet he can deny neither himself nor his word. If he reproaches thee with being a sinner, justify him in doing so; but plead with him, in return, that he is the Savior

of sinners. Confess that he is in the right, when he
sets before thee thy unbelief, thy wretchedness, and
and thy unworthiness; and set his word before him,
' Seek, and ye shall find; knock, and it shall be opened
unto you.' When he was an infant, he was wrapped
in swaddling clothes; and his promises are now the
cords of love by which we may hold him fast. And
the best of all is, he holds us fast; otherwise timid
Jacob would have taken to flight at the first attack.
O how lovely! he was afraid of his brother Esau, but
not of the Son of God, even when he dislocated his
thigh.

' Let me go.' How wonderful, that he declared himself vanquished at the very moment when Jacob was
unable to do any thing more! As long as Jacob, resting on his feet, was able to defend himself, his antagonist also did his best against him. But no sooner are
his feet no longer of any use to him, and Jesus must be
alone and entirely his support, than he becomes so
wholly and solely; and Jacob, when unable to do any
thing more, can now do all things through Christ, who
strengthens him; in whom he has righteousness and
strength, and who himself deprived him of his own
strength.

In the Divine life the same thing is wont to occur.
At the commencement, we are generally able to do
many things; we form noble resolutions, and expect
to fulfil them faithfully, in which we succeed to a tole-
rable extent. We arm ourselves with a multitude of
laudable maxims and noble motives. We hear and
read the word of God with unction and devotion. We

pray much, and with fervor.   If we commit a fault, we
repent of it bitterly, and renew our good resolutions.

But what generally happens afterwards.? The fervor in prayer expires, and the oppressed heart can
scarcely relieve itself by sighs and ejaculations; it can
seldom shed a tear, and must experience, to its sorrow,
that the Word is in the right to speak of ' stony hearts.'
Gladly would the individual feel the right kind of sorrow at it; but he seems to himself to be hardened.
And if he prays, where is the fervor ? where the faith ?
And yet no prayer is heard, unless it be offered in
faith. - Where is devotion ? when even the reception
of the holy sacrament itself cannot restrain the wander-
ing mind, however much he may strive to occupy himself only with good thoughts.

And the good resolutions ? Oh, he no longer knows
himself, whether they are altogether sincere ! He
feels, indeed, self-love, unbelief, and hardness of heart ;
but how to alter it, unless the Holy Spirit does it ; and
how to obtain Him, when he prays so wretchedly, is
then the question.

The Christian then feels like Jacob did, when his hip
was out of joint.   He supposes he must irrecoverably
fall a prey to the wretchedness which he fears. · If
Jesus does not accomplish the work entirely ; if he be
not the beginning, middle, and end ; if we are not
saved by grace alone ; there is at least nothing more
for him to hope for. · The name of Jesus alone, and the
word grace, sustains him in some measure, while
every other support gives way.

But how does the faithful Shepherd act under these

circumstances ? This is the real time of mercy. O what does the poor man now perceive! His Savior and his Gospel. He recognizes his supreme faithfulness in having humbled him, although he thought his Lord and Master acted strangely, and intended evil towards him. He now finds that the Lord permitted him to succeed in nothing, although he could not conceive before why he did not listen to his anxious supplication. He now understands that the Lord hedged up his way with thorns, to make him take the right one ; and led him into the desert, that he might speak kindly to him.

After having suffered the loss of his own strength, he now succeeds in the very same way in which Jacob succeeded, whilst casting himself entirely upon Him who is all to us.

' Let me go.' This is like the sporting of Eternal Wisdom in the ' habitable parts of the earth,' which she often repeats, in order to have her delights with the good conduct of the children of men.

A similar circumstance is mentioned concerning Moses, in Exod. xxxii. This man of God remained a long time upon Mount Sinai, on which God had given his law. At length the people said, ' We know not what is become of the man ;' and induced the brother of Moses to make them a golden calf. He did so, and they honored it as their God—ate and drank, played and danced, around it. The Lord informed Moses of it and said to him, ' I see that this is a stiff-necked people ; now therefore let me alone, that my wrath may wax hot against them, and that I may consume them ; and

I will make of thee a great nation." Without the consent of his servant, the Lord would do nothing ; and
Moses so adroitly took advantage of this condescension,
that he took the forgiveness of the people's sin with
him from the Mount, And how ably did he oppose
the Lord with his own weapons ! He confesses the
wickedness of the people, but pleads with him also his
word, his oath, and the honor of his name : and binds
his arm, as it were, although already lifted up to pun- .
ish. For God always acts only in accordance with
his word.

The Syrophenician woman is also a remarkable instance of this. It was assuredly only to help her, that
the Savior took a long journey to the borders of Tyre
and Sidon. But just as if he would have nothing more
to do with helping and delivering, he went into a
house, and would not that any one should know he
was there ; but, fortunately, he could not continue hid.
His arrival became known ; and, happily, a poor
afflicted Canaanitish woman heard of it. She besought
him, pitiably, to help her ; but Jesus did not even look
back, much less answer her a word. He let her cry
on, and walked unmercifully forward. But could his
heart have been seen, it would have been evident how
it melted with compassion. The disciples, highly astonished at the extraordinary behavior of their Master,
intercede for the poor woman ; but they are repulsed,
and that in a manner which would have deprived even
the distressed mother of all courage, had not the Lord
continued secretly to impart fresh courage to her; 'I
am not sent,' said he, 'but to the lost sheep of the

house of Israel ;' and not. to people like this woman. But she will not take a refusal ; she blocks up
his path, falls at his feet, and exclaims, ' Lord,. help
me !' She had even now to sustain the severest test,
and is told in reply, ' It is not meet to take the children's bread, and to give it unto dogs.' ' Yea, Lord,'
answered she, ' it is certainly not right ; do not treat
me. therefore as a child, but as a dog, to which the
crumbs are given which fall from the table.' Jesus is
now overcome ; ' O woman,' he exclaims, ' great is
thy faith ! Be it unto thee even as thou wilt.'

After his resurrection, he joined himself to the two
disciples going to Emmaus. He spake to them in such a
manner, that their hearts began to burn with love and
joy whilst he expounded the Scriptures to them. He
holds their eyes, and they walk forwards with him, and
listen to him, without knowing who he is. At length,
towards evening, they arrive at the inn. His love is
too great for him to leave them, and yet he wishes to
have the pleasure of being invited by them. . He
makes therefore as if he would go further, whilst rendering it impossible for them to let him go. They
urged him to remain, or more properly, they compelled
him ; which gratified him much. He remained therefore. Whilst breaking the bread, their eyes were opened. They knew him, and the same moment he vanished. . Their joy was too much for. them alone : they
hastened back to Jerusalem, and there all was joy,
animation, and triumph. He was risen indeed. .

Lazarus, his friend, dies ; although he is informed of
his sickness, and sends word that it is not unto death.

He remains quietly in his place : he suffers the-friend whom he loves to expire. Lazarus is buried, and lies four days in the grave. All hope is at an end. Jesus suffers Mary and Martha to weep and mourn, although he loves them also, and does not once visit them. He even almost confuses their faith : for Lazarus is dead, although he had said, ' The sickness is not unto death.' At length he comes, but too late ; and now stands and weeps with them, although he might have helped them. ' Ah, Lord, if thou hadst been here, my brother had not died,' says Mary, and falls weeping and almost heart-broken at his feet ; and no one can refrain from weeping, not even he himself. All at once he exclaims ' Lazarus, come forth !' and the dead man again comes to life, after he had been dead four days. For Christ's word and promise must be fulfilled, whatever happens : and Abraham went by no means to too great lengths, in hoping, after receiving the Divine promise, where nothing was to be hoped for.

'Let me go.' If many of those who belong to Christ, who surrender themselves to him with heart and hand, are to be sirnamed Jacob and Israel, as we read in Isaiah xliv., they will have to pass through a similar conflict to that described.

'Let him go,' says the world and sin, at first, to the heart which is desirous of resigning itself to Jesus; as if we should fare better in the service of sin, than in following Jesus. It may violently and variously incite and tempt us to withdraw our hearts from Jesus, and no longer strive against it, but submit ourselves to it. The world advises us to let Jesus go, and whispers, 'Why wilt thou renounce the company and amusements thou hast hitherto enjoyed, and trouble and shorten thy days? Consider what others will say to it. Who can live in such a manner? It is not even necessary; and if it were, it is still time enough. It seeks to gain only a particle of our hearts, because all the rest easily follows. If Jesus himself was obliged to endure such temptations, as when it was said, ' All this will I give thee, if thou wilt fall down and worship me!' we must also be satisfied to bear them, and show ourselves as good soldiers of Christ.

Satan also says, ' Let him go,' even as he deceitfully promised Jesus himself the whole world, if he would let God go, and serve the prince of this world. As long as he is able, he takes away the word from the heart of man. When he can no longer succeed in this, and the individual begins to think with all earnestness of his salvation, he then tries to depict godliness as much too difficult; the heart of Jesus as full of wrath and displeasure; and to persuade him that it is now too late, and that it will not avail, whatever trouble he may give himself; he is either too great a sinner, or is much too small a one in his own eyes. ' Trouble not the master,' therefore; what will it avail? pacify thyself as well as thou art able, and let the serious thought of Jesus and thy salvation go. And he may even go so far as to quote what the despisers say in Mal. iii. 14, ' It is vain to serve God, and what profit is it that we have kept his ordinance, and that we have walked mournfully before the Lord of hosts?'

Yea, even as Jesus once said to his disciples, ' Will ye

6

also go away ?' and here said to Jacob, ' Let me go ?' he also informs us, that if we will follow him, we must deny ourselves, and take up our cross ; that the path is narrow on which he leads us, and that we must not expect continued enjoyment, but also sensible sufferings. If he often lets us pray a long time before he comes to our aid, or conceals himself anew, when we supposed we had really found him, and when we cannot perceive by his guidance that he loves us, cares for us, will do all things well, but seems, on the contrary, to be opposed to us, as in the case of Jacob—he then, as it were, says to us ' Let me go.'

In such a situation, the Christian has a fine opportunity of giving a proof of his estimation of Jesus, and of his earnestness in seeking salvation, of showing what is the object of his desire and choice, what he clings to, and what he is willing to offer up. Job went so far in this as to declare, that he would rather die than part with his integrity. Abraham was ready to sacrifice his son Isaac, the dearest and the best he had in the world. The Apostles, and many thousands of other Christians, did not shun bonds and imprisonment—nay, even every torture, and the most horrible death, to win Christ.

The Savior is not only able, but frequently really gives his people such an insight into his heart, so full of love, grace, and truth, that, like Jacob, they clearly perceive that they may ask in his name what they will, in the certainty that he will grant it them ; and, in a certain sense, must do so, for his faithfulness and his truth's sake.

Their hearts become so enlarged, that they feel the

entire emphasis of the passage, ' He that spared not his own Son, but freely gave him up for us all—how shall he not with him also freely give us all things !' ' Whatsoever ye shall ask the Father in my name, he will give it you.' Jacob's heart expanded so much at the words, ' Let me go,' that he answered, ' I will not let thee go, except thou bless me.' But more of this another time. At present I only add:

If you are desirous of becoming true and sincere Christians, let not your heart be troubled, neither let it be afraid. Ye believe in God—believe also in Jesus Christ. If sometimes your path is strange, incomprehensible, and painful, you have no reason to fear. Be not dismayed, when you can accomplish nothing more by your own strength; for Christ makes you weak, only that his strength may be perfected in your weakness. But, whether courageous or fearful, do not forsake Jesus.

' Faithful is he who hath called you, who also will do it.' Amen.

SERMON IV.

GENESIS XXXII. 26.

And he said, I will not let thee go unless thou bless me.

WE read, in 2 Kings xiii. 14, that Elisha, that great
and remarkable prophet, at length fell sick, and drew
near his end. Joash, the king of Israel, came and visited him : and when he saw how dangerous his illness
was, the king wept, and exclaimed, ' O my father, my
father, the chariot of Israel, and the horsemen thereof !'
Thou art near death, who wast more to Israel than a
whole army, and often delivered it out of its distresses !
What a loss ! especially at a time when the Syrians
were pressing Israel sorely.

The sick prophet had pleasing news from the Lord
for the sorrowing king, which he communicated to him
in a symbolical manner. He told him to open a win-
dow, and shoot out of it. The king shot, and the prophet said, ' This is an arrow of the Lord's deliverance
from Syria.' He then told the king to take other ar-
rows, and smite upon the ground with them ; which
was again intended as a pre-intimation of successful occurrences ; as Joash might have inferred from the first
sign. But he smote only thrice, and then ceased. The
man of God was then wroth with him, and said,
' Thou shouldst have smitten five or six times ; then

hadst thou smitten Syria till thou hadst consumed it ; whereas now thou shalt smite Syria but thrice.'

Such is the history. What does it teach us ? That we should not stop half way in the spiritual course, but press forward to the mark. Even in spiritual things we may stop, after having smitten thrice, when we ought to have done it six times. Some satisfy themselves entirely with the externals of religion ; and are contented with having smitten once, so to speak. Propriety of conduct, going to church, and the reception of the sacrament, constitute the whole of their religion. They ought, however, to go on to repentance and faith, and thus smite five or six times. Some smite the ground twice, and add to their outward observances, attendance at meetings, and a greater degree of prayer ; they also feel a little distressed, and are then a little relieved, and are like the foolish virgins who carry lamps without oil ; are ever hearing and learning, and yet do not attain to the knowledge of the truth. Others possess genuine grace, poverty of spirit, sorrow for sin, and a hungering and thirsting after righteousness ; and yet, like Joash, they do not obtain a complete victory, although they obtain salvation : their faith rests upon their feelings, and is as mutable as the latter. It depends upon the consciousness of the characteristic marks of a state of grace, and is founded more upon the grace in them, than that which is in Christ Jesus ; and hence they are never comfortable ; they smite the ground twice or thrice ; they do not proceed in a direct line towards Jesus ; and resemble a man who looks at a star through a telescope held by a

6*

trembling hand—he sees it sometimes, but not at others, and must then seek it again.

. There are also some who, like the Corinthians whom Paul reproves, are . soon satisfied. They have had some experience in religion, their acquaintance with which induces them to reckon themselves amongst the children of God, notwithstanding all their present coldness and estrangement from Jesus ; and to regard it as faith, and even strong faith, that they do not doubt of their state of grace. But believing in Jesus is certainly something else than the belief in our own state of grace ; and salvation is promised, not to the latter, but to the former. If we are in the vine, where is the sap ? They have ceased to smite, when they ought to have continued to do so.

But there are others who look steadfastly unto Jesus, and do not receive him half, but entirely ; not occasionally, but continually ; and maintain an uninterrupted intercourse with him. They are wholly sinners in their own esteem, and let Jesus be their entire Savior ; and thus they smite five or six times, until they consume the Syrian host.

Jacob, terrified at the wrath of his brother Esau, has recourse to the Lord in prayer. Scarcely has he begun to do so, when a man lays hold of him, in the darkness of the night, and struggles with him. He endeavors not only by bodily strength to expel him from the place, but also to drive him from the throne of grace, by setting before him his sins ; both, however, solely with the intention of exercising his faith, and occasioning him a new victory. Jacob resists with his bodily powers, and especially by his tears and prayers, according to Hosea. (xii. 4.) The struggle becomes more violent, so that the patriarch's thigh is dislocated by the touch of his antagonist. But the very moment in which he was unable to continue the conflict, in consequence of being deprived of his strength, and when compelled to sink down completely overcome, so that he must necessarily fall into the hands of Esau, he throws himself upon the neck of his opponent, who then declares himself vanquished; thus he is in Jacob's power, and cannot depart unless the patriarch voluntarily releases him. Wonderful procedure! As long as Jacob possessed strength he was overcome, and conquers at the moment when it forsakes him. 'When I am weak, then am I strong.' To them that have no might, increased power is given, whilst the strong grow weary and fall. Who can understand it, or comprehend the wonders of the kingdom of God? Only they to whom it is given. To others it is a stumbling-block, and foolishness. Jacob perceived very clearly what was implied in the words, 'Let me go;' he perceived that his opponent was in his power, yielded himself to him, and virtually said, 'Ask of me, and I will give thee the heathen for an inheritance, and the uttermost parts of the earth for a possession.' And he faithfully took advantage of this when he answered, 'I will not let thee go unless thou bless me.'

We consider,

What the blessing implied:

Jacob's resolution not to let the Son of God go, before bestowing it; and lastly,

The result.

The Lord, in his word, has opened the door of grace
to us to an astonishing extent.   If we had faith, and,
like Jacob, made a due and bold use of it, we should
experience marvellous things.   It is said in general,
' Ask, and ye shall receive.   Ask, and it shall be given
you, that your joy may be full.'   And there is no limit-
ation prescribed, either in asking or in giving ; on the
contrary Christ says, ' What things soever ye desire,
when ye pray, believe that ye receive them, and ye
shall have them;' and adds, ' Have faith in God.   For
verily I say unto you, that whosoever shall say unto
this mountain, Be thou removed, and be thou cast into
the sea ; and shall not doubt in his heart, but shall be-
live those things which he saith shall come to pass : he
shall have whatsoever he saith.'   What a bill—if I
may speak in a mercantile manner—has He whose
name is Amen, here drawn upon himself !—and since
his riches are unsearchable, there is no doubt of the
payment.   ' Yes,' says Paul, he is rich unto all that
call upon him.'

It is however said, ' Have faith in God !' and there
is great want of this upon earth.   The testimony of
man is received ; but the testimony of God, which is
greater—dreadful thought !—no man receiveth.   But
he that receives it, sets to his seal that God is true ;
and he that does not, deprives himself of eternal life.
(John iii. 32, 33.)

In how many different ways the Savior seeks to encourage boldness in prayer!   He asks parents whether
they would give a stone to their children when asking
for bread, or poison instead of food ; and teaches us to

draw the conclusion, that God who is gracious, and even love itself, is certainly ready to bestow blessings which cost him nothing, since men are capable of doing good, though they are evil, and though it costs them something. Is it possible, that a friend can show kindness to another, when urgently entreated, although it occasion him trouble; and you will not place a similar confidence in God, who, by a mere nod, can communicate the greatest blessings to you, without being the least incommoded by it? You think it possible that a haughty and unrighteous judge, who neither fears God nor regards man, may be induced, by the persevering entreaties of an inconsiderable widow, to grant her request; and yet imagine that your kind and gracious Father will unfeelingly suffer you to supplicate him in vain?—He who says, 'Call upon me in the day of trouble; I will deliver thee.' Be ashamed of your incredulity! If he has given up his Son—the best, and dearest, and most excellent of all he possessed—shall he hesitate about infinitely inferior benefits? Will he not rather, with him, freely give us all things? Is it not irrational, absurd folly and sin to cherish the smallest doubt of it? Ah, Lord, teach us how to pray! for it is a wonderful art to be able to pray aright.

We know neither how we ought to pray, nor what we ought to pray for as we ought. But the Spirit maketh intercession for us with groanings that cannot be uttered. And certainly prayer is a very different thing to the sound and arrangement of the words that are used; and it is a question, with respect to many, whether ever they prayed in their lives, however often they thought they prayed and seemed to pray ; whilst others pray very-powerfully who believe they cannot pray at all. ' But if ye abide in me, says the Savior, and my words abide in you, ye shall ask what ye will, and it shall be done unto you.' (John xv. 7.)

Jacob understood all this. He perceived that he had the Son of God in his power, and could request as great a blessing of him as he wished. Hence he declares that he will not let him go unless he bless him.

But what is the meaning of blessing ?

It means, amongst men, wishing them every good, particularly of a spiritual kind, from God through Christ, in a praying and believing frame. The blessings which Isaac, and afterwards Jacob, pronounced upon his sons, were prophetic announcements, and therefore of a very peculiar kind. The first-mentioned description of blessing is pleasing and salutary.

Pleasing are the good wishes of one towards another, when springing from a loving heart, which is turned towards God through Christ ; for they are proofs and signs of love, and consequently expressions of the image of God. They are therefore beautiful and sacred, and only true Christians know how to bestow them—and they do so too. How many salutations does the New Testament contain ! The sixteenth chapter of the Epistle to the Romans consists almost entirely of them ; and saluting or greeting means nothing more than affectionately blessing, and consists not in the sound of words, but in the emotion of the heart. It is an exercise becoming Christians ; for they are priests, whose province it is to bless. Hence Paul took pleasure also in mentioning the salutations of others, which he by no means looked upon as inconsiderable trifles. St. John likewise does not fail to communicate the salutations of pious children, with which he had been charged, as his second Epistle proves. But he looks upon such salutations very earnestly and closely, when, in the same Epistle, he enjoins that those who do not bring with them the doctrine of Christ—the doctrine of the Father and the Son—shall not be received into the house, nor even be wished God speed; for John possessed as much holiness as love, respecting which we must not imagine that it consents to every thing, although it doth not behave itself unseemly. God himself is a sea of love; and yet his anger burns, his lips are full of fury, and his tongue a consuming fire. For even as love attracts that to it which is like itself; so also it violently rejects that which is unlike. Hence Jesus also, on the day of final judgment, will say, ' Depart from me, ye evil doers; I never knew you.' Even as he also said to Satan, ' Get thee behind me.'

The salutation or blessing of real Christians is likewise something salutary and powerful, when it is bestowed as it ought, with a believing elevation of the heart to God through Christ. We believe in the communion of saints. It consists not merely in that sincere and heart-felt love which so infallibly prevails amongst real Christians, that John adduces it as a characteristic of having passed from death unto life; and adds, ' He that loveth not his brother abideth in death.' It consists not merely in contributing to their support with our outward substance, and ministering to them

with our spiritual gifts, such as instruction, encouragement, and consolation ; but we have also reason to believe that our labor is not in vain in the Lord, when
you bless me in spirit, and I, in return, bless you, and
when we mutually supplicate for each other grace and
salvation from God.   For the Lord fulfils the desire of
them that fear him.   Nay, it is even a reciprocal duty.
‘ Pray for the peace of Jerusalem,’ it is said in Psalm
cxxii.—an expression synonymous with wishing prosperity to it.   ‘ They shall prosper that love thee.’
‘ We bless you in the name of the Lord,’ is the conclusion of Psalm cxxix.   And Paul says, ‘ Pray for one
another ;’ and also requests the intercessions of the
church on his own behalf.   Let us also mutually exercise this, that the body of Christ may be edified.   Our
blessing, however, is powerless in itself, and is only
effectual when our hearts are incited to it by the Lord,
and accord with His will.

Jacob desires to be blest by the Lord himself; and
the blessing of the Lord does not consist in mere words,
but in the real communication of grace and gifts.   The
Lord left this world whilst lifting up his hands in the
act of blessing ; but we do not read that he uttered
any thing on the occasion.   He imparted real life to
his disciples ; which enabled them to return to Jerusalem without the visible presence of Jesus—not with
sorrow, but with joy.

Every thing, in the kingdom of God, has reference
to that which is real and substantial.   The world, on
the contrary, is a kingdom of falsehood.   It promises
pleasure and delight, and even rest ; but it does not

keep its word. What it gives is shadow, which may for a season deceive, so that the mistaken individual himself imagines that he is wonderfully well satisfied. But before he is aware, the delusive prospect fades from his view, and he finds himself enveloped in darkness. The world deprives him again of all the dignities, pleasures, property, and happiness it had afforded him, in order to bestow them upon others. It pays no attention to his ardent desire for the further possession and enjoyment of them, nor to his great unwillingness to part with them. Inexorable death deprives him of every thing; reduces him to dust; and hurries him, naked and bare, into another world, where he meets with none of the objects which had been lent him for a time; where the man in authority is no longer respected, and where the rich man no longer possesses anything; because nothing avails then, but the new creature, which after God is created in righteousness and true holiness, which he does not possess; and in faith which worketh by love, of which he is destitute. Poor deceived mortal!

Thus the world is a kingdom of lies, and we ourselves are also full of deceit, which misleads the understanding as well as the desire to seek happiness in vanity. Hence the individual must be born again; from being carnal, must become spiritual; from being earthly, must become heavenly; and from being an unbeliever, must become a believer; and thus enter into the kingdom of God, which consists solely of truth and reality. When in the latter, anything is termed good or evil, it is really so, and will manifest itself to be so. · The things are

really as it describes them. When it says, ' Seek that !'
it is really worth while. When it says, set not your
affections upon that particular object,' it is not worth
the while striving for it. In short, it always advises us
for the best. Its promises also are true and sure.
When it says, " The blood of Christ cleanses the conscience from all sin, and renders us happy," it proves itself to be so in our minds; even as many thousands, in
every age, have found it confirmed in their own experience. If it tells us, " The Lord careth for you," it
proves that it is the case in all who receive the saying.
Its joys are real and substantial; and when once it will
appear what we shall be; all our expectations will be
exceeded. In short,

> " Who seeks this world, a burthen finds,
> Which firmly on his back he binds.
> Upon the chaff and wind he feeds,
> And a most wretched life he leads,
> Until at length he feels, too late,
> The misery of such a fate.
> A friend in need, in death a stay,
> A comfort during all the way,
> Unfailing, thou wilt find in none,
> On earth or heaven, but God alone."

With all its wisdom, the world is nothing but deceit,
when it presumes to put in its word upon spiritual things,
because it knows nothing of Christ. But upon him who
enters into the kingdom of God the true and marvellous
light arises, and he sees what was otherwise hidden
from his eyes. When Jesus blesses, he actually imparts
' all things that pertain to life and godliness.'

What is it, therefore, that we call blessing? It is the

opposite of curse. As the latter comprehends in it all
that is evil, with respect to body and soul, in time and
eternity ; so blessing, on the contrary, comprises in it all
inward and outward temporal and spiritual prosperity.
Outward prosperity, that is, perfect health, disturbed by
no sickness, pain, or indisposition ; in the enjoyment of
which, the body possesses all possible perfection, so
that no weariness oppresses it, no tedium troubles it,
and every sense is capable of uninterrupted and exalted
enjoyment. We must certainly take into account, at
the same time, the infinite period after the resurrection ;
but in the kingdom of God a thousand years pass for a
day, and Jesus as a perfect Savior renders at length both
body and soul perfectly healthy and happy ; as an infallible pledge of which we know that he himself dwells
in heaven with body and soul.

Blessing, in a spiritual sense, is a perfectly tranquilized mind, an understanding endowed with all perception,
a heart thoroughly pervaded by God, and entirely one
with God, which may be experienced even here below,
in a good measure. It is true we live here by faith and
not by sight, and are saved and sanctified by hope, and
are not yet in perfect possession and enjoyment. The
blessing, the life, however, which takes its commencement here, is an eternal blessing, an eternal life ; and
becomes in us a well of water springing up to everlasting life. Let it suffice you, that you are kept, through
faith unto salvation ; and that all things shall work together for good to them that love God. Rejoice that
your names are written in heaven, and that a mansion
it already prepared for you. The heavenly Joshua is

able to conduct you through the wilderness, and not to let you want either bread or water; and even if you must have flesh, he knows how to procure it; only take care to leave the world its onions and its garlic.

What has been premised sufficiently proves, that blessing comprehends in it the entire appropriation of salvation, from the first gentle inclination of the man's will towards God—of which he himself may perhaps be unconscious—to perfect felicity before the throne of the Lamb; from the being called with a holy calling to the being glorified in heaven; for it is one blessing, something entire. Hence Paul represents it, in Rom. viii., as in a chain or series of blessings; 'Whom he did foreknow, he also did predestinate to be conformed to the image of his Son. Whom he did predestinate, them he also called; and whom he called, them he also justified; and whom he justified, them he also glorified. What shall we then say to these things? If God be for us, who can be against us?'

Earthly benefits are also a species of blessing, which certainly ought not to be overlooked. The abundant harvest of the present year forcibly draws our attention to this view of the subject. The field and the garden preach to us concerning the goodness of God, by presenting us with the enjoyment of it, with respect to which we ought not to be unsusceptible, but to lift up our eyes to the God of blessing, who opens his liberal hand, and satisfies the desire of every living thing, and on whom our temporal prosperity as much depends as our spiritual. But we call whatever belongs to our temporal prosperity only a species of blessing; because

even the wicked partake of it; whilst the godly not unfrequently obtain only a small share. God causes his
sun to shine upon the evil and the good, and his rain to
descend on the just and the unjust. Temporal benefits
are only a curse to the wicked; and in the end they
fall into the most bitter poverty, as we see in the example of the rich man. What does it profit a man, if he
gain the whole world and lose his own soul? What
avails all participation in the things of the present world,
without having part in that which is to come? And
how lamentable is the folly of neglecting eternal blessings, whilst seeking after transitory good; and yet,
alas! how common!

The triune God is the source of all blessing. ' The
Lord bless thee and keep thee! The Lord cause his
face to shine upon thee, and be gracious to thee! The
Lord lift up the light of his countenance upon thee, and
grant thee peace!' From him, as the Father of lights,
comes down every good and perfect gift. No man can
receive anything, except it be given him of the Father.
It is not of him that willeth, nor of him that runneth,
but of God that showeth mercy, and of his free will. It
is in vain to rise early and sit up late, unless the Lord
give his blessing with it. In vain is the watchfulness
of the watchman, unless the Lord keep the city; or
the industry of the builder, unless the Lord co-operate.
With all his rapidity, the swift may fail in the race, because he either applies it too early or too late. With
all his ability, the merchant may miscalculate, and fail,
notwithstanding all his prudence. Strength alone is
not sufficient to secure victory in the combat, nor does

expertness in anything render the individual acceptable.

Success belongs to a jurisdiction which receives no
laws from princes, since they are themselves the subjects of that which men call time and chance; but we
Christians, ' Divine Providence.'   Be careful for nothing, and know at least that it is of no avail.   The case is
the same with spiritual things, and in a still greater degree.   The Lord bless thee! Thou art then blessed indeed.

The real cause of blessing is Christ crucified—his
priesthood—and, primarily, his expiring on the cross.
The blessing had departed from us, and it was necessary to regain it for us.   The curse had come upon us,
and must be removed.   Both were too great and too
difficult for us to accomplish.   The price was such, that
we should never have been able to procure it.   God
then sent his Son into the world.   He came attired in
such a manner that no one regarded him for what he
really was but he to whom the Father revealed it.   A
simple son of man, in fashion as other men, few only
beheld his glory, the glory of the only begotten Son of
the Father, full of grace and truth.   In the form of a
servant, it was easy to take him for any thing else than
the Lord from heaven.   And what was the end of him ?
He died in the flower of his years—died without having
apparently accomplished any thing—died in the most
wretched, painful, and ignominious manner, as a condemned malefactor, as a defamer of Divine and human
majesty, and was buried.   What shall we say to these
things?   The disciples knew not what to say, and wept.
The Jews thought they understood it.   " If he were

not a malefactor; if there were any truth in the thing; if it were only half true what he affirmed as entirely so with an oath, that he was the Son of God; he could not possibly have been crucified." But a mystery lay, and lies, in the whole affair—a mystery that was hidden from the beginning of the world; but which is revealed to us by the Apostles; a mystery which was unknown to the rulers of this world; a wisdom of God with them that are perfect; in one word, the mystery of the cross of Christ. And what mystery is that? Paul declares it in Gal. iii. 13, when he says, ' Christ hath redeemed us from the curse of the law, by becoming a curse for us, which is proved by the manner of his death; for it is written, Cursed is every one that hangeth on a tree.' And Christ hung upon the tree, that we might receive the blessing already promised to Abraham. Jesus is therefore, by virtue of his death, the true high priest, who pronounces the blessing upon us; from Him we must seek it, even as Jacob did.

But what are the means for obtaining the blessing? Not works. If you seek it thus, you will nevertheless continue under the curse; (Gal. iii. 10) and though you torment yourselves day and night, you will advance no further. Jacob had also wrestled mightily; and such must be the case, and it must be continued with all earnestness, as long as we are able to accomplish anything. At length we are obliged to stand still. Jacob had at last no alternative, after his thigh was put out of joint, than passively to cast himself upon the neck of the Son of God; and then only it was that ' he blessed him there.'

By faith, says Paul elsewhere, we are to receive the
promised Spirit; and calls the Galatians, who had understood it otherwise, foolish and bewitched. Read the
chapter in which this occurs—yea, the whole Epistle;
but do it as a humble scholar, do it with a prayerful
looking unto the Lord, that you may learn from himself the true method of becoming a partaker of his blessing; for our own reason will be here of no avail, but
the sentiment conveyed in the words, 'I thank thee,
Father, that thou hast hid these things from the wise
and prudent, and hast revealed them unto babes.'

We need say little respecting the necessity of this
blessing. It might be imagined, that every one would
clearly perceive it. Or are ye the people, who, after
having sown or planted any thing, can yourselves
cause it to spring up and increase? Or are there
princes anywhere, to whom we may apply, in order to
obtain sunshine, rain, or healthy seasons? Are you
yourselves the wise, and able, and powerful people on
whom the direction of success and the seasons depends?
If so, we will confess that you are little gods. Can
you impart to yourselves the impulse to all that is good,
and hatred to all that is evil? Are you able to expel
from yourselves sin, self-love, envy, self-interest, and
unbelief? Can you render yourselves meek, humble,
benevolent, patient, heavenly minded? If so, we must
confess that you are really the whole that need not a
physician, and the righteous, who require no repentance; confess that you have some other progenitor
than Adam the sinner, and that consequently you can
reasonably do without the second Adam; that Paul's

assertion, that 'there is no difference, for all have sinned, and come short of the glory of God,' does not extend to you; and that you make an unheard-of exception. As for us, we believe that it is God who worketh in us both to will and to do; that we are not sufficient as of ourselves to think anything good, but that our sufficiency is of God; are of opinion that it is the work of God, when we believe on the name of the Son of God; and think that Jesus is quite in the right, when he says, 'Ye are not able to make a single hair either white or black.'

When we call ourselves sinners, we do so because we really know not by what other term to designate ourselves, and thus nothing is left us but to have recourse to Him, on whose neck Jacob hung; and to declare with him, 'I will not let thee go, unless thou bless me!' Do you know any better way? God himself said, 'I know of none.'

Finally, we have still to remark the possibility of obtaining this blessing, and the certainty of it for all who are of Abraham's faith. 'Seek, and ye shall find.' This cannot be said with so much certainty of earthly blessings, otherwise we should have a greater number of rich people. But with respect to this blessing, we are empowered by supreme authority, even by the King of kings, to assert that he that seeketh findeth. Let him therefore, who esteems it a matter of importance, betake himself to the search; and let him who is seeking it, say with Jacob, 'I will not let thee go, except thou bless me.' Of this, therefore, we have still to speak: but this we will leave till another time.

See to it, therefore, that ye receive not the grace of
God in vain. There is something terrible in the words,
' He refused the blessing, and chose the curse, therefore
it shall come upon him.' Terrible are the words which
are spoken of every transgressor of the law: 'Let him
be accursed.' ' This people that knoweth not the law
is accursed.'

Beware of esteeming earthly blessings too highly,
and spiritual ones too meanly; and know that you
have long lain under the curse, unless you believe in
Jesus Christ. See to it betimes, that the sentence of
death and damnation already pronounced upon you be
not executed, and that by the mediation of Christ it be
transformed into a sentence of justification unto life.
What will otherwise become of you? Wrestle for the
blessing like Jacob, with all your strength, and with all
your energy. Say, I must and will know how it stands
with reference to my soul's salvation; otherwise I will
not rest. You will never repent the labor, although it
may be painful to you, even as Jacob also experienced
labor and pain. But how glorious was the result; when
it is said, ' He blessed him there.' How happy you will
esteem yourselves; with what thankfulness and joy you
will point out the hour, the opportunity, the place,
where you will be assured of the blessing, become partakers of it, and be translated from the kingdom of lies
into the kingdom of truth, and yourselves experience its
wonders! The Lord will then remain with you, and
guide you safely through the wilderness, until at length
you are present with the Lord. Amen.

SERMON V.

GENESIS xxxii. 26.

'And he said, Let me go, for the day breaketh. And he said, I will not let thee go, except thou bless me.

On a recent occasion, we considered the former part of the subject contained in the words of our text. We have still to meditate upon the conduct of Jacob expressed in the words, 'I will not let thee go, except thou bless me.'

This blessing comprises in it, generally speaking, the appropriation of the salvation purchased by Christ, from its first scarcely perceptible commencement in the individual, to its completion in heaven; from the first inclination of the will towards God and his truth, to the standing before the throne of the Lamb; from the anxious inquiry, 'What must I do to be saved?' to the being satisfied with Divine felicity as with a stream; in which appropriation there is a commencement, a continuation, and a completion observable.

Jacob expresses a strong and ardent desire for this blessing. He does not however mean its first beginnings; for he had no doubt of the favor of God, of the forgiveness of his sins, and that the renewing of the Divine image had already been commenced in him. He had no doubt of the validity of the blessing received from his father, although not in an entirely correct manner; since not only his father, but God himself, had confirmed it. He had not the smallest hesitation with regard to the Divine sealing of the promise he had received, but appeals to it in the twelfth verse, with all boldness. He did not consider himself as one in whom the Lord had hitherto had no pleasure, but although entirely unworthy of it, as the favored object of his mercy and loving kindness, of which he had received the most visible and affecting proofs.

But still he was not satisfied. He longed to be blessed in a superior, more inward, and profound manner than before. And the Lord himself had excited this desire, this hunger, and this longing within him. The Lord had awakened in him the feeling of necessity for a superior blessing, for a more substantial impartation of grace. He had inflicted a deep wound upon him, not only outwardly but inwardly also, which rendered him desirous of being healed. He could no longer exist in the manner he had done hitherto, nor be any longer satisfied with his state of grace. He wished for more. From being Jacob, he desired to become Israel. The eagle felt its wings and wished to soar aloft with with them. It was with him as with the grain of wheat in the lap of earth, whose germ bursts the husk, and springs forth. He felt as though what had been said to his grandfather Abraham, had been also said to him: ' Walk before me, and be thou perfect; for I will make a covenant between me and thee.' From being a youth he wished to become a man.

When a soul is called from an inferior to a higher

state of grace, and to a more perfect faith, and when Christ is to be more completely formed in the soul, a certain pressure precedes it. This was also the case with Jacob; and the Lord employed a variety of means to produce in him this necessity for and craving after a superior communication of grace and blessing. He first gave him the command to return to the land of Canaan, where his father dwelt, and also his brother Esau, and gradually conducted him to the scene of conflict where we have hitherto contemplated him, and where wonderful but glorious things occurred to him. In Mesopotamia he had no reason to trouble himself about his brother's fury, although he had something to suffer from the convetousness of his father-in-law; but now he himself, with all that was dear and valuable to him, was at stake, and he was cast, as it were, to the lions. It was not his own choice; for this would have been fool-hardy, and he would have been unable, in this case, to have made God his confident. It was the Lord's own guidance. To this Jacob appeals in the ninth verse, ' Thou saidst unto me, Return unto thy country.' The Lord had also promised him, saying, ' Behold, I am with thee, and will keep thee in all places whither thou goest.' (ch. xxviii. 15.) His own reason and his own will would have been no good guide, nor do they lead any one aright. Hence the promise is, ' I will guide thee with mine eye;' ' I will lead thee into the wilderness, and speak comfortably unto thee.' (Hosea ii. 14.) Hence David prays, ' Let thy good Spirit lead me on a plain path;' and again, ' Turn from me every false way, and grant me thy statutes.'

However, Jacob was not enabled to conduct himself under these circumstances, on approaching his brother, in a manner consistent with the promises he had received. By the Lord's wise permission, a dreadful fear of his enraged brother takes possession of his soul, and under its influence he acts, in some respects, too much like a natural man; but in others, in an exemplary manner. The feeling of fear was not only painful in itself, but one might have supposed it could not have seized such a man as Jacob. Doubtless he himself regarded it as something unbecoming, improper, and even absurd, and for which there was no cause, and by giving way to which he might act derogatorily to the faithfulness, power, and promise of the Lord. But these · considerations were insufficient to tranquilize him; his reason looked too much at that which was seen, and too little at that which is invisible —too much upon Esau, too little upon God; and he could not divest himself of it. And what was the result ?—a struggle, and the desire that the Son would make him free. Until he obtained this, he acted with too much human prudence. Hence his humble message to his brother. Hence his submissive and excessive courteousness, in commanding Esau to be always called his Lord, but himself his servant ; hence the prudent division of his family and his flocks into two parts, in order to save at least one of them ; hence the placing the present intended for him in the first rank, and the instructing all his domestics to address Esau in a highly complimentary manner. He did everything to rid himself of his fear, and yet it is said, ' Jacob was greatly afraid and distressed.' . And certainly, it was not for him to deliver himself from it ; this honor belongs to the Son of God alone. Jacob's anxiety was doubtless rendered still more painful by the reproaches of his enlightened understanding on account of it, which prescribed an entirely different line of conduct to him, and a deportment consistent with the many proofs of Divine favor which he had received, and which were similar to those expressed by David in Psalm xci. : 'Though a thousand should fall at thy side, and ten thousand at thy right hand, yet it shall not come nigh thee. Only with thine eyes shalt thou behold and see the reward of the wicked. No evil shall befall thee, neither shall any plague come nigh thy dwelling, for he hath given his angels charge over thee to keep thee in all thy ways.' How much had Jacob in his favor!—his father's blessing, which God himself had confirmed ; the remarkable vision of the heavenly ladder during his flight ; and the glorious promise of the blessing, which should extend itself to all nations through the medium of his posterity.

The many temporal blessings which the Lord had bestowed upon him in such a visible manner, during his residence with Laban ; the express command to return, with the promise of protection ; the wonderful change produced in Laban, who, notwithstanding his furious rage, was not permitted to speak an unkind word to him ; the meeting of a host of protecting angels at Mahanaim ; and yet to be the subject of fear—of such great fear—was evidently not right, was a proof that Jacob did not yet possess a perfect faith ; that he had

not apprehended this golden chain of promises as he
ought. There were promises enough, but not sufficient
faith. 'He that feareth,' says John, 1 Ep. iv. 18, 'is
not made perfect in love. Fear hath torment; but per-
feet love casteth out fear.' Perfect faith does not make
haste, nor does it flee, through fear. He that can say
with the Psalmist, 'God is my refuge and strength'—
can also say, 'Therefore will we not fear, though the
earth be removed, and though the mountains be carried
into the midst of the sea.' But Jacob had not yet attained this standing; we must beware, however, of
supposing that perhaps only a single saint in a century
attains to it, and that it cannot be attained by others
because we ourselves have not yet arrived at it. For
such thoughts are base, derogatory to God and his
grace, and resting-places for the flesh.

Jacob was conscious that his faith was not in accordance with the promise. All his prudent measures were
unable in the smallest degree to expel his fear, which
laughed, like Job's leviathan, at the shaking of the
spear. All his endeavors to compose and tranquilize
his mind were fruitless, and only increased his fear and
disturbance, instead of lessening it. O happy failure of
his own, self-potent striving to help and amend himself!
Happy is he whose own strength, wisdom, and righteousness is dislocated in the struggle, and who has no
other alternative than to cast himself entirely into the
arms of Jesus!

Thus it fared with Jacob. His distressing condition
outwardly, and his still greater inward distress, which
he was unable of himself to remove, compelled him to

have recourse to the Lord by prayer; in which he un-
folds the state of his mind, and candidly confesses that
he was afraid of his brother Esau. At the same time
he intreats a superior communication of grace. Perhaps it was more in the manner of groanings which cannot be uttered, than of clearly experienced and plainly
expressed requests—a moaning of the new creature—
which against its will lay in bondage to vanity—after
the glorious liberty of the children of God; a longing
after something better, of which he could not himself
form any clear conception.

But He who searcheth the heart, well knew what
was the mind of the Spirit. He himself had implanted
in him this superior hunger after righteousness, and
produced this urgency of spirit in him. Even as the
hart panteth after the water-brooks, so his soul panted
after God. His soul thirsted for God, for the living God,
that he might come and appear before God, to see his
power and his glory, so as he had seen it in the sanctuary. His heart would have been delighted to have
been able to praise the Lord with joyful lips. He
sought retirement. He prayed and wept, as Hosea
says; he could not properly say what he required; it
was not merely fear, but also its peculiar source, of
which he wished to be divested. His heart, not yet
established in perfect faith, and still unable properly to
apprehend God in his promises, travailed, as it were, in
the spiritual birth—as the Savior says—by which
something new was to be produced in the soul.

But it was only after the Lord had laid hold of him
in such a manner, that his travail really commenced.

8*

The Lord himself struggled with him. His sin and unworthiness was deeply unfolded to him; but at the same time his cleaving to the Lord, and his craving for a blessing, became so urgent that he could not refrain, whatever might be the result. Although in the most wretched plight, and deprived of all strength, he still exclaimed, "I will not let thee go, except thou bless me? I cannot possibly let thee go without it; I will and must have a special blessing."

The Lord was also willing to impart it, and he therefore prepared him for it, by depriving him of every other support, that the Lord himself might be his rod and his staff. He divested him of all strength, that he might find it in the Son of God alone. It was necessary that he should feel the impossibility of expelling fear, notwithstanding the Divine promise which had been given, and likewise that he might seek and expect the changing of his heart, the pacifying of his soul, and everything else from the Lord alone. He decreased, and Christ increased; he became little and nothing, that the Lord might be great, might be all; thus on his dying-bed he was able to confess and say, ' He hath redeemed me from all evil,' and not I myself; even as he expressed his whole inward state in the words, ' O Lord, I wait for thy salvation!'

In a similar manner the Lord has acted towards others, to whom he intended to manifest his glory more fully. Take, for example, the disciples. The Lord had still much to say to them, but they could not then bear it, they were not able to apprehend it. It would have appeared irrational to them; they could not have received it; the Savior therefore was wisely silent, and **had** patience, until the Spirit should come and lead them into all truth. But what took place in their souls before this more glorious manifestation of Christ? The Lord himself hints at it in John xvi. 21, where he says, 'A woman, when she is in travail, hath sorrow, because her hour is come; but as soon as she is delivered of the child, she remembereth no more the anguish, for joy that a man is born into the world. And ye now, therefore, have sorrow; but I will see you again, and your heart shall rejoice, and your joy no man taketh from you.' And Paul says to the Galatians, 'My little children, of whom I travail in birth again, until Christ be formed in you.' The disciples, in consequence of the sufferings of Jesus, were themselves plunged into profound and unwonted suffering. The entire edifice of their hopes was overthrown, and nothing remained but the foundation which God himself had laid in them. But the other foundation of sinful nature also manifested itself in them, in a manner they could not have believed. They had long indeed regarded themselves as sinners; but at the same time, as far better men than they were now obliged to acknowledge. They were offended at Jesus, who had, nevertheless, pronounced him blessed who should not be offended in him; they were offended at Jesus, although they had regarded it as impossible; and therefore pertinaciously contradicted him, when he told them beforehand, that such would be the case. "That will never happen," answered they, "we are too much devoted to thee." But when put to the test, they all forsook him, and endeavored to keep it a secret that they had ever been his disciples; they

were afraid of their Esau-brethen, and apprehensive lest
their mother's children should smite them; nay, they
even began to consider their hope, that Jesus would deliver Israel, as groundless, and to suppose that the Jews
had succeeded in their devices against him to an extent he had not anticipated.

All this took place in their old man, in their natural
heart and understanding. . But what was the new man
doing meanwhile ? It mourned and wept, as Jesus
had predicted; it travailed in birth, but there was no
strength to bring forth. It would gladly have elevated
itself to a higher degree of faith; but both the requisite
power and light were wanting for this purpose. They
mourned and wept in the distress and anxiety of their
hearts, and were like a ship upon the stormy sea,
tossed hither and thither by the waves, without an anchor, and without any harbor in sight. There was an
end to the cause of Jesus, and to them along with it.
. A man wrestled with them, to drive them from the
spot, and to confuse them with respect to God, to Jesus,
to the kingdom of God, to all the promises, and to
themselves. The Bridegroom was taken away from
them, and the time to fast had arrived. But what followed ? A superior manifestation of the glory of
Christ; a view which they had not previously possessed; a faith, of which they were before ignorant;
a knowledge of the Scriptures, of which they had till
then been deficient; a humility and a confidence, a
resignation and a wisdom, to which they had before
been utter strangers.

'I have chosen thee in the furnace of affliction,' says

the Lord, by the prophet (Isa. xlviii. 10.) He who desires to be raised with Christ, must first be taken captive with him in the garden of Gethsemane; bound round about with grief, so that he cannot move, that he may be absolved before a Divine and human tribunal; be condemned by the law and his conscience, that he may be pronounced righteous; and be crucified and slain, in order that he may live unto God. True felicity does not consist in words, but in the fruits of repentance and faith; in the essential experience both of sin and faith; of self and the living God. Such is also the experience of all those Christians who are predestinated and called to become conformed to the Son of God. After they have passed through the first stage of repentance—after entering through the narrow gate into the kingdom of God—after being joyfully assured of the forgiveness of sins, and believing in Christ and his grace—much is given them to enjoy. The Bridegroom is with the children of the bride chamber; therefore how can they mourn? A beautiful robe is put upon them, and shoes on their feet; a feast is prepared, and singing and dancing are heard. Their assurance of their state of grace is firm; their joy is heartfelt; and they say to others also, ' Come hither, ye that seek God;' they feel a power which induces them to use the confident language of Paul, ' In all these things we are more than conquerors, through him that hath loved us;' a courage which shuns no reproach of the world, no suffering, no death, no devil; a heavenly-mindedness, which feels a disgust at all that is vain; a relish for reading the Scriptures, that induces them to break off many an hour even from sleep; a delight in prayer, so that hours fly like moments, and they leave it with regret; a communication of grace, which their mortal tabernacle is scarcely able to endure; a readiness to suffer, which makes them willing to beg their bread, and to give all they have to the poor; a disgust at sin, which borders upon indignation; a facility in every good work, which causes them heartily to recommend the yoke of Christ as easy and his burden as light. O how happy do they then feel! They think they must tell it to every one, that others may also set out in quest of such a felicity; they desire that all should possess it, and even torment the still unconverted members of their households with unceasing persuasions to be converted: just as if it were the work of man; and they exclaim, 'Ho, all the world, come hither! here ye may see that God is gracious without any merit of your own!' If experienced Christians put in a word, and tell them that a change will take place with them, they cannot believe it. But how should they fast, as long as the Bridegroom is with them? Rather call unto them, and say, 'Rejoice, thy King cometh!' The Lord, by his only-begotten Son, has caused their mountain to stand strong. They say, We shall never be afraid; but when He hides his face they are troubled. This is, as it were, the welcome on entering the kingdom of God. Like the children of Israel, after their departure from Egypt, and their passage through the Red Sea, they come to Elim, with its twelve fountains of water, and its seventy palm trees, and encamp there. But from thence the whole congregation removes into the desert, which leads them to Sinai (Exod. xvi.) The refreshing seasons decline, and often intermit with times of great barrenness. The individual at one time feels great strength, and finds himself at another in the most deplorable impotency. At one time he possesses great courage, and at another the same degree of timidity; at one time he can call Jesus his, and at another not; at one time he feels himself very able to make a sacred surrender of himself, and at another by no means disposed for it. He at length becomes extremely weary of this continual vicissitude, and inquires if it be impossible for the heart to be established; if only a Paul could say, ' I know in whom I have believed,' and am persuaded and assured; if that faith be unattainable which the Apostle describes as the ' substance of things hoped for, the evidence of things not seen;' if we ought not in the present day, according to the rule laid down by the Apostle John, to believe the love which God has towards us in Christ, and experience that fear is not in love, and must be expelled by the latter; and if we may have boldness even in the day of judgment: and then he asks, " Shall I only be unable to attain to it, seeing that with God nothing is impossible, although in myself I am incompetent to any thing that is good, and inclined to all that is evil? Is that state of grace, described by the Apostle, no longer attainable in the present day, in which the individual is free from an evil conscience, and is able to come boldly to a throne of grace; and where he speaks of a rest in God, and a cleaving to the Lord, by means of which we become one Spirit with him ?" In short, he is compelled to believe that there is something higher, more glorious, and blissful in religion, than what he, or even others, have yet experienced; and he feels within him an ardent longing after this substantial and permanent state, although he sees and acknowledges himself unworthy of it; although it rests with the Lord's free-grace whether he be pleased to lead him out of his present straitened and contracted position into greater liberty; and he counts those elect souls particularly happy, who through grace have attained to it; from whence he learns to believe, that the most honor is frequently put upon those members which are thought to be less honorable, and that no one has reason to despair on account of his unworthiness, because the reward is not of works, but of grace.

Those souls, which in an especial manner hunger and thirst after righteousness, and to whom the promise is given that they shall be satisfied, experience a disgust, a certain dissatisfaction with their former standing in godliness; and in all their good exercises, they feel much poverty, and can no longer continue them in their customary manner; they see too clearly the self-love and self-righteousness which intermingle themselves in every thing; they detest their own working, although they cannot yet give it up; they also perceive that pleasing feelings do not constitute the essential part of religion. They languish until the Son makes them truly free, till salvation shall come upon Israel out of Zion, and the Lord deliver his captive people. The man here obtains a much deeper insight into the corruption and depravity of his own heart, into that dreadful self-love and self-righteousness which pervades us, into the amazing unbelief in which we are immersed, and is compelled to consider all that proceeds from himself as a mere hindrance. The case is now the same with him as with Jacob, when his hip was out of joint, and when he was thus deprived of all ability to stand and to continue the combat; so that only the choice was left him either to fall helpless into the hands of his infuriated brother, or to cast himself upon the neck of his opponent. Nothing now remains for him but to place his hope and confidence entirely upon the Lord, and to say with Jacob, " I will not let thee go, except thou bless me—bless me with a superior light than has hitherto shone upon me, by which I may duly view thee, my Savior, as elevated upon the cross, with a stedfast peace, which shall keep my heart and mind in Christ Jesus instead of the constant mental disturbance I have hitherto experienced: with a complete faith, which receives out of thy fulness grace upon grace, and abides in thee as the branch in the vine; which affords an entire and constant assent to the work of redemption, and perseveres in it, so that I have a sure confidence that thou wilt bless me with such a real fellowship and intercourse with thee, as to enable me to pray without ceasing, offer thanks unto thee, and thus glorify thee."

Such is Jacob's prayer, ' I will not let thee go,'—a prayer to be used not only in the beginning, but also in the progress of the life of grace. Happy is he who employs it in both cases, and to whom light rises in darkness!

May the Lord bestow his blessing upon us all ; begin his work in those souls where it is not yet commenced ; and where it is already begun, carry it on until the dawning of the perfect day. May complete knowledge and faith, a perfect cure and perfect love, be, by grace, the lot of all of us ! Amen.

SERMON VI.

GENESIS XXXII. 27. ·

And he said unto him, What is thy name? And he said,
Jacob.

JACOB had assured the Lord, that he would not let him
go, without first receiving his blessing; and, in the
words of our text, we find the preparation for the reception of that which he desired. The Lord's sole intention was to impart to the Patriarch a superior blessing to anything he had previously enjoyed. But observe what a singular way he takes for this purpose.
It seems as if he intended his entire ruin—nay, it not
only seems so, but is so in reality. Jacob is driven
more and more into straits. He is afraid of Esau, and
the promises he has received, no longer serve to tranquilize his mind. In this way, many an individual
miscalculates, upon whom the promises are impressed
in a particularly lively manner. He looks upon them
as a capital, upon which he can draw in the season of
distress, and carefully notes them down, in order to refresh and encourage himself with them when he requires it. But the manna thus laid up, refuses to perform its office. The word, indeed, continues the same;
but, as the Spirit is not with it, it produces no more
effect than in the case of Jacob, who was afraid notwithstanding; and this is likewise productive of good.

In the most pitiable situation, and whilst hanging on the neck of his opponent, his desire for a superior blessing is increased ; and it is then suggested to him, to let *him* go, who can alone bestow it. Thus it may also seem, as if Jesus did not trouble himself about the grief of soul which the individual experiences, and it seems as if he would be suffered to remain in it. But the Lord's intention is to make the man thoroughly acquainted with the real source from whence every blessing flows, deeply to convince him of the insufficiency of all self amendment, and to heal him of it.

Jacob now implores a blessing, but he does not receive it instantaneously ; for the Lord enters into a conversation with him, which causes delay. Pious souls must also be satisfied to wait in like manner. They easily suppose, that when they have prayed once or a few times, with earnestness and fervor, for some particular blessing, it must immediately be bestowed, or else they become apprehensive that their prayer is not of the right kind, and their state of grace uncertain. But, friend, though thou knowest it not, thou art perhaps not yet poor—not yet humbled enough. Look at Jacob ! When does he conquer ? When is he blest ? Only when his hip is dislocated, and no more strength is left him. Probably the Lord intends by it 'that thou mayest remember, and be confounded, and never open thy mouth any more, because of thy shame, when he is pacified toward thee for all that thou hast done.' Thou must, therefore, force thyself to be content, whether thou wilt or not.

'And he said unto him, What is thy name ?' Who

was it that asked the question ? It is remarkable, that in 1 Kings xviii. 31, it is said, that 'the word of the Lord' uttered this. We call this remarkable, because John, as is well known, calls the Son of God, our Lord Jesus Christ, by this appellation. We are, however, already acquainted with the inquirer.

He asks the name of the Patriarch—not from ignorance, as if he knew not his name, since he had known and loved him from everlasting, and by his providence had so arranged it, that this name should be given him; and he put the question for Jacob's sake, in order to instruct him respecting the signification of his name, and to induce him to reflect upon the occasion of its being given him; which was, that at his birth, he held his twin brother Esau by the heel. His birth reminded him of the word of the Lord, which had been spoken to his mother—'The elder shall serve the younger;' which Rebecca had certainly not concealed from him, but had probably made the chief inducement for him to consent to the surreptitious mode of obtaining the blessing in preference to his brother Esau. But if Jacob had forgotten, the Lord was not unmindful of it; if Jacob could not cleave firmly to it, the Lord held himself bound by it: 'For the mountains may depart, and the hills be removed; but my kindness shall not depart from thee, neither shall the covenant of my peace be removed.'

The Patriarch was to derive encouragement also from the signification of his name. It means a supplanter. Hence his brother said of him, after he had deprived him of his father's blessing, ' Is not he rightly named Jacob, for he hath supplanted me these two times. He took away my birthright, and behold now he hath taken away my blessing.' (Gen. xxvii. 36.) This name ought therefore to have imparted courage and confidence to the Patriarch, that Esau would not overcome him. But when we are in difficulties and darkness, what do we think of? Chiefly of that only which is calculated to increase them—the law and its threatenings; and if we call the promises to mind, they . take no effect, however sweet they may have been to us.

Jacob might also think thus with himself: "How canst thou derive encouragement from thy name, which chance and human choice has given thee? If God himself had ordered thee to be called so, the case would have been different." Thus many act also with the promises. They think that they only accidentally occur to them; that they have read or heard them somewhere, or learnt them by heart. But it would be strange, and at the same time a loss to the diligent readers of the Scriptures, if they were not at liberty to derive benefit from those promises, with which they are already acquainted. David acted otherwise. He ·pleaded the Lord's word with him, and then expected, in a prayerful frame, its fulfilment. But why should promises be suggested to us, if we are not enabled, at the same time, duly to act upon them?

Jacob perhaps also thought, "Why this question? I ask for a blessing, and he inquires my name. I should have preferred no such delay, but the immediate fulfilment of the desire of my heart!" But he was never-

9*

theless obliged to consent to, it. God does all things well in due time, and this must be waited for, however inconvenient it may be. Mary said, ' They have no wine;' and received for answer, 'My hour is not yet come.' Strange arrangements are then made; wine is wanted, and large vessels are filled with water; but in the end, wine is furnished of the best quality. It often goes to great lengths, before a very favorable result. The sick daughter of Jairus dies before Jesus affords his aid. Lazarus not only dies but putrefies, before it is manifest that his sickness was not unto death. The individual imagines that his help is arrived, and begins to sing hymns of praise; but whilst supposing that the path will now lead to the right, his guide turns to the left, until he at length learns to let himself be led, without seeing before him, or caring whether the pillar of cloud and of fire goes forward or rests.

' What is thy name?' Was the Lord ignorant of it? and if not, why did he ask, and appear as if he knew it, not? We may well ask, " Why does the Lord often seem to renounce his own attributes, and suffer us to pray and cry as though he heard us not; even as the Syrophœnician woman cried long before a sound was given her in reply? But how does this agree with his promise in Psalm i. 15: ' Call upon me in the day of trouble; I will deliver thee.' And that in Isaiah lxv. 24; ' Before they call I will answer.' If he is so full of mercy and compassion, why does he exercise many with the severest sufferings, and heed neither cries nor tears? If his ability is so great and his strength so inexhaustible, why does his church still find reason to

complain : ' O thou, the hope of Israel, the Savior thereof in time of trouble, why. art thou as a stranger in the
land, and as one that tarrieth but for a night ?. Why
art thou as a man astonished, and as a strong man that
cannot help ? Yet thou, Lord, art in the midst of us
and thy name is invoked by us.' (Jer. xiv. 8, 9.)
David prays, ' Look upon my affliction,' as if the Lord
did not sympathize in it. The being placed in such
circumstances may well occasion grievous pain, and yet
they are certainly not without excellent fruit, though it
be sown in tears. · Although the Lord may act as a
stranger for a time, yet we must not let this surprise
us ; for he has the best intentions towards us.

' My name is Jacob,' answered the Patriarch, in the
simplicity of his heart. How simple and childlike may
we converse with Jesus Christ, our Lord and Friend ;
particularly under the New Testament dispensation, in
which, not a servile, but a filial spirit reigns, whereby
we cry, Abba, Father ! There is nothing that we are
not permitted to tell him and complain of ; nor need
they be always matters of importance—they may be
also trifling things, for a mother listens gladly to the
lisping of her children. How wisely we act, when we
apply to him under every circumstance, and say to him,
in few words or in many, " I am at a loss ; I need advice ; what shall I do ? how shall I act in the most
proper manner ?' This might well be called holding
converse with the Lord ; habituating ourselves to him.

' My name is Jacob.' If the Lord knew the name of
Cyrus, the heathen king, and named him a century
and a half before his birth, how much more may we

believe that he knows his children according to their
names, residences, situation, necessities, and circumstances.   If he has numbered the hairs of their heads,
shall he leave more important matters unnoticed?

When Jacob told him his name, a new light probably rose upon it, that rendered its signification clear to
him in a pleasing manner, and strengthened his faith.
For it often requires only a little word to shed light and
peace in the soul, and whole sermons may be heard,
whole volumes read, and yet the individual may continue unedified, as the Lord pleases.   Many a one is
childish enough to think, 'If I had but heard this
sooner; if it had only occurred to me sooner.'   But
when the time arrives, the help we previously sought in
vain, comes also.   Jacob now found an encouragement
in his name, which he had not perceived before; and
thence saw likewise, that in our gloomy hours, everything is hid from us, which might have encouraged,
and which was otherwise so clear as to be almost tangible to us.   We then foolishly imagine we shall never
doubt or despond again.   But what have we left, when
he hides his face?   The lamp of our souls burns only as
long as the heavenly householder feeds it with oil.
We cannot ascribe anything to ourselves; all that is
good remains the Lord's property, over which he retains
the right of disposal.   According to Heb. viii. 3, he is
a minister of the true sanctuary.   No man can receive
anything, except it be given him from heaven.   'So
God ascended from Jacob,' it is said in ch. xxxvi. 13,
and did not suffer himself to be detained.   To this we
gradually accustom ourselves, and are only glad that

the Lord is that he is, however much he may change ;
nay, in the end we perceive that we are in no respect
more, when adorned with his gifts, or less when he
withdraws them from us.

'My name is Jacob,' said the Patriarch. His parents
had given him this name at his circumcision, and whatever it might signify, it reminded him of the covenant
of grace, of which circumcision was the seal, and
the substance of which was the promise, 'I am thy
God.' In this respect, we enjoy the same privilege
with Jacob. The names which were given us at our
baptism, are to us this seal of the new covenant, which
rests upon far more excellent promises. An ambassador
in Christ's stead has named us, and sealed the new covenant to us in the name of the Father, the Son and the
Holy Ghost. What more do we require or wish for ?
What bold claims we may found upon God even from
our names, since they remind us of the covenant which
God, for Christ's sake has established with us. We are
sinners it is true ; but it is also true, that Christ is willing to wash us with his blood and Spirit from all our sins,
and renew our natures after his image. But certainly it
is a great insult for a person to bear the name and yet disregard the covenant. Happy is he whom God brings into such straits, amd presses so closely, that he is glad to
take refuge in the covenant of grace, and seek the real
communication of the glorious blessings which are promised him by it. Lo ! God is willing to be thy Father,
and thou shalt be his child. All that the Son of God
has purchased by his sufferings and death, shall be thy
own. The Holy Spirit shall be thy teacher and comfort-

er. How is it possible, therefore, that thy salvation should not be perfect, since the sacred Trinity itself has undertaken its accomplishment? Be ashamed of thy unbelief.

Jacob doubtless also felt a sacred confusion, when reflecting on the uncommon condescension of God, in entering into such a glorious alliance with such a worm, in which he in reality requires nothing, although the contrary may seem to be the case—and is willing to to give everything; and when he says, ' Walk before me and be thou perfect, he first directs the eye of faith to himself as the all sufficient God. He is willing to care for us, to cleanse us from our sins, and to instruct and comfort us. We therefore need only keep our minds in a tranquil frame; and even if we are incapable of doing so, he will also bestow this upon us. We are encouraged to cast all our care upon him, and if we cannot rid ourselves of care, we are permitted to inquire and say, ' How long shall I take counsel in my soul, having sorrow in my heart daily? How long shall my enemy be exalted over me?' (Psalm xiii. 2.) ' Ask of me,' says the Lord, ' and I will give thee the heathen for an inheritance, and the uttermost parts of the earth for a possession.' (Psalm ii. 8.) What a gracious alliance is this, in which everything is promised! Well may it be said, ' I am not worthy of all the mercy and the faithfulness thou hast manifested towards me.' Who does not feel a desire to enter into such a precious covenant, in which it is said, ' Blessed are the poor, for theirs is the kingdom of heaven! Blessed are they that do hunger and thirst after righteousness, for they shall be filled; and in which only the rich and those that are full have

no part.   When this is duly perceived, it. plunges us
into the sweetest confusion, and excites a gratitude of a
very peculiar kind.   'For I saw thee lying in thy
blood, and said unto thee, Live!'   Wonderful mercy!

Jacob felt also a sacred confusion at his timidity.
"What," he would think, "if God be for us, who can
be against us!   If Esau had four thousand men instead
of four hundred, what could he do to me?   God himself has been unable to prevail against me, because his
omnipotence could not act otherwise than in accordance with his promise, 'I will do thee good.'   "O,"
he would think, "how little do I know him—how little
do I still apprehend of him!   What am I without his
light, but darkness itself—without his grace, but weakness itself?   And what am I in him?   I have all and
enough!"   How he would finally feel, when he reflected and thought, "who gave me courage for the conflict, and strength to persevere?"   How wise was the
whole mode of treatment!   Truly he might well call
the place a Peniel.   And humble souls still experience
things of a similar nature.

"My name is Jacob," said the Patriarch.   And
what are we called?   Our names are, in some respects, very disgraceful, and in others very consolatory
and even glorious.

Our names sound very disgraceful; and because they
are given us by the true and faithful word, we cannot
deny their correctness, without making the true God a
liar; and what a horrible sin would that be?   But
what are we called?   Oh, we might adduce a long
catalogue of such evil names: we are reproved as be-

ing unrighteous sinners, ungodly backsliders, and diso-
bedient; and many other such evil titles are applied
to us.

What shall we do in this case? Deny them? This
would be only rendering them still more heinous.
Caring not for them will also not avail; for those
names carry all of them their sentence along with them.
We ought not to be indifferent to them, but they ought
to produce in us a troubled spirit, and to render us humble and contrite in heart; until we are induced to confess our transgressions to the Lord, justify him in oppo-
sitiou to ourselves, and confess that we are what these
names indicate, and nothing else. He is then faithful,
and will strengthen us, and preserve us from the evil
one. But ah! how much is requisite before we attain
to this. How many attempts are usually made, in order
that we may deserve the appellation of pious, and what
distress and sorrow it occasions when we do not succeed! We strive to rid ourselves of our sins by praying, struggling, and distressing ourselves. And such
attempts are the more useful, the more earnest they
are; for by them the individual learns to know himself
the more thoroughly, to seek his salvation in Christ the
more exclusively, and to believe, with the greater confidence on him who justifies the ungodly. But certain
it is, that if we wish to understand the name of Jesus,
we can do so in no other manner than by previously
becoming well acquainted with our own name of " Sinner." The more fully we assent to the latter, the more
inestimable will the name of Jesus be to us, who alone
can save the sinner.

When this name has once become truly precious to us, the consolatory names which are applied to us will also refresh us. And which are they? The name of sinner stands foremost here also, as a very consolatory appellation. But in what respect? If God himself calls us by this name, he proves by it that he expects nothing else from us, as of ourselves, but what is in accordance with this name, and thereby encourages us to present ourselves before him in our poverty and nakedness. And what promises are connected with it! so that in reality I need be nothing but a sinner to appropriate to myself the most glorious things; for the name of Jesus stands opposite to it, with the promise to save such characters; and this is a faithful saying. When this become apparent to the troubled mind, that which previously distressed it, will impart courage to it, and it will find in Jesus all that is sought for in vain in itself. If he saves sinners, they will certainly be saved, or else Jesus is no perfect Savior. The more, therefore, a person feels and knows himself to be a sinner, the greater confidence may he have that Jesus will save him from all his sin and misery.

How consolatory, in a certain sense, is the appellation of ungodly—for God pronounces them justified; of lost—for Jesus seeks such characters; of needy—for he will supply all their need; of afflicted—for he will comfort them; of captives—for he liberates them. In short, if we can only apprehend Jesus at the same time, all these names will only serve to encourage us. If Jesus therefore asks what we are called; and we can reply in simplicity, and with a full assent, that we are

sinners : a lovely light will rise upon us, even as upon
Jacob, on mentioning his name.   But if we resist, if
we seek to have a hand in saving ourselves, and
refuse to entrust ourselves solely to Jesus—we shall
find nothing but wretchedness and sorrow of heart in
our way.   But tne practice of this is not so easy as it
appears.   Only make the attempt, and you will find it
to be so   We are much too wise, proud, and righteous
in our own esteem, and many a stroke of the hammer of
the law is requisite, before the rock of our heart is broken

But those who, renouncing everything of their own,
seek everything in Jesus, bear at the same time more
glorious appellations, which are written in heaven.
One of the most excellent names which they bear, and
which comprises in it every other glory, and is perfectly Scriptural, is that of Christians.   We read that God
changed the names of Abraham and Sarah, by adding
to them a letter from his own name, Jehovah, by which
he received them into a degree of fellowship with his
glory.   But by our being called Christians, we are
placed in fellowship and relationship with Christ; and
this implies much.   With respect to ourselves, we are
sinners ; but in Christ we are righteous before God :
in ourselves we are weak ; but united with Christ we
are strong and invincible : in us we are wretched ; in
him we are happy and glorified.   But the mere ima-
gining the thing, is here of no avail—it must be truth
and reality.   What, therefore, is thy name ?   But art
thou that which thou callest thyself ?   If so, what
happiness is thine !   Christ must be dethroned, sooner
than anything evil can befall thee.   If the Lord is thy
shepherd, thou shalt not want.   Amen.

SERMON VII.

'No one is crowned, except he strive lawfully,' observes Paul, in writing to Timothy (2 Ep. ii. 5.) This he said in reference to the Grecian games. An individual might have used the greatest efforts in striving: yet if these were not in accordance with the rules and laws of the conflict, he did not obtain the prize, however much he excelled in other respects. Such is also the case in the spiritual course. Augustine says, 'Halting forward upon the right path brings us further than running out of it ;' and this expresses, in other words, the meaning of Paul. A person may strive against that which is evil ; he may use great exertion ; he may even seem to accomplish great things, and yet all be in vain, because his efforts are not in accordance with the rules of the spiritual conflict. 'I fight,' says the Apostle, 'not as one that beateth the air,' by which no man is wounded.

What should we expect to effect in natural things if we used improper weapons; and endeavored, for instance, to destroy bees with the sword; which is effected only by smoke: or if we did not use our weapons in a proper manner, and expected to wound our foes with the hilt, instead of the blade of the sword ? It is certain, that in the spiritual conflict, persons frequently act thus inconsistently, and therefore accomplish nothing in

reality, even when they appear to succeed, or else are
conscious that they do not really hit the enemy. And
are not the frequent complaints of the little which is
effected, and the slow progress which is made in the
spiritual course, all of them proofs that those who thus
complain do not strive in a regular manner? He that
does not, will not obtain the crown, as his own conscience already tells him. The enemy will always renew the challenge, and mock at him. He will perceive
that there is some cursed thing in him, in whatever it
may consist, and hence he cannot stand against his foe.
And this accursed thing is so deeply hidden, that the
man himself does not perceive it, until the Holy Spirit
reveals it to him, and shows him, at the same time,
wherein he is deficient, which is a great mercy, since it
is also connected with instruction how he ought to
fight, in order to gain one victory after another, and to
go from strength to strength. When Jesus calls his
yoke easy and his burden light, every complaint of religion being a wearisome thing only proves that we do
not rightly understand the taking upon ourselves his
yoke. And yet many seem to think more highly of
complaints of religion, than of thankfulness; and of
anxiety, than of peace. We betake ourselves to the
conflict, without considering whether it is advisable with
ten thousand men to oppose him who comes against us
with twenty thousand; and whether it be not more
prudent, either to make peace with him, while he is
still afar off; or, if that cannot be, to look about us betimes for a powerful ally. Jehoshaphat acted thus.
'In us,' said he, 'there is no strength; for we know

not what we ought to do.' But instead of desponding-
ly complaining, he adds, ' But our eyes look unto thee,
O Lord !'

Let us consider our combatant Jacob, and see whether
we can learn of him how to strive aright.

GENESIS XXXII. 28.

*And he said, Thy name shall be called no more Jacob, but
Israel ; for as a prince hast thou power with God and with
men, and hast prevailed.*

WE recently considered the question put by the Lord,
' What is thy name ?' and the direct reply of the Patriarch ; ' and he said, Jacob.' The Lord now gives
him a new name, and says, ' Thou shalt no longer be
called Jacob, but Israel,' and mentions the reason for
it ; ' for as a prince hast thou power with God and
with men, and hast prevailed.'

By names, we indicate persons and things, in order
to distinguish them from others. If the thing becomes
changed, it also receives another name. Water when
frozen, we term ice, snow, and hail ; when it falls from
heaven—rain ; when it descends at night upon the
plants—dew ; and when it dissolves into small particles
—mist.

Man, according to his age, receives the name of a
child, a youth, a man, and an old man. With reference to God and his kingdom, he is either a sinner, a
wicked man, or even a child of the devil and an enemy
of God ; or else he is an awakened person, a penitent,
a believer, a righteous man, a saint, a perfect man, a

10*

child and heir of God. Some true Christians are called children; some, young men; and others, fathers. Some are called carnal, others spiritual. The disciples, whilst Jesus was with them, could not bear many things of which they were afterwards susceptible; and until that time, Jesus was silent, though he told them of their limited state. Paul says to the Corinthians: "Hitherto ye were not able to bear it, neither yet now are ye able. I could not speak unto you as unto spiritual; but as unto babes in Christ. I have fed you with milk." Hitherto the Patriarch Jacob had been called a supplanter; and this name corresponded more with his defective state of grace up to that period, than that which was now appropriated to him. He had held his enemy as it were by the heel, but had not previously overcome him. He had received glorious promises, but could not duly tranquilize himself with them. He still looked too much at the things which were seen—at his brother and his four hundred men; at the misfortune which might possibly befall him, and at his defenceless condition. He was still too prudent, and lingered too much at natural causes and effects; and hence he regarded it as possible, that he, together with his children, might be slain, although God had assured him that through him and his posterity, all the nations of the earth should be blessed. He felt a great degree of fear: and John says, "He that feareth is not made perfect in love." But still, he was a real child of God, and would therefore have been saved, if he had not attained to that higher standing to which the purpose of God had predestinated, and also called and prepared him.

The Apostle says to the Corinthians in the close of the preceding, "Now ye are full." There is accordingly, even on this side eternity, a being blissfully satisfied, which is promised to those who hunger and thirst after righteousness. The seed of the righteous shall not suffer hunger. "I shall not want," says the Patriarch, "It is enough," said Jacob. But that satiety which is injurious, is when a Christian is so satisfied with his state of grace, that he supposes he has experienced everything that is to be experienced, and judges everything according to his experience, and that with so much self-esteem, as if everything that was above and beyond it was imaginary. This is a great mistake, and entirely opposed to poverty of spirit. Paul therefore says also, "Whosoever thinketh himself to be something whilst he is nothing, he deceiveth himself." If we are really nothing we must learn to know ourselves aright, and this is just the chief thing. "He that humbleth himself shall be exalted." He that supposes he knows anything, is still ignorant of everything, and thus it is with other things. Only look at Jacob. In which way did he become Israel? In that of humility. Every support was taken away from him, his hip was dislocated, and, instead of every other stay, the Son of God is alone left him, and when he is willing to fall into the hands of his enemy he must throw himself into the arms of the angel of the covenant. And at the moment when all is over with him he conquers. His former name was now no longer suitable for him. The Lord had worsted him in poor grace; the guilt of his faith was now quieted from the dross attached to it; and thus he obtained a new name.

'Thy name shall be called no more Jacob.' Fear shall never again take possession of thy heart in the same degree, because thy soul will cleave to me, and thus imbibe my vivifying and peaceful influences. Thou shalt never more experience such great vicissitudes of fear and hope, anxiety and joy; thou shalt be more perfect in me!

People often miscalculate in their religious course. If they have happily escaped from a gloomy vale, and again rejoice in their state of grace; if the mists of doubt disappear before the lovely beams of the Sun of Righteousness, they often think they have now attained, and believe that in future they will not be so timid. But does not a degree of presumption lie in such an idea, as if the individual could do this or that of himself? and Jesus, who has said, 'Without me ye can do nothing,' is too jealous of his honor, and of the maintaining of his promises, of his Jesus-name, to endure such presumption in his favorites. He will therefore sit as a refiner, and purify the sons of Levi, even as gold and silver is purified, until his gold attains the purity he has intended. Perhaps he dislocates their thigh, and brings them into such straits that they feel incompetent to strive without Him, against a doubt, whether great or small; and are compelled to give full assent to his assertion, that they can do *nothing*.

But what then? 'Thy name shall no more be called Jacob, but Israel;' this is that magnificent title which no one ever bore except Jacob. It means a prince of God! God makes a show of Jacob, as it were, and boasts of him, because through him he had accomplished so much. Thus. God acts also towards his people, when he says, ' Fear not, thou worm Jacob! I will help thee. Thou shalt thresh the mountains, and beat them small. like chaff.' If a worm can thresh mountains, it is only possible through God, who receives all the honor of it. Thus Jesus boasts respecting his sheep, " That they shall never perish, and no one shall pluck them out of his hands." This excites the world, together with the hosts of hell. The most specious errors, the vilest temptations, fire, sword, martyrdom, imprisonment, and death, are called forth to see whether defenceless sheep cannot be destroyed. Whole · hosts of wolves attack them ; and what do they accomplish ? Nothing ; except that they prove the faithfulness of Jesus, and increase his fame. And here even God strives with a weak and sinful man, and cannot overcome him! ' In all these things we come off more than conquerors, through Him that hath loved us.'

' Thou shalt be. called Israel.' What are all the titles, however high-sounding, which men may bear ? They dissolve, at length, into smoke and vapor, of which the age in which we live has furnished astonishing proofs. In themselves they are no protection ; least of all against the wrath of God, to whom that which is highly esteemed amongst men is an abomination ; and who chooses, by preference, that which is weak, simple, despised, and nothing, that he may confound that which is wise, mighty, and noble ; yea, and things that are not,

to bring to nought things that are; that no flesh may
glory in his presence, and that the abundant power
may be of God, and not of us. What a foolish direction
is given to the ambitious feeling implanted in us by God,
when we seek honor from men, instead of that which
cometh from God; when we seek earthly possessions,
and are not rich in God! A bruised reed in the kingdom of God, is more than those who are 'regarded in
the world as stately oaks; and a glimmering taper in
the temple of Jesus Christ, more than burning torches
out of it. Esau far exceeded Jacob in earthly possessions. He could take the field with four hundred men;
and his sons were princes. But God loved Jacob, and
not Esau. Of what avail, therefore, was all his superiority? Be not deceived, for that is only valuable
which appears so in the eyes of God.

'Thou shalt be called Israel.' The Patriarch doubtless received this name with reference to the remarkable individual whose progenitor he was to be, and in
whom all the nations of the earth should be blessed—
Jesus Christ, to whom the name of 'Prince of God'
peculiarly belongs. It is also said in Jer. xxx. 21,
'Their prince shall be of themselves, and their gover-
nor shall proceed from the midst of them, and he shall
proceed from the midst of them, and he shall approach
unto me.' King, Prince of Life, Lord of Glory, are
his titles; 'And upon his vesture and his thigh he has
a name written, King of Kings.' He indeed strove
with God, with men, and with devils, and overcame,
and has received a name which is above every name.
Without his conflict, all our wrestling would be lost

labor; but through him we come off more than con-querors.

The wondrous man also adduces the reason why he changed the name of Jacob into Israel; ' For,' says he, ' as a prince thou hast power with God and with men, and hast prevailed.' The name Jacob—supplanter—was also a very instructive and encouraging name; but the Patriarch, from want of light, had not found much encouragement in it : hence the Lord gives him the requisite instruction respecting his new name. ' In thy light,' says the Psalmist, ' we see light :' and prays, ' Open thou mine eyes, that I may behold wondrous things out of thy law.' We require the Holy Spirit to guide us into all truth, not less than the disciples of the Lord, who, nevertheless enjoyed his instruction. Without his light, ' We see men, at the best, only as trees walking;' and therefore indistinctly and confusedly. Hence Paul not only taught, but prayed also, that the Ephesians might comprehend the height, and breadth, and depth, and length of the love of God.

God bears witness to Jacob that he had wrestled; and we have been spectators of the conflict. He had engaged in the contest with all the energy—outwardly of his body, inwardly of his will. And thus it ought to be. The slothful man dies over his wishes, and his hands refuse to labor. Let such a one go to the ant and learn of that little insect, if he cannot see it in Jacob, how to exert all his strength, and employ every means. Let him do his uttermost, and not lie down to sleep too soon upon the pillow of human inability, which he is acquainted with only from hearsay. Jacob

would certainly not have received the new name, if he
had immediately fled, under the idea that he had no
power to resist. But he was compelled to struggle,
because his life was now at stake. How many are
there who take up the words of Jesus, and say, " We
can do nothing without him," without really believing
it, because they have never tried · how far' their own
strength extends. Assuredly the Scripture - does not
call upon us in vain to strive and fight, to fear and be
diligent, to work and do violence ; and these things are
equally as true, as that ' in quietness and confidence
shall be our strength.'   ' I write unto you, young men,
because ye are strong, and the word of God abideth
in you ; for ye have overcome the wicked one.'   However, every thing has its time. What has been said,
has reference to the first station, if I may so speak,
on the journey to Jerusalem ; ' Six days shalt thou labor and do all thy work ; but on the seventh, the sabbath of the Lord, thou shalt rest.'

Such was Jacob's case. He wrestled and strove;
but at length his struggling was at an end, since his
thigh, the soundness of which was indispensable to his
wrestling, was dislocated. There was now an end to
his striving, because he had no strength left. He then
fell into the arms of his God ; and conquered then, and
not before ; he was blessed then, and not till then.
Fight therefore, O man ! who desirest to be saved.
Fight with all thy might. Do not give way a hair's
breadth. Watch, pray, read, and hear. For lo ! Esau
marches against thee with four hundred men ! With
four hundred men !—and Jacob was alone. Danger-

ous situation! For what assistance could he derive from his wives, his children, or his shepherds? He was compelled to fight with men. To Mesopotamia he dared not return; for God would not have it. Proceed he could not. What fool-hardiness, to march out alone, against four hundred men! Therefore, weep, and lament, and mourn, and despair!" Not so. He believed in an Almighty and merciful God; be believed in his promise, 'I will do thee good.' However, his faith was at that time not sufficiently strong to enable him to say, ' Though a host should encamp against me, I will not be afraid'—or to think and say with calmness, " God, who enjoined Laban to speak no otherwise than kindly to me, is still the same, and is able and willing to turn the heart of Esau in such a manner, that he shall be unable to act cruelly towards me, seeing that God hath promised that in my descendants all the nations of the earth shall be blessed." Could he have acted thus, how glorious would it have been! But this was not in accordance with his previons state of grace. He was afraid, because his reason still reflected too much, and looked more at the things which are seen, than at those which are not seen. But his faith was the victory which overcame the world. This faith softened his heart, so that he wept, as Hosea says; and much is already gained, when we acquire a contrite spirit, and when the hard heart dissolves. His faith opened his mind and his heart; so that he was able to pray, as Hosea also informs us. His faith took refuge with God. What! shall God work a miracle? How miserable, to be

11

only able to oppose prayer to four hundred armed men! Certainly this is not rational, but still it is of faith. And to the believer are given all the promises of a living God, who overrules all natural and accidental events according to His good pleasure.

It was thus he wrestled with men, in the most prudent manner, by taking God to his aid against them; for if God be for us, who can be against us? And oh, how evangelically wise we all act, when we commence our spiritual conflict—not in our own wisdom and strength, but draw the Lord himself, by faith and prayer, into the conflict; he will then fight for us, whilst we shall hold our peace. If we go·out to the battle without God; if we think that in our own wisdom and strength we are sufficiently equipped—we should act as foolishly, as if Jacob had believed that he alone was able to face four hundred men; and that which we think we have accomplished, is only self-deception. But with God, it might be all one to Jacob, whether his brother came out against him with four hundred or four thousand men. For he that without Christ can do nothing, with him can do all things; and it is the same to the Lord, to help with many or with few.

Thus Jacob wrestled, like a prince, against men. He did not despair on account of the might and multitude of those who were against him, and looked not at his littleness and inability. Nor did he trust to the fragile staff of his own strength, which indeed he was unable to do; for it was broken. Reason showed him nothing but ruin and death, and nature was afraid, but faith helped him through. By its means, he honored God as able to help, where there is no other aid ; and although he did not understand by what means, yet he left this with God's all comprehensive wisdom. He said, " Wilt thou not do it, Lord ? I know no other measure, and can do nothing more, and see myself compelled to resign myself to thee and thy good pleasure, with all that are mine, and what thou hast otherwise given me. Do with me, therefore, as seemeth thee good."

Nature, indeed, trembles, when it feels compelled to seek help of God, because it is no where else to be found, and is more inclined to fear its total ruin, than to expect help and deliverance. But the Holy Spirit here turns the scale. He holds the soul fast, so that it declares, ' I will not let thee go, except thou bless me !' This is the real inward conflict and travailing in birth, during which the soul cries to God, out of the depth of its distress, and then ascends on high when the time arrives. This is in reality no trifle, and it may be said with Solomon, ' A wounded spirit, who can bear !' But these are, at the same time, paths which terminate in the desired end :—' The Lord hath done great things for me, whereof I am glad.'

' Thou hast had power with men, and hast prevailed,' said the Lord to Israel. He came off more easily with Laban. He fled, and prudently took advantage of the absence of his father-in-law, as the fittest moment for his flight. However, that he might not ascribe all the success to his prudence, Laban ascertained his flight early enough to hasten after him. He did so,

and took with him his brethren ; which however did
not betray the most friendly intentions towards Jacob,
and overtook him on the seventh day.   But God came
to Jacob's aid, by a dream, in which he turned the
heart of Laban in such a manner, that he was not permitted to do him any harm, but only spoke harshly to
him ; and at length retired, after taking a friendly
leave.   Jacob, in this instance, came off easily, and
with a slight degree of terror ; for God usually leads
his people step by step, and exercises those whom he
calls to severer conflicts, previously in easier ones.   For
a period, they are able by their own strength and reflection to accomplish much ; but at length both go to
the bottom.   Waves cover the little vessel, and the
cry is heard, ' Master, save ! we perish !' and then the
help is near at hand.

Such was also the case with Jacob.   After the departure of Laban, he was greatly comforted, and received a powerful invigoration to his faith ; for he was
met by the angels of God.   This circumstance was
highly remarkable and encouraging ; and because the
art of writing was at that time not understood, he called the place where it happened, ' Mahanaim,' the
Lord's host : for when he saw the angels of God, he
said, ' This is God's host.'   This afterwards assisted
him in his conflict.   If any one is delivered out of six
troubles, he cherishes the hope that in the seventh he
shall not be forsaken ; ' for experience worketh hope
and hope maketh not ashamed.'   Christ said to Peter ;
' Thinkest thou that I cannot now pray to my Father,
and he shall presently give me more than twelve le-

gions of angels ?' Thus Jacob saw that God could at least send two hosts of angels to his aid. But when he was in straits, all sensible supports gradually gave way, and Jacob remained alone with God.

The affair with Esau was a much more serious one than that with Laban. But defenceless Jacob did not overcome even him by armor and weapons, not by humble messages, not by presents, nor any other means which his prudence might have dictated : but by his humble, believing prayer, or rather by God himself. God softened the heart of the infuriated Esau, who had sworn his brother's death, to such a degree, that when he came in sight of his brother, he ran to meet him, cordially embraced him, fell upon his neck, and wept. But Jacob saw in his brother the face of God. He perceived in his whole deportment the wonderful over-ruling power of God, who had blessed him. He saw with his eyes, in the most striking manner, that a man's actions do not stand in his own power ; that he can purpose saying something, and yet that it depends up-on the Lord whether he is suffered to utter it. Jacob ascribed nothing of it to himself, as the consequence of his prudence ; nor could he indeed do so. He gave God alone the glory, and saw in Esau's whole deport-ment only the power and faithfulness of God ; he there-fore bowed himself seven times to the earth, more be-fore God than before his brother. Hence he called him his lord, as he was in reality. For naturally Esau, with his four hundred men, could have done with Jacob what he pleased ; although in reality only as God pleased. Thus, with his dislocated limb, through God's

11*

help, he overpowered Esau with his four hundred men.

But we will here break off. This is wrestling so as to gain the victory : for faith is the victory that over- cometh the world. This does not take place in our own strength, nor to our own praise. God receives all the glory. 'No one is crowned, except he strive lawfully.' See to it, how you will stand against four hundred, or whether you are able to go forth with ten thousand against him who comes towards you with twenty thousand. But 'if the Son shall make you free, then are ye free indeed.'

SERMON VIII.

'Is there no balm in Gilead—is there no physician there?' inquires the sorrowing prophet Jeremiah, chap. viii. 32. He previously complains of the lamentable state in which his people were placed—a state which would draw after it one still more lamentable. 'Where is the man,' he asks, 'who does not gladly rise again after his fall? and who, after going astray, would not gladly return to the right path? But this people hold fast deceit, and refuse to return?' However much understanding men may have in natural things, they manifest the very reverse in spiritual things. Even the birds of the air, as he observes in verse 7, put men to shame in this respect. At the same time they were haughty, and said, 'We are wise, and the law of the Lord is with us?' which, however, they did not understand. Self-conceited individuals refuse advice, and therefore cannot be assisted. But must this wretched state of things continue? Is there no physician there! Or if there is, is there any want of medicine? Oh no! A physician is there. He possesses all the requisite knowledge. He perfectly understands the method of cure. He is a faithful, patient, gentle, and a kind physician. He knows the nature and real seat of every disease; knows whether he ought to use the knife or the plaster; to cut, burn, or heal. A physician therefore is there; but is there a want of medicine—is there no balm in Gilead? Oh yes: this physician is at the same time the medicine; or if you will, his blood and Spirit is the balm. Was he able formerly to heal every disease—he can do so still. Was he able, when on earth, to raise the dead— he does so still, as he has proved in the cases of many of you, and doubtless will continue to do so. Many amongst you are already healed; but why not all? Some suppose they need no physician; others do not think their diseases sufficiently dangerous, and endeavor to heal themselves, by which the evil is made worse; others prescribe to the physician the method in which they wish to be treated. Some do not understand how to buy the balm; and seek for money, although it is to be had for nought. The majority will not suffer themselves to be cured of their own piety, and even think the physician must promote it; but they are much mistaken: ' He maketh sore and bindeth up; he woundeth, and his hands make whole.'

GENESIS XXXII. 28.

For as a prince thou hast power with God and with men, and hast prevailed.

WE lately considered how Jacob wrestled with God and with men, and prevailed. Let us now contemplate the manner of his struggling with God, and prevailing; and consider,

I. The conflict; and

II. Its result.

'Thou hast power with God,' said he who had wrestled the whole night with Jacob. Unequal conflict! God against man! Unheard of, incredible result! The man overcomes! Jacob now learnt with whom he had to do—not with a foe, but with his best friend. How is the soul astonished, when at the end of the darkest paths, in which it was inclined to think that God had in wrath forgotten to be merciful, and to say, 'Is his mercy clean gone for ever?' it perceives in these very paths the most striking condescension of the Lord, and the greatest kindness in a guidance which seemed only to aim at its destruction. Then indeed a wonderful and glorious morning dawns.

He wrestled with God. God, therefore, seemed in some respects not to be for him, but against him. God seemed not to be for him; for why was it otherwise with him with regard to Esau, than it had been with regard to Laban? Why did fear obtain such possession of his mind, without his being able to defend himself against it? Why did it not depart at his humble prayer and thanksgiving? If God intended to do him good, why did he expose him to so much danger—and he at the same time so defenceless? If he loved him, why did he ask him to let him go? And why did he put him so entirely to shame? If the Lord be with us, why is all this befallen us? This question of Gideon's, the children of God are often inclined to ask: "If I am really regenerate, whence these sinful inclinations in me? If the Lord loves me, why does he place me in these particular circumstances? If my prayer is acceptable, why does it not produce greater effect ?　If God is for me, why is there so much against me ?''　But the end of the ways of the Lord is better than their beginning, and the soul at length receives a very·satisfactory answer to these questions.

The Lord, however, seemed to be entirely against Jacob; against him with words; for he must have said bitter things to him; otherwise why did he weep ? as Hosea informs us.　He must have reproached, reproved, rejected, and threatened him; otherwise why did he entreat him ?　Did he not, in after-times, compare the Canaanitish.woman to a dog, and mention what was proper and improper in the treatment of such ?　And is it not often the case with individuals, that when desirous of comforting themselves with a promise—a command, a threatening, a reproof meets them and snatches it away, as it were, from their lips ; and this continues until the covering of Moses falls off from the heart and the soul looks into the perfect law· of liberty ; until Christ becomes the end of the law ; till the whole of holy writ becomes a Testament, and the covenant of grace beams forth as such.　But what is chiefly necessary in order to this ?　The Lord plunges Jacob, in a certain sense, into despair, when he says ' Let me go— I will depart.'　And does he not often withdraw himself, whilst the soul resolves to cleave to him, whatever be the result ?

It did not rest in mere words: actions are added to them.　He increases Jacob's distress by wrestling with him; and that so violently, that Jacob, according to the expression of Hosea, is obliged to resist with all his might. He chooses, for this purpose, the night, a season the most appalling of all; and the period when Jacob's distress had, besides that, reached a terrific height, and when his fear was great. By the dislocation of his thigh, he deprived him of all strength, and rendered it impossible for him to continue the conflict, although the ceasing from it was equally impossible. He caused him pain. He casts him, as it were, defenceless before his enemy, by making escape impracticable.

Jacob therefore found it necessary to defend himself, and to strive against his adversary, be he who he might. And the Lord bears him witness that he had struggled with God, and had prevailed. With God? How wonderful! What!—does God act in such a manner with men? Does he so degrade himself as to wrestle with a man—as man against man? It is not credible! Not credible? Thou shalt see still greater and more unaccountable things than these. How wilt thou believe the latter, if the former are incredible to thee? Go to Bethlehem; there thou wilt find him lying in a manger, as a little needy infant. Go to Jerusalem; there thou wilt see him in the hands of the wicked, who nail him to the cross; there thou wilt behold him crucified between two malefactors, hear him complain of being forsaken of God, see him die, and witness his interment.

What sayest thou to these astonishing mysteries? If thou canst not believe the less, how will it be with the greater? Does God act thus towards men? Why should he not? If not a sparrow falls without the will

of God, what do we think can befall the children of
God without their Father's superintendence? Even
the very hairs of our head are all numbered; every one
of them is precious to him; and how can it be otherwise, since he has paid such an inestimable price for
them? · How wonderful! Does his love assume such
a form as we here see it in the case of Jacob? Does
he distribute benefits in such a manner? Does apparent injury also belong to his method of doing good?

In what manner did Jacob wrestle with God? Certainly not in the sense in which Stephen said to the
Jews, 'Ye do always resist the Holy Ghost, even as
your fathers did, so do ye.' The Patriarch defended
himself not merely by struggling with his body—this
was only the effect; the cause lay deeper, lay within;
and that was faith. This faith was not exactly a sensible faith, nor a perfectly satisfied faith—for he was
afraid; but distress excited it, and the best kind of
faith is when the individual, in the consciousness of his
utter poverty, does not look so much at his faith, as at
Jesus. Faith is that which is Divine in the Christian;
which by a strong impulse seeks that which is Divine,
and is invincible. It manifests itself in taking refuge
with Christ under the strong attraction of the Father;
in not casting away our confidence, which has great
recompense of reward. Jacob clung with such firmness to the Divine promise, which his distress compelled him to do, that he was so little confused by the
adverse conduct of the Lord as to refer him to his own
promise, 'I will do thee good,' and adhere firmly to it.'

Jacob wrestled with God, first, with the exertion of

all his powers, in the most determined struggle, as long as he felt any power in himself; but this only served to convince him, that we do not gain the prize by our own efforts, and that the kingdom of peace is not taken by violence. This mode of wrestling was rendered impracticable to him, since he was deprived of the requisite power for it by the dislocation of his thigh. The conflict was now obliged to be continued in an entirely different manner—that is, by a passive conduct, which the circumstances pointed out. The paralyzed combatant had no alternative than that of casting himself into the arms of him who had thus disabled him, and instead of exerting himself, to let himself be carried ; in other words—instead of caring for himself, to cast his burden upon the Lord—to believe, and to turn from the law to the Gospel. And when he began to do this, the Lord saw that he could not prevail against him, and took his part. The struggle then assumed a very different aspect ; it then became a reposing, such as Isaiah speaks of in ch. xxx. 7 : ' Their strength is to sit still ;' and in another place, ' In quietness shall be your strength.'

Thus we see in Jacob how legal exertion at length gives way to the evangelical sabbath of repose ; and that in the latter, that is attained for nought and without labor, which is sought in vain from the most strenuous efforts ; for according to Psalm cxxvii. 2, ' He giveth it his beloved, sleeping.' Wonderful ! When Jacob was unable to struggle any longer, ' the Lord saw that he prevailed not against him.'

12

But why did God enter into such a conflict with Jacob?

First, because it pleased him. *Secondly,* to give a particular proof of his condescension, how minutely he concerns himself about his people—a subject of which our ungodly hearts so often doubt, and so seldom confide in, to the extent we ought, if we only give ear to the single injunction of the Apostle when he says, ' Be careful for nothing.'   But the unbelieving corrupt nature requires one proof after another, and still remains incredulous; as Job says, ' If I had called and he had answered me, yet would I not believe that he had hearkened unto my voice.' (ch. ix. 16.)   We prefer caring for ourselves, although we accomplish nothing by it, and only occasion ourselves fruitless labor.

We have certainly much greater and more striking proofs of the uncommon condescension of God to man in the Holy Scriptures, than this to Jacob; but the latter is not to be despised.   When should we have done, were we only in some measure to go through the history of Jacob's posterity, both during their forty years' journey through the wilderness, and their actual residence in Canaan, in order to show how God often so visibly interfered; and what would it avail the old man, who would have recourse to the subterfuge, " though God did these things formerly, yet he does them no longer."   Just as if he either did nothing, or must do obvious miracles, and as if he were bound to one particular mode of acting.   And even when miracles were really performed, there were prudent people enough, who said, " Master, we would gladly see a separate sign from thee, which should not merely convince the vulgar, but us also." "Ye shall have a sign," replied the Master; "I will rise again after ye have slain me." This took place; they knew of it in a manner which ought to have been perfectly satisfactory to them. But what did it avail? They continued in unbelief; for when the kingdom of God comes, outward phenomena do not contribute to it; unless the individual receives the spirit of faith, he does not believe though one rose from the dead. He that knows God, sees him not only in the thunder and the storm, or in manifest wonders, which certainly may compel even Egyptian magicians to acknowledge his hand; but also in the lot, and the hair of the head, and in events unimportant in themselves, by which he is the most honored. God therefore gives, in this conflict with Jacob, a proof of his uncommon condescension.

It serves also, *thirdly*, as a representation to others of the ways by which the Lord may lead them, in a similar manner to Jacob. It is true, the Lord will scarcely think it needful to enter into a bodily conflict with any one, although he is able, and really does, exercise his children by temporal occurrences. There are instances in which, from the time the individual was converted to God, success no longer attends him, but sickness or misfortunes befal himself or his family; nay, it may even be the case, that he himself is deprived of his natural ability to take charge of his affairs, and they fall into confusion, however much he may exert himself, and however cautiously he may act; so that even in natural things he is put to shame. In his domestic and family circle, the words of Christ may be verified—'A man's foes are those of his own household.' Quarrels may arise with respect to religion, between husband and wife, parents and children, where unity previously prevailed. It may happen, that a person, on account of his religion, may become the object of an almost universal hatred, calumny, and ridicule; nay, he may be occasionally ill-treated, as was the case with the Holy One himself.

Generally speaking, those to whom the Lord is willing to manifest himself more intimately, as he did to Jacob, experience many trials and much adversity for a period; and at length an Esau stands in their way, who threatens them with destruction—nay, not only an Esau, but the Lord himself. They are brought low in themselves, that the Lord may be magnified. They desire to be holy, strong, righteous, wise, believing, and good; they pray and labor as much as possible; but instead of advancing forward, they go back. They increasingly exert themselves like Jacob; but only dislocate their limbs the more. Whatever they lay hold of, eludes their grasp; what they seek, they do not obtain. Jesus makes sinners of them without mercy, and their sin appears extremely sinful to them by means of the commandment, however much they may moan and groan on account of it. At length, their very hip is dislocated; they can no longer maintain their former footing; and nothing is left them but to yield themselves to the Son of God at discretion, and creep, as chickens, under his expanded wings. O glorious result, but highly disagreeable path to nature, to which nothing is left, and to which nothing ought to be left! Here it is manifest, that the mystery of godliness is great.

But what was the result of the conflict? It is described in the unparalleled words, 'Thou hast had power with God, and hast prevailed.' How absurd to reason! How apparently impossible to prevail over God! What strange things are related in the Scriptures! Certainly they are strange; no rational soul can deny it. How absurd it sounds, when it is said, for instance, 'He that will be wise, let him become a fool;' 'God justifies the ungodly;' 'When I am weak, then am I strong;' 'Having nothing, yet possessing all things;' 'I am not come to call the righteous, but sinners;' and many more such paradoxical expressions; on which account, Paul calls the whole Gospel foolishness, for which all that are wise, justly regard it; but to us, who believe this foolishness, it is become the wisdom of God, and the power of God, after it is given us to believe it.

Jacob, therefore, gained the victory over God; nay, he gained it of necessity. And why? God could not strive with him as the Almighty; or as the Holy One, because he had bound his own hands by his truth, and by his promise, 'I will do thee good.' God had rendered it impossible for him to strive with Jacob in such a manner, as would have resulted in his ruin. This would have been at complete variance with his truth, the thoughts of peace he had towards him, and with the whole contents of the covenant of grace, as well as the spiritual espousals of the Lord with his church.

12*

He could, therefore, only strive against him in love, and do him no further injury than the glory of God and Jacob's salvation necessarily required. Under these circumstances, therefore, Jacob could not fail to succeed. He saves sinners, and justifies the ungodly. Now, since he has said this himself, he cannot treat those who are sinners and ungodly in any other manner.

' As a prince thou hast power with God.' Wherein consisted his princely conduct ? He was sincere, and did not wish to appear before God better than he really was. He confessed his sins, by frankly owning that he was afraid. He believed the word which the Lord had spoken.

And oh, how much may such a sincere confession accomplish ! When David at length said, ' I will confess my transgressions unto the Lord,' he forgave the iniquity of his sin. But as long as he kept silence, his bones waxed old through his roaring all the day long. (Psalm xxxii. 3—5.) He prayed and laid all his burden before the Lord, whilst seeking all his help from him, and not from himself. He believed, and that from faith to faith ; so that he suffered nothing to confuse him, and was bold enough at length to cast himself into the arms of his opponent, when every other mode of acting was rendered impracticable. And to him that believeth, all things are possible, even the overcoming of God himself.

" Ah, but who is able to act in a similar manner to Jacob ?" Be it so ; but we must remark that the Hebrew language has something in it very peculiar ; so that it is not only said, ' Thou hast prevailed,' but at the same time, " Thou art rendered fit, able, and competent, and wilt be made competent to prevail." The whole affair is now clear. It is now conceiveable how Jacob could have acted thus, although it would otherwise have been incomprehensible how a weak and sinful man could have conducted himself in such a manner. Now the whole glory reverted, as it ought, to the Lord. It was sufficiently honourable for Jacob, that he was enabled to act thus; and a cause of sufficient joy, that the Lord had thus condescended to him.

But what a carte-blanche for the future—" Thou shalt be made competent !" What was left him, therefore, but to believe, to hang upon his neck, and suffer him to carry him !

How confidently might he now look forward to whatever might occur ! If he had no sufficiency for it beforehand, he did not need it. ' Take no thought what ye shall say, or what ye shall do; it shall be given you at the time what ye shall speak.' ' If ye abide in me, and my words abide in you, ye shall ask what ye will, and it shall be done unto you.'

SERMON IX.

The Epistle of James is a remarkable piece of Holy Writ, although it is somewhat difficult to understand it aright. Its object is, that those whom he calls brethren, should be perfect and entire, wanting nothing; and that their faith should be unfeigned. Hence he endeavors to overthrow all that is not sincere and genuine: and because trials are a blessed means for this purpose in the Father's hands, he wishes them to esteem it all joy when they fall into divers temptations, and counts him happy who endures the test. He then points out the source of every good and perfect gift, which is the Father alone; and entreats them not to err in expecting any thing from any other quarter. He then recommends prayer; because God giveth liberally, and upbraideth no one. Every one pretends that he prays; but the Apostle inquires whether his prayer possesses the true properties? Is it offered in faith? If not, let no one suppose that he shall receive any thing of the Lord. Faith, again, is a thing of which it is easy to say, "I possess it." Be it so; let us look at thy faith. The devils also believe, and Abraham likewise. Which of the two does thine resemble? Thou seest that with Abraham it was not a lifeless matter, but enabled him to offer up Isaac on the altar; and hence it is evident that man is not justified by faith alone, but that justifying faith must necessarily be living faith, and the man must prove his faith by his works. If he does not, his faith is available neither before God nor man, nor even before the man's own conscience, who says, 'I believe,' much less before the all-penetrating eyes of God.

But, says one, "I have faith and works also;" these are again subjected to a test. Dost thou do all the good thou knowest to be such? For 'to him that knoweth to do good, and doeth it not, to him it is sin.' But art thou deficient in no single point? For supposing that thou didst keep the whole law, and yet didst offend in one point, thou art guilty of all. How does it therefore stand with thee; especially with regard to love, this royal law? Does that which thou doest arise from compulsatory motives, or to procure thy salvation? Thou probably judgest others, and art therefore not a doer, but a judge.

In this manner the Apostle shakes the foundation of every thing in its turn. He first of all attacks prayer, then faith, and then works. For what purpose? A house that is built on a rock must be able to withstand the winds and the waves; if it falls, the foundation is bad. 'When a man is tried, he shall receive the crown of life, which God has promised to those who love him.' He mentions Jesus Christ only twice; and if we join with it the word Lord, only five times in the whole epistle: whilst Peter, in a much shorter one, names him upwards of twenty times. James acts in a proper manner with the kind of people he had before him. Nothing is effected by the mere talking about

Christ, faith, and good works. The individual must first become acquainted with his natural state; his boasting of prayer, faith, and works, will then be at an end; and he will become wretched, so as to weep and mourn. When in this school, he must learn patience; in due time he will also be able to look into the perfect law of liberty, and then be blessed in his deed.

We find this confirmed in the history of Jacob.

GENESIS XXXII. 29.

And Jacob asked him, and said, Tell me, I pray thee, thy name. And he said, Wherefore is it that thou dost ask after my name?

LET us more closely consider the meaning of these words, and investigate,

    I. The Patriarch's inquiry; and,

    II. The Lord's reply.

The Lord had asked Jacob how he was called, not as if he did not know it, but in order to give him a name more in accordance with his present state of grace. Jacob, meanwhile, feels emboldened to ask his antagonist his name. It may be that he was desirous of knowing how the Lord ought properly to be called. He was usually called 'Elohim'—the most High. God himself had said to Abraham, 'I am the El Shaddai, the almighty or all-sufficient God.' He was also called simply El, the Strong One. But these appellations no longer satisfied the patriarch after his recent experience. They all expressed something of the Divine glory, but none of them the whole of it. There was probably an ardor in his soul, which would gladly have poured itself out in hymns of praise, but for which he could not find words. He that can worthily praise God, must be God himself. When the Son said, ' Father, I thank thee,' he was perfectly praised; but all the praises of all created things are called a silence, because they fall far short of their infinite object. It is like the praise of a little child, that commends some one for being wise or rich; but to which praise no one pays particular attention, because a little child knows so little what it is to be wise or rich. Such is the case with us in comparison with God. We are however able, on our part, to adduce a perfect praise of God, of which angels are incapable; since Jesus Christ, the God-man, is made unto us righteousness and sanctification, and we in him are the righteousness of God.

But Jacob doubtless was not anxious merely about the name, when he said, ' Tell me, I pray thee, thy name.' I think he meant to say by it, " Lord, how shall I call thee ? I know not what to think, much less to say. Such a condescension as that which thou hast shown to me, who am but dust, is more than my heart could have remotely anticipated. I know and confess, that thou, O Lord ! art wonderful and gracious. I know how thou hast condescended to my forefather Abraham, and didst converse with him as one friend with another. I know that thou art wonderful, as thou didst show thyself, when desiring my father Isaac as a sacrifice. I know, from my own experience, how gracious thou art. Thou didst once appear to me in a dream, and thou hast impressed promises upon my heart, which I cannot doubt proceed from thee. Thou hast blessed me outwardly, so that I am become a rich man. But what hast thou now done to me? Thou disguisest thyself in my flesh and blood, and becomest like one of us; thou feignest thyself to be my opponent, in order to do me good! Thou even wrestlest with me! Thou grievest me, only to console me! Thou breakest down all my strength, in order to declare that thou art in my power. Thou givest me a new name, which represents me as the conqueror and thee as the conquered, and which renders that which is impossible real. Thou art not ashamed to declare that I, a worm, have striven with God, and have prevailed; although all victory lies in thy hands. Thou entreatest me to let thee go; as if I could compel thee to remain, and to do what I please. It was thou who madest me competent to all this, and yet commendest me, as if I, a poor timid creature, had done it of myself. Thou, who art the Holy One, sufferest thyself to be embraced by my unholy arms; thou, who art Almighty, to be overcome by one so weak as I! This is too much, this is too wonderful and too lofty; I cannot comprehend it. Tell me, what is thy name? What shall I say of thee? for I know not. Who, indeed, can know how he ought to bless, praise, exalt, and extol thee as he ought, when he learns and is conscious of what thou doest to thy children?"

If it had been said to Jacob, thus filled with God, "This that the Lord hath now done unto thee, is something very trifling compared with that which he is willing to do for thee. He has, in this instance, assumed the human form only for a short time; but in the fulness of time he will really be born of a woman, and not spend merely a few hours, but three and thirty years, upon earth; suffer in body and soul the most extreme anguish; and even die for Israel, that they may live. And the people will not meet him, as thou hast done, with prayers and tears, but with great wrath and bitter fury will they do him all conceivable injury; whilst He, from love, will bear it as a lamb." If the Patriarch could then have been told these things—which were not fitted, however, for that period—" Oh," he would have exclaimed, by God's grace, " I can believe it! I can believe it! What can be too much for Him to perform ?" Had he been told that he would be called Love, he would have exclaimed, " That is his true name!" And who can say what an insight Jacob may have obtained into the mystery of salvation during this event, and of which he uttered many things in his parting blessing ? . At least, Jesus says of Abraham, ' He saw my day, and was glad.'

It is also certain, that when the Lord's people have spent a period of profound trial and inward suffering, he is often wont to refresh them in a very especial manner. The darker and more anxious the previous night, the more reviving, the more ravishing is the light which succeeds; the more profound the complaint, the more exalted the praise; and the Lord is never more fervently praised, than by deeply humbled souls. ' He will regard the prayer of the destitute,

13

and not despise their prayer.' (Psalm cii. 17.) 'Return unto thy rest, O my soul ! for the Lord hath dealt bountifully with thee. For thou hast delivered my soul from death, mine eyes from tears, and my feet from falling.' What shall I render unto the Lord for all his benefits towards me ? I will take the cup of salvation, and call upon the name of the Lord. Thou hast loosed my bonds.' (Psalm cxvi.) He perceives, in the humiliating paths by which he has been led, the faithfulness and kindness of the Lord, in the most particular manner. He finds that they lead to nothing but blessing, although he perhaps thought at the time, that, if the Lord loved him in any degree, he would have acted very differently. But now everything becomes clear to him, and he thinks he will despond no more, however strangely it may go with him. But whether he will be able to keep his word or not, is another question; certain it is, that when God withdraws his grace, nothing but sin and weakness is left us, and the being willing to learn this is also wisdom and grace. But "tell me, I pray thee, thy name. Reveal thyself more intimately to my soul." Such a desire is very laudable. Christ declares that ' this is life eternal, that they might know thee, the only true God, and Jesus Christ whom thou hast sent.' Paul found so much comprised in the knowledge of Jesus Christ, that he regarded everything else in comparison with it as loss and dung. Moses also once experienced such a strong desire, that he prayed, saying, ' If I have now found grace in thy sight, I beseech thee show me thy glory.' And the Lord really granted him his request, as far as was possible.

In the Old Testament dispensation, the general inquiry was, ' Watchman, what of the night ?' The prophets who prophesied of the grace, which was still to be revealed, searched diligently into the meaning of their predictions, and longed for the period, when the knowledge of the Lord should become general. An acquaintance with all the blessings we have in Christ Jesus, invigorates faith, as Paul writes to Philemon ; and it is very desirable that the morning star should arise in the dark place of our hearts, and the day dawn ; that thus the path of the just may increase in brightness, ' even as the shining light, which shineth more and more unto the perfect day.' (Prov. iv. 18.)

' I am known of mine,' says Jesus. O glorious acquaintance, in which everything may be met with which can strengthen, delight, cheer, and tranquilize us, and which Jesus justly declares to be eternal life. An acquaintance, which is like an inexhaustible mine, from whence we receive grace upon grace ; a knowledge irrespective of which, there is no rest for the soul. The Old Testament church—and with it, the heart of the awakened individual—longs and languishes for light ; until it is said to the cities of Judah, ' Behold your God.'

How can it fail, that he who finds an inward rest for his soul, and whose inward powers and faculties are collected from a state of multiplicity into a state of unity ; who enjoys intimate intercourse with Jesus Christ, and is acquainted with him as made of God unto him wisdom, righteousness, sanctification, and redemption ; should be satisfied even in the midst of poverty and barrenness, since he has all in Christ ?

Who would not long for such an acquaintance, and pray, " Make thyself known to me; cause thy face to shine upon me; make me acquainted with thee!" especially since we have the promise, 'Thou shalt know the Lord.' Certainly, this is a pearl worthy of the whole of our poor property; a treasure, for the sake of which, we may well sell every thing in order to obtain it. But it is only in the light of God that we see light. Blessed are the eyes which see what ye see. 'Flesh and blood has not revealed it unto thee, but my Father which is in heaven.' But as long as the Christian is not duly acquainted with his Lord and head, he feels like Noah's dove, which found no rest for her foot. If he finds rest, he is soon again disturbed; if he thinks he possesses something, it is soon taken from him again, because he still desires to possess it in himself, and not in Christ; if he falls into straits, he is again embarrassed as before; for he still looks to himself, because Moses and Elias have not yet disappeared, so as to leave Christ alone.

But the Lord replied, 'Wherefore is it, that thou dost ask after my name?'—and with this he breaks off. This is strange! When Manoah, the father of Samson, besought him to tell him his name, he acted almost in a similar manner, and replied, 'Why askest thou thus after my name, seeing it is secret?' (Judges xiii. 18.) Moses also entreated him to tell him his name, in order that if the children of Israel should inquire what was the name of the God who had sent him, he might be able to give them an answer. To which the Lord replied in a singular manner, 'I AM THAT I AM.

Thus shalt thou say unto the children of Israel, I AM hath sent me unto you.' (Exod. iii. 13, 14.) . God afterwards called himself Jehovah; which name comprehends in it the ideas, He is, was, and shall be, and of which God says, in chap. vi. 3, 'I appeared unto Abraham, unto Isaac, and unto Jacob, by the name of God Almighty; but by my name Jehovah was I not known to them.' But he was then desirous of being known and honored under this title. In the days of Moses, the first syllable of this name, ' he shall be,' was the most important. Hitherto he had revealed himself in an intimate manner only to individuals; but then, he wished to show to all lands, and to the people of Israel in particular, by a multitude of great and mighty wonders, what kind of a being he was. They were to be continually in the full expectation of the things that should come to pass, until they should at length be able to exclaim, ' Unto us a child is born, unto us a son is given,' until the times should be fulfilled that he sent his Son.

But even in the New Testament, the name Jehovah —' he that shall come'—is still in operation. Hence it often appears in the revelations of St. John, not indeed as the word itself, but the translation of it, ' He that was, and is, and is to come;' because the New Testament church also continually waits for new revelations of the glory of God in the hearts of the elect, and in the coming of his kingdom; until at length, after the complete accomplishment of all the Divine counsels, and after the new Jerusalem shall have descended out of heaven from God, it shall be said, ' It is done!' And, what will then occur, no eye hath ever

seen; for this name Jehovah flows on through all eternity as a beautifying stream.

'He was,' is the second syllable, and shows us that
Moses preached to them, not a new, but the old unchangeable God.   He is ever the same in himself, in
his covenant, in his manifestations—a God of perfect
blessedness; whilst without him and his fellowship,
there is nothing but delusion, deceit, and unhappiness.

But why does not the Lord answer Jacob's question,
since he himself excited it in his heart?   The Lord
often acts in a manner according with his name '.Won-
derful.'-   What was the reason why he said to Mary
Magdalen, who by his appearing was most joyfully astonished, and doubtless fell upon the ground before him
in order to embrace his feet—why did he say to her,
'Touch me not! for I am not yet ascended to my Father;' although, immediately afterwards, he suffered-
the other women whom he met, to touch him in this
manner?   Why did he break off so unexpectedly from
her, as here from Jacob?   Why did he vanish from
the eyes of the two disciples in Emmaus, at the very
moment when he made himself known to them, as if
unwilling that they should express their feelings towards him; not to mention the singular answers which
he frequently gave to the Jews: for instance, on their
asking by what authority he did those things, he replied, 'I will also ask you one thing; and answer me.'
To their question, Who art thou then? he replied,
'Even I that speak unto you.'   At their urgent inter-
rogatory, How long wilt thou keep us in suspense; if
thou art the Christ, tell us plainly? he answered, 'I

have already told you, but ye believe not; for ye are not of God.' But frequently he told them far more than they wished to know, and were only offended by it.

His name is 'Wonderful.' Jacob, Mary, and the disciples at Emmaus, probably saw afterwards the wisdom of the behavior of Jesus towards them, although it might appear strange to them at the time. If the Lord is willing fully to satisfy the desire which he has implanted in his children, he must make them partakers of the whole blessing, which he purchased for them on the cross. He is also willing to do this, according to his name; ' He that shall be ;' not here below, but in paradise. Hence we must learn to be content and satisfied with our daily bread. Nor must we be astonished, if, when enjoying some gracious communication, something all at once intervenes, whilst we believed more would have been added. Here we still dwell in Meseck, and are not yet at home in the Lord, but in patience wait for him. And this waiting is an essential part of religion, in which the Lord has exercised his church from the beginning even until now.

The Lord does all things well in due time, in general, as well as in particular—He only knows also the proper manner ; and hence we must be content to be told, ' my hour is not yet come.' Jacob's question was also fully answered ; eternity, however, is destined for its further elucidation. Israel thought he might then become acquainted with the whole mystery of redemption ; but a couple of centuries must elapse ere it was fully made known. Israel was obliged to learn to. wait—to see the promises afar off, and to be satisfied with it. He was satisfied, and held his peace.

This waiting continued until it was proclaimed, 'Behold, I bring you glad tidings of great joy, which shall be unto all people'—and then again, when it was said, 'It is finished!' the waiting recommenced, until it was said, 'The Lord is risen indeed!' Again the people of God began to wait, and expressed their expectations, in the question, 'Lord, wilt thou now restore the kingdom unto Israel;' and were exercised by the reply, 'It is not for you to know the times or the seasons, which the Father hath put in his own power.' It therefore happened unto the disciples almost as it did to their forefather Jacob. Jesus ascended up into heaven, and the church was again instructed to wait, when the Lord sent word from heaven, saying, 'This same Jesus shall so come in like manner as ye have seen him go into heaven.' (Acts i. 11.) Since that time it has continued to pray, for nearly two thousand years, 'Thy kingdom come!' Often indeed was the inquiry made, 'Lord, wilt thou not at this time restore the kingdom to Israel?' under the idea that it would be the case; but the same reply was again given, 'To you it is not given to know either the day or the hour.' It now continues quietly to wait, assured that He will accomplish it in his time. It must not be taken amiss of the church, that it has frequently miscalculated in its joy, and been compelled to wait afresh; which is certainly painful, since the thing is so desirable for which it hopes. But if it tarry, wait for it. It will certainly come, and will not tarry. Although with regard to determining the time, every year may have witnessed a similar mistake to that of the disciples, yet the thing itself remains true, and we continue to pray, ' Thy kingdom come,' until we, or our descendants, are enabled to say, ' Thine is the kingdom.'

Such is also the case with individual Christians. They must wait—not merely for perfect salvation and glorification, but also, for being made meet for it. It is often very painful, when, though possessing the will to perform what. is good, the ability is wanting ; when, although we clearly perceive that we might be far more happy and courageous in our spiritual course, yet we are unable to attain to it ; when we see how comfortable those are, who can hold confidential intercourse with the Savior, who believe in a child-like manner, who pray without ceasing, cast all their care upon the Lord, rejoice in him continually, and confide themselves without anxiety to his guidance and providence ; and when we clearly perceive, that this is not only something very blissful and very sacred, but also possible, and by God's grace attainable ; but yet are compelled at the same time to say, " Ah, who will give me the wings of an eagle !" and are obliged to confess, that this is not attainable by human effort, and that no one can receive anything except it be given him from heaven.

But when it is not yet given the individual, and a more intimate manifestation of the Lord to his soul is still denied him, this state is more painful than those are able to conceive of, who are already full, and, as the Apostle says, ' reign without us.'

However, 'faithful is he who hath called you, who also will do it.' If it be once given you duly to apprehend, believe, and understand the words, 'Who also will do it'—your peace will flow like a river, and your righteousness as the waves of the sea. Yea, he will do it! O bless the Lord! Amen.

WHEN Paul says, that his preaching consisted not in excellency of speech or human wisdom, he states something that is applicable to the whole of Scripture, which presents to darkened reason a labyrinth, out of which it sees no outlet, and something that also very frequently applies to the ways in which God leads his people. Whet deep complaints are uttered by the man after God's own heart in Psalm xxxviii.; from which, however, we will only adduce the tenth verse, where he says, ' My strength faileth me.' Strength is necessary in order to labor; and he who does not possess it, is incapable of the latter. The Christian must labor much. He must watch, pray, deny himself; preserve himself unspotted from the world; lay aside the sin which so easily besets him, and renders him slothful, put on the armor of light; believe—because without faith it is impossible to please God; love—because only he that loveth abideth in God, and God in him; in short, to say every thing in few words, he must ' work out his own salvation with fear and trembling.' Let us not think to excuse ourselves with the idea that we are unable to do this; for the debtor mentioned by our Lord, was delivered over to the tormentors, just because he was not able to pay.

David was able to do it. It is true, he never imagined he did it perfectly, but confessed that no one can understand his errors; yet he succeeded. What did *he* not possess, whom Saul called a stripling, whose form was more pleasing than great; what courage did he possess, and how much did he accomplish! A lion and a bear once attacked his flock, and carried off a lamb; but the little beautiful boy ran after him, smote him, and rescued the lamb from his jaws; and on its attacking himself, he caught it by the beard, smote it, and slew it. O pleasing type of Christ! The fair and ruddy youth had courage enough to go forth against the Philistine, whose height was six cubits and a span, when every one else fled before him. His brother Eliab angrily reproached him for being presumptuous, and thought he would do better to go and tend the few sheep in the wilderness. But it was not presumption; it was confidence in the living God. The fair-faced courageous youth probably did not at that time anticipate that he should ever compose such a Psalm as the 38th; and lament in it that his strength failed him. If his strength had departed, he was no longer able to accomplish that which he could otherwise have performed, and which was at other times easy to him; it was now become difficult, and even impracticable. 'I am feeble, and sore broken,' says he in verse 8; 'I have roared by reason of the disquietness of my heart;' according to Psalm lxxvii., he was so troubled that he could not speak, much less accomplish anything. What was the reason of so much wretchedness? His iniquity was the cause of it; on which account he at length says, ' I know, O Lord, that thy judgments are just, and that in faithfulness thou hast afflicted me.'

. What was it that failed him ? Not *all* strength in the general, but his own strength. ' *My* strength faileth me.' Before, he had been able to do much that was good ; but this is now at an end. No wonder that he began to be troubled about his sin. In verse 17, we are told he was ready to halt. This was a severe trial to self-love, self-righteousness, and to the life of self. But whom the Lord loveth, he overthrows in this manner, and gives them over unto death.

What was the result of this guidance ? He never obtained his own strength again, nor did he wish for it ; God has no pleasure in the strength of a man. Nothing was left him, but to declare his iniquity, and to hope in the Lord; who according to Psalm lxviii., gives his people might and power. His own strength was then no longer needed ; he was then strong when he was weak, and great, by being humbled. Then he no longer said, ' I care ;' but, ' I lay me down and sleep in peace, for thou, Lord, only causest me to dwell in safety.'

Strange beginning ! glorious end ! Such is also the case in the history of Jacob.

GENESIS XXXII. 29.

And he blessed him there.

Jacob now receives the blessing on the very spot on which he had been obliged to wrestle. We will consider this a little more minutely.

14

Israel had entreated a blessing, and that with a fervor and resolution which would take no refusal : ' I will not let thee go except thou bless me.' This was the Lord's own work in the soul of his servant. It was a prayer according to his will; and '·if we ask any thing according to his will, he heareth us.' This prayer flowed from a profound and vital feeling, from a heartfelt consciousness·of the necessity of a superior communication of grace. It was a hungering and thirsting after- righteousness, which Jesus pronounces blessed, on account of the satisfaction attendant upon it, and to which the latter is secured.

What was it that Jacob particularly desired in imploring a blessing ? He had already a sufficiency of earthly wealth ; and in spiritual things he probably did not regard himself as one who has no part in the Divine blessing, and who is not an object of the good pleasure and love of God; by no means. He intended by it, *first*, a confirmation of the blessing received from his father, in virtue of which he was to be the progenitor of the promised Savior of the world. This is prov-ed by his high esteem and love for the Redeemer. Esau, his brother, might have had the first claim to it, on account of his being the first-born; but he thought so little of the Redeemer, that he sold his birth-right, with all its privileges, for a mess of pottage ;—a figure of all those who esteem temporal blessings, and sensible and sinful delights, more highly than the favor of God. Esau obtained what he sought—earthly prosperity ; and in this respect far exceeded Jacob. The latter had only a sufficient number of servants, whilst Esau could take the field with four hundred armed men; which was at that time a great number. The children of Esau were immediately termed princes, (ch. xxxvi.), and they were numerous. Two of them were called Eliphaz and Teman; and as these names were applied to Job's friends, it is evident that they were the descendants of Esau. As they make no mention whatever of the Redeemer in their discourses with Job—to whom the latter bears such an excellent testimony, and who is also mentioned by Elihu—we justly conclude that Esau troubled himself little about it, and that his descendants followed in his steps; who, in the case of Job, only regarded temporal prosperity as a sign of Divine favor, and the being deprived of it as a proof of the Divine displeasure; and hence declared Job to be an ungodly man, by which they at the same time proved their own righteousness; according to which they regarded their temporal prosperity as a reward of their virtue, and inferred from Job's affliction, that he possessed no virtue. They were hirelings; hence the Lord said to Eliphaz the Temanite, ' My wrath is kindled against thee and thy two friends, for ye have not spoken of me the thing that is right, as my servant Job hath:' ' My servant Job shall pray for you, for him will I accept; lest I deal with you after your folly.' If before, they would only hear of their own righteousness, and not of a mediator, they were now obliged to be content to accept of Job's mediation, and hear that the Divine displeasure was kindled against them, notwithstanding their great wisdom and virtue, in which they thought they so much excelled Job; and they were in great danger of experiencing the most painful proofs of it. God regarded all their boasted wisdom as folly, however much they had said that was true and excellent ; and testified, respecting his servant Job, whose whole wisdom was at last comprised in this single expression, ' I know that my Redeemer liveth,' notwithstanding all that he had uttered in his haste, ' Ye have not spoken of me the thing that is right, as my servant Job hath.'. We must hope that in this manner, their own wisdom and righteousness were in mercy put to shame, and that they learnt with Job to comfort themselves with a Redeemer, and with Elihu to look unto the One of a thousand, who says, ' Deliver him from going down to the pit.'

Esau and his posterity soon established themselves in Mount Seir, and had already kings of their own, whilst Israel's descendants were still in circumstances of difficulty ; as a proof that the Divine favor and temporal sufferings may not only well exist together, but that the cross generally accompanies grace, and that those are not necessarily the children of God, with whom every thing succeeds according to their wish. Jacob called his life a pilgrimage, and thus proved that he sought a country beyond the limits of the visible world. He gladly chose Christ, even with the cross ; which mind was afterwards manifested very gloriously in Moses, that true Israelite, when he chose rather to suffer affliction with the people of God, than to enjoy the pleasures of sin for a season !

But what ideas must Esau have had of the blessing of God, on comparing himself with Jacob ? The lat-

ter called him 'his Lord,' and himself 'his servant.'
And such it really seemed, according to outward appearance. "Ah," may Esau have thought, "what a
superstitious fool I was, to attach so much value to my
father's blessing, as to weep because my brother fore-
stalled me in it! How little reason I had for doing so!
How every thing succeeds according to my wish! And
my brother, how does it fare with him and his blessing?
It is only superstition. And according to reason, he
was in the right. But did Jacob think so too? Did
he think, "What am I profited in being preferred to
Esau? Wherein consists my preference? In suffering, in persecution, in misfortune?" Did he think,
"The blessing was of no importance, and it was very
unnecessary for my mother to have been so anxious to
appropriate it to me?' O no! His Redeemer was his
treasure, which he would not exchange for any consideration. He regarded all he possessed as a gracious
present of the good pleasure of God; and this made the
little more precious to him, than the abundance which
Esau possessed, and respecting which, it was doubtful
whether he possessed it in wrath or from favor. David preferred spending a day in the courts of God's
house, to a thousand in the tabernacles of the ungodly.

Israel desired the confirmation of the promised blessing, by which, according to the assurance given to his
predecessor Abraham, all the nations of the earth
should be blessed in his seed. This he preferred to
everything else; and that justly. 'I have enough,'
said Esau; but Jacob, 'I have abundance; for whom
have I in heaven but thee, and there is none upon earth

14*

that I desire beside thee.   Though flesh and heart fail,
yet God is the strength of my heart, and my portion.'
This confirmation was Israel's primary wish.

The *second* thing of which he was rendered desirous
was a deeper establishment in grace, greater liberty in
it, a greater facility in boldly resigning and committing
himself to it, by which he might be divested of a multitude of anxious cares.   He had received the blessing
from his father : he had experienced repeated confir-
mations of it from the Lord ; he had received glorious
promises, and the most striking proofs of his kind providence and goodness ; but all this had not produced
the effect upon his state of mind, befitting such gracious
intimations.   He was still subject to much anxiety and
fear respecting Esau.   One would be inclined to think
and say, .' How is it possible, that with such marks of
favor, and after such experience, he could still be apprehensive that Esau might slay him, together with his
children, since the promise of God would then be rendered void ?"   Jacob was fully sensible how painful
and unbecoming this was, without being able to alter
it ; and felt compelled to apply to God in prayer, that,
together with the promise, he would grant him the
ability duly to co-operate with it.

Such is also frequently the case with the Christian:
After having been so often enabled to receive the promise of the Gospel, and Jesus Christ himself, with joyful confidence, and to swear, ' In the Lord have I
righteousness and strength ;' after having been a hundred times translated from darkness to light, and from
pressure into peace ; after having been most firmly as-

sured of his having been received into favor, and frequently inundated with consolation, and been so often able to trust in the Lord, that he will surely perform what he has promised, he becomes in some measure ashamed of always doubting of his reception to favor, as he did at the beginning : yet still he possesses no real peace and rest for his soul, and cannot yet fully commit himself, with filial confidence and resignation, to God, and all his concerns to the Lord, and still feels occasionally fear and anxiety. There are many, indeed, who think it cannot be otherwise here below ; and that every one must satisfy himself with it as well as he is able. There are also others who have a superior idea of grace. They know, beyond a doubt, that grace is more powerful than sin ; that the heart may be established with grace ; that the knowledge of Jesus Christ may be exceedingly abundant, so as to cause us to count all things but loss for it ; that the law of the Spirit of life in Christ Jesus, may make us free from the law of sin and death ; that we may be purged from an evil conscience, and that we may find rest for our souls ; that from being children we may become men and fathers in Christ, and that our hearts may be knit together in love, unto all the riches of the full assurance of understanding, to the acknowledgement of the mystery of God, and of the Father, and of Christ, in whom are hid all the treasures of wisdom and knowledge. In short, the individual is compelled to form no mean, but great ideas of a really evangelical and New Testament state of grace, with respect to enlightening peace, sanctification, and power, as is only just and rea-

sonable.   And not only so, but he also feels a powerful hunger and thirst after righteousness—after this perfect liberty, faith, and love; and finds himself compelled
to declare with Jacob, 'I will not let thee go, except
thou bless me.'

It is therefore no longer single, transient enlighten-
ings and seasons of refreshment which he desires, but a
dwelling and abiding of Christ in the heart, a walking
before him and in him, and a being rooted in him. Be
it that the soul is not clearly conscious of this; yet still
there is an impelling principle of the Spirit of God
within her, which desires, with David, to be translated
out of a strait place into a large room.   Thus it manifested itself also in the disciples, when they prayed,
'Lord, increase our faith!'   'Lord, teach us how to
pray!' because they could no longer be satisfied with
their former mode of believing and praying.   'Lord,
shew us the Father, and it sufficeth us,' said they; and
Jesus promised them the Holy Spirit, who should satisfy
all their desire.   Paul was not satisfied with the believing Corinthians, but calls them babes and carnal;
nor with the Hebrew Christians, ' for when for the time
they ought to have been teachers, they needed that one
should teach them again, which were the first princi-
ples of the oracles of God.'   He says to the Galatians,
that he must travail again in birth with them, until
Christ be formed in them. Christ reproves his disciples
for being so devoid of understanding; and Peter says,
' Grow in grace, and in the knowledge of our Lord and
Savior Jesus Christ.'

No one, however, can add one cubit to his stature,

nor make a hair white or black. Without Jesus, believers can do nothing, not even think any thing good. It is God that worketh in us both to will and to do that which is well pleasing to him. Our nature is never to be trusted, however pious it may appear to be, and then even the least of all; for from motives of mere self-love and self-complacency it may seek to grow and be something superior; hence also it is said, ' Mind not high things.' We ought not to take pleasure in ourselves. Our self-love is shrewd enough to take pleasure in making a display of gifts, grace, and a lofty standing, to regard them as a prey, and to let itself be seen by others in such array. It will gladly pass with Simon the sorcerer for some great one. This desire to become something may be the motive for much labor, effort, and diligence, in things which in themselves are holy and good ; and a long time may elapse before the individual himself perceives it. We may be, or seek to be, superior Christians in our own eyes or those of others, and yet it may all be nothing ; for what is highly esteemed among men is an abomination in the sight of God But the gracious path he takes, is always that of bringing to nought that which is, in order that he may be all in all.

When was Jacob blest ? When did he receive the new and glorious name ? When was he commended ? Only after the wondrous conflict. And what occurred in the latter ? Did he become increasingly stronger ? Thus we naturally imagine it ; and, according to our opinion, such is the mode of procedure. First, the individual succumbs under the power of his adversaries ;

he then begins to struggle; whilst doing so, he increases in strength; at length he rises up, and treads
his foe beneath his feet. Such is the idea reason forms
of it. But with Israel, the case was entirely reversed.
He begun the contest with his whole strength; which
however gradually decreased; at length it entirely
disappeared when his hip was dislocated. The conflict did not indeed cease then, but was changed into
an entirely different method of warfare, which consisted
in his throwing himself upon the neck of his opponent,
who now became his only support. And the very moment when his strength forsook him, his wondrous antagonist saw that he could not prevail over Jacob, and
declared himself vanquished. This is extremely
strange; but the ways of the Lord are right. Thus the
Lord continues to annihilate that in his children which
is, that he may be all in all.

On the whole, we must recollect, that real, genuine
religion consists in a very essential experience of sin
and grace, of our own misery and God's glory, of our
own weakness and God's strength, of our own blindness and God's wisdom; and remember, at the same
time, that in reality we understand nothing more of it
than what we experience. We must learn to know
that God has interwoven the cross into all his providential dealings, and that the old man gradually bleeds to
death upon it under them. The Scriptures speak of a
salutary crucifixion and a dying with Christ, as well
as a rising and being made alive again with him.
Even as the latter is something very sacred and glorious—so the former, on the contrary, like every other

mode of being put to death, cannot take place without
anxiety and distress, as little as Jacob's conflict could
be carried on without pain and tears. Before Israel
was delivered out of Egypt, their distress „had reached
its height; and Paul always bore about him the dying
of the Lord Jesus, that the life of Christ might also be
manifested in him.

When the disciples were about to be elevated to a
higher state of grace, enlightening faith, and sanctification, their souls fell previously into great spiritual
travail at the sufferings and death of Jesus Christ,
in which they wept and mourned. It is extremely
easy to talk of religious subjects and exalted states,
and self-love can take great pleasure in so doing.
But where essential grace exists, there all that is mere
talk infallibly ceases; because all foundation for it
is taken away, and if the individual be inclined to
glory, it must be in his weakness. 'I thank thee
that in faithfulness thou hast afflicted me and help-
est me.' A life of believing dependence, in which
the individual boasts only of the Lord, is in truth
and reality a rare phenomena.

Now if the Lord has wrought in a soul an ardent
hunger after a genuine state of grace, he conducts.it
thither in the way which is best pleasing to him;
and, by means which his manifold wisdom selects for
the purpose—means and ways which mostly seem to
Reason any thing else than suitable, and appear to
her ever the very reverse. For they are in conform-
ity to the saying, 'He that humbleth himself shall be
exalted.' Reason, which is blind in the ways of God,

·hopes to become increasingly richer and stronger in
itself, and to require less and less the help of the Lord.
But it is just the contrary! Christ increasingly becomes the one and the all, the Alpha and Omega, the
first and the last; so that out of him, we can neither
believe nor love, neither think nor desire anything
good, neither hope nor be patient; and yet we are able
to do all this, and even more, through Christ which
strengtheneth us. Thus Jacob also, in the end, could
neither stand nor walk. And it is then that praying
without ceasing becomes easy to us, and that all that
is necessary to life and to godliness is given without
ceasing to us, and that the Christian has nothing, yet
possesses all things, is weak and yet strong, is nothing,
and hence is able to do all things.

The Lord blessed Jacob. This was an actual reply
to Israel's question, ' Tell me, I pray thee, What is thy
name ?' The Patriarch experienced it internally. His
former fear departed from his soul, like the dawning of
the day expels the shades of night. Even as by its
pleasing light the refreshing dew descends upon the
grass—so a heavenly peace descended soothingly into
the distressed soul of the weary Patriarch. The wild
animals retired into their caves, and instead of their
horrifying roar, the birds of heaven chanted their morning hymn, and Jacob's terrific idea of ruin and destruction dissolved into confident hope. The thought of
threatening Esau and his four hundred men, no longer
terrified him; he was overcome; and Jacob, more defenceless than yesterday, was to day, although lame, as
bold as a young lion. He no longer needed to look at

the armed host. He knew in whom he believed, though Esau were to march against him with four thousand instead of four hundred men. His heart was enlarged in peaceful confidence in his God.

·Thus the Lord blessed him, not in word, but by an essential impartation of his inward grace, which far exceeds all reason.

O glorious communication, more precious than if his mind had been refreshed by words, and literal promises, the effect of which is seldom wont to be of long duration! .O what mercy, when it is not single alleviations that are vouchsafed to us, and which are soon followed by new distresses ; but when it is given us to " come up out of the wilderness like pillars of perfume,' and to lean upon our beloved ; and when it is said, " How beautiful are thy feet with shoes, O prince's daughter !" What mercy, when it is granted us in future to act in a becoming manner towards' the Friend of our souls, and to come boldly to the mercy seat; quietly to walk forwards in the profoundest poverty of Spirit, in genuine sincerity and complete faith; and when our state is like that of the Apostle, described in the words, 'I am crucified with Christ. Now I live; yet not I, but Christ liveth in me ; and the life which I now live in the flesh, I live by the faith of the Son of God, who loved me, and gave himself for me.'

In this blessing, every thing is comprehended which is requisite for our commencement and progress, and our awakening and deeper establishment ;—in a word, the essential appropriation, by the Holy Spirit, of the blessings of salvation purchased by Christ, and the Holy

15

Spirit himself. When Jesus, at the close of his residence on earth, and as a pre-intimation of his employment in heaven, lifted up his hands, and blessed his disciples, they no longer hid themselves behind .closed
doors from fear of the Jews; they began to praise and
give thanks; they assembled together openly of one accord in the temple, for prayer and supplication. Thus
the Lord first awakened in the mind of the Patriarch an
urgent craving after the blessing, so that he could af-
firm and say, 'I will not let thee go, except thou bless
me.' The Lord then let him wait awhile, that he might
be the more profoundly conscious, that it is not of him
that willeth, nor of him that runneth, but of God that
sheweth mercy; and in order that he might be the
more completely emptied of all his own activity: and
then he blessed him there, on the very spot where he
had been obliged to wrestle. Hence the place became
very memorable to him, and he called it Peniel—the
face of God.

It was indeed worth the while; for such a blessing
is every thing. In earthly things it causes the seed to
grow, the fruit of the vine not to deceive the hope,
business to succeed, and prevents loss and injury; for
the race is not to the swift, nor the battle to the strong;
ability is not sufficient for the procuring of a mainten-
ance, nor prudence for the acquisition of wealth. If
the Lord do not build the house, they labor in vain
that build it; unless the Lord keep the city, the watchman waketh in vain. It is in vain to rise up early, to
sit up late, to eat the bread of sorrows; for he giveth it
his beloved sleeping. In vain thou weariest thyself in

the multitude of thy ways, and takest thought in vain to add one cubit to thy stature. But the Lord's blessing maketh rich, and addeth no sorrow with it : everything then comes as of itself. 'Bless me also,' cried Esau, and yet did not obtain the blessing ; as a proof that even earnest and real longing after the blessing is the Lord's work in the soul. Ah, Esau the elder still seeks to have the blessing, and to be something great and powerful ; seeks to compel God to regulate the way of salvation according as he thinks best, and to be righteous and perfect in himself. But in this he will never succeed ; he will not obtain the blessing, however much he may murmur and complain. The less, the younger, the new man receives it, but only when the hip of self is dislocated, when it is at length said to him, ' I have chosen thee, thou art mine.'

To Him be the kingdom, and the power, and the glory; for ever and ever ! Amen.

SERMON XI.

It was an unparalleled, wonderful, and incredible method, in reference to which it is impossible to find language sufficiently glorifying to God, that king Jehoshaphat employed, when he went forth to war, and gained the victory; on which occasion it pleased God to manifest his glory in such an extremely striking manner, as we read in 2 Chron. xx.

In the enemy's great superiority of power, which constrained Jehoshaphat to confess and say, ' We have no might against this great company that cometh against us;' and which placed him in such a dilemma that he exclaimed, ' Neither know we what to do;' and which urged him to call upon God, saying, ' Our eyes are upon thee;' we see, at the same time, the object of all the afflictions through which we are called to pass. We are by them to be rendered lowly, little, nothing, impotent, and helpless, and to give God the glory; even as Jehoshaphat said, ' Wilt thou not judge them?' How desirable, that we should also be brought, from heartfelt conviction, to say, ' We have no might;' and be enabled at the same time to lift up our eyes unto the hills, from whence cometh our help. How admirable is the power of faith! Its basis is the promise, ' Thus saith the Lord.' Its object is God: ' The battle s not yours, but God's.' Its effect is peace and com-

posure : ' Ye shall not need to fight in this battle ; set
yourselves, stand ye still, and see the salvation of the
·Lord, who is .with you.!'   It also produces deep humility.   The king prostrates himself with his whole people.   It excites to thanksgiving and praise, and the
ground of thankfulness is this, ' His mercy endureth for-
ever.'   It terminates in complete victory.   Behold
what power God can give to those, in whom there is
no might, and who know not what they ought to do.
He can enable them still to believe in the Lord, and to
feel safe, when everything appears against them ; and
can cause them to thank and praise ' with a .loud voice
on high,' not merely after having obtained the victory,
but even before the commencement of the fight ; for the
Lord is wonderful in his believing people, and glorious
in his saints.

Oh, if we could only .believe, and do nothing else but
believe !   For all things are possible to him that believeth.   But this is only learnt in those paths in which
Jehoshaphat learned it : ' Not in us, but in thy hand is
the might and the power.'   In this manner the Patriarch Jacob also learned it.

15*

GENESIS XXXII. 30, 31.

And Jacob called the name of the place Peniel; for I have seen
God face to face, and my life is preserved.   And as he pass-
ed over Peniel, the sun rose upon him, and he halted upon
his thigh.

THE Lord had blessed Jacob; therefore he now let
him go.   He inwardly felt, that though the Lord might
visibly disappear from him, yet he remained with him
and in him.   Such was also the case with the disciples
at the ascension of Jesus.   He departed from them bodily, but spiritually and essentially he remained with
them, and continues with us even to the end of the.
world.   And of this we are conscious from his Spirit,
which he hath given us; and from the peace, joy, and
power, which operate in us.

The whole affair with Jacob deserved a memorial.
He instituted this, by giving a new name to the place
where this remarkable event occurred.   Nature presented him with an emblem of it—the rising sun; and
he had a memento of it in his own body—he was lame.

The Son of God had given Jacob a new name.   The
Patriarch could not apply a new name to God in return, since his goodness is every morning new, ever
alike fresh and lovely.   He therefore gave the place
a new and suitable name, by calling it Peniel—that is,
the face of God.   He explained what he meant by this
new name, by adding, ' I have seen God face to face;'
and the effect of this was, ' My life is preserved.'   But
God himself instituted a memorial of the event, which
shall last as long as the world stands, by causing it to

be recorded by His servant Moses, and to be called to mind by the Prophet Hosea. But what am I saying? —as long as the world stands? To all eternity will Jacob himself be a memorial of this event; and even as he was so here by his lameness, so he will be there by his glory.

Peniel. This world possesses many uncommonly glorious places. The natural man finds those the most remarkable, where Nature manifests herself in peculiar splendor and majesty; where lofty mountains yield delightful prospects, and smiling plains exhibit the blessings of heaven; where majestic rivers roll along, or the wide ocean expands itself like an eternity before the eye, which seeks in vain its limit. The scientific man lingers with pleasure on the monuments of ancient and modern art; he gazes with admiration at the enormous dome which ancient times reared heavenwards, or is ravished with the productions of the painter or the statuary, which animate, as it were, the lifeless canvass and the solid marble. He admires the magnificence and beauty of princely palaces, and lingers astonished at the works of art. The historian loses himself in reflection, when visiting the scene of former important events; when coming in sight of ancient Rome, with all its reminiscences; or when upon a field, where memorable battles have been fought. Who, at this present period, does not think with admiration of Wittenberg, and its royal chapel; of the Wartburg, of Zurich and Geneva, and of the names of Luther, Zuinglius, and Calvin, because they remind us of a multiplicity of events connected with them?

The Christian has also his memorable spots and
places in the world; Bethlehem, Capernaum, Jerusalem, Calvary, and the Mount of Olives, are these remarkable spots. Formerly they were personally visited
by the piously superstitious pilgrim, whilst his heart,
perhaps, was far from God. His bodily eye saw the
remarkable places, whilst the eye of his Spirit remained closed against the wonders which there took place
for the salvation of sinners. His feet wandered in what
is called the Holy Land, where Abraham once sojourn-
ed; which the Son of God touched with his sacred
feet, and even with his face; which he bedewed with
his tears, his bloody sweat, and his atoning blood; in
which his lifeless body slumbered three days, and
where he again rose to heaven from whence he had
come down. There the foot of many a pilgrim wanders, whilst it is not given him to walk in the steps of
faithful Abraham, and to know the way of peace—
nay, whilst rejecting the Son of God, by thinking to
render his own works effectual as an atonement for his
sins. These places are Peniels to believers, revelations
of the glory of God, since his faith and love find the
pastures of eternal life in that which there took place.
And has not every Christian his particular Peniels, in
which God revealed himself to him in an especial manner ?—his closet, a sermon, a book, a company, a
solitary hour, and the like, which continue ever memorable to him.

Jacob called this remarkable place Peniel—not as a
memorial of himself, nor of that which he had there
performed and accomplished: but of that which he had

apprehended and experienced of God, and of the gracious benefit bestowed upon him. You see here the character of all God's children. The world is proud, and boasts that she has done this or accomplished that; she desires to be regarded and commended for it, and to be honored for zeal, prudence, and ability. Her own glory is her aim, and the being denied it her most sensible mortification. Like the Pharisee in the Gospel, she ascribes it to herself, that she is not this and that, and that she is and does the other; she will not give her glory to another, and feels much offended if any one seeks to possess it in her stead. Even when the Son of God says, ' Without me ye can do nothing,' he has only contradiction to expect from her; and when Paul says, ' Not of yourselves, it is the gift of God,' the proud world is insulted by it. The Lord knows how to produce a different effect in his children, even though he be obliged to deprive them of their strength. He does so, in order that if any one will glory, he may glory in his weakness, and in the Lord; and that all glorying in himself, may cease and perish.

Jacob gives the reason for the appellation of this place in the words, ' For I have seen God, face to face.' Here we find a complete explanation who it was who wrestled with Jacob, dislocated his thigh, gave him a new name, and blessed him. It was not a mere angel. With these Jacob was well acquainted. During his flight with his brother, when sleeping solitarily in a wilderness upon the earth, with a stone under his head for a pillow, he saw in a dream the angels of God ascending and descending upon a ladder, on the top of which stood the Lord himself; on his return, he was again met by two hosts of angels, and he called the place where this occurred, Mahanaim. Here, however, it was no created angel, but God himself—that person in the Divine Being, who is called the Messiah, 'the sent of God,' Jesus Christ, who in the fulness of time was really manifested in flesh and blood. If we ask, by what it was that Jacob perceived with such certainty that it was a Divine person with whom he had to do, we answer, He was assured of it in the same mysterious manner as the weeping Magdalen at the sepulchre was assured by the single word, 'Mary!' that it was not the gardener, but Jesus himself, who was conversing with her; and as the disciples on the sea of Tiberias were so perfectly convinced it was the Lord, that none of them needed to ask him, 'Who art thou?' 'The Spirit beareth witness that the Spirit is truth' (1 John v. 6.) The Christian's conviction is something peculiar. It is a consciousness that it is really so, a certain confidence which does not and cannot doubt; whilst, on the contrary, a mere human belief thinks, it may be so, or may be otherwise.

Jacob now said, 'I have seen God face to face.' Paul calls God, 'The Invisible' (1 Tim. i. 17;) and in ch. vi. 16, he says, 'God dwelleth in a light, which no man can approach unto; whom no man hath seen, or can see.' Still, we read in Exod. xxiv. 9, 10, that Aaron and his sons, and the seventy elders of Israel, were ordered to ascend Mount Sinai, and worship afar off. But Moses alone drew near to the Lord. And when they went up (ver. 10) 'They saw the God of Israel; and

there was under his feet, as it were, a paved work of a
sapphire stone (which is azure, with golden spots,) and
as it were the body of heaven in its clearness." Isaiah
also saw the Lord 'sitting on a throne, high and lifted
up, and his train filled the temple' (chap. vi.); and he
whom he saw was Jesus Christ, as we see from John
xii. 41.

The people of Israel sinned by idolatry, soon after
the giving of the law. When Moses came down from
the Mount, and saw and heard with what tumultuous
joy the people worshiped the golden calf, he dashed in
pieces, in his anger, the two tables of the law, which he
had brought with him from Mount Sinai, and on which
God himself had written the commandments; he was particularly irritated against his brother Aaron, who made
the calf; but to the people he said, ' Ye have sinned a
great sin; and now I will go up unto the Lord, perad-
venture I shall make an atonement for your sin, he ascended the Mount, and said, ' O Lord, this people have
sinned a great sin; yet now, forgive their sin; but if
not, blot me, I pray thee, out of thy book, which thou
has written.' ' What?' answered the Lord, whoever
hath sinned against me, him will I blot out of my book:
Lead the people unto the place, of which I have spoken
unto thee; behold mine angel shall go before thee. I
will not go up in the midst of thee; for thou art a stiff-
necked people, lest I consume thee in the way.' This
did not please Moses, and he humbly interceded once
more; and as God for some time had only called the
children of Israel ' the people,' Moses said, ' consider
that this nation is thy people;' and the Lord then de-

clared, saying, 'My presence shall go with thee, and I will give thee rest.' Moses eagerly caught at this, and said, 'If thy presence go not with me, carry us not up hence. For wherein shall it be known that I and thy people have found favor in thy sight, except thou goest with us? And the Lord said unto Moses, I will do this thing also that thou hast spoken, for thou hast found grace in my sight, and I know thee by name.' This emboldened Moses so much, that he said, 'I beseech thee, shew me thy glory?' The Lord answered, 'I will make all my goodness pass before thee, and I will proclaim the name of the Lord before thee ; and I will be gracious to whom I will be gracious, and I will shew mercy on whom I will shew mercy. But thou canst not see my face; for there shall no man see me and live. But thou shalt see my back-parts.' And thus Moses beheld the glory of the Lord from behind, and the face of Moses shone in consequence, so that the children of Israel could not look at him without a veil.

Jacob also said, 'I have seen God face to face.' But in reality he only saw the human form which the Lord had assumed for a season. In the fulness of time, he took upon him our nature, in personal union with his Divine. The infinite surrounded himself with bounds, and the invisible became visible—God became man. Without controversy, great is the mystery. With what rapture shall all his elect eventually behold him, be like him, and see him as he is ! 'Blessed are the pure in heart, for they shall see God.'

But even here below there is a seeing God in grace, in a spiritual manner, and superior to sense.

The earth, the sky with its splendid and majestic lights, the beauty of the spring, the blossoming trees, the waving corn-fields, the rolling of the thunder in the clouds, the genial dew—all remind us of an overruling providence. But Job at length says, after the Lord had taught him from a whirlwind, ' I formerly heard thee with the hearing of the ear ; but now mine eye seeth thee ;' and the consequence was, ' Therefore I abhor myself, and repent in dust and ashes.' Hence the knowledge that Job obtained after his affliction was more profound and perfect than before ; even as we receive a much clearer idea of a thing, which we see with our eyes, than by merely hearing of it.

Such was also the case with Jacob. Distinguished light had risen upon him by means of this conflict, such as he had never possessed before. He became much more intimately acquainted with his God than previously ; even as when we see the face of some one whom we had only known before from report. Now if it be eternal life to know the true God, and Jesus Christ whom he hath sent ; if life consist in righteousness, peace, and joy, he had evidently increased in all these in a remarkable manner ; Christ in the struggle, had become more perfectly formed within him, although painful distress had preceded it. ' In thy light we see light,' says David, and prays : ' Open thou mine eyes, that I may behold wondrous things out of thy law.' He also confesses that the law of the Lord is perfect, rejoicing the heart, and making wise the simple. But Peter says, ' Grow in grace, and in the knowledge of our Lord and Savior Jesus Christ.' Now this is not accomplished by reflection, studying and reading; by these the head may indeed be filled with orthodox thoughts and ideas; but this, as Paul says, is only ' the form of sound words.' It is like undigested food, which may indeed puff up, but cannot strengthen or nourish. Hence the same apostle says, 'Knowledge puffeth up, but love edifieth.' The instruction which Jesus imparts, is given us by the Holy Spirit on the path of experience, by means of a variety of providential dispensations, afflictions, consolations, impartations and privations, disturbance and peace, strength and weakness. Thus he teaches sinners in the way, he guides the meek aright, and teacheth the humble his way. It is thus that he instructs them respecting sin and grace, until with Job they are able to renounce themselves entirely, and give God all the glory; the path which was rugged before, then becomes straight and even.

Jacob then also mentions the effect of this seeing God, and adds, ' My life is preserved.'

He was delivered. His former state was an oppressive one—fightings without, and fears within. Esau with his four hundred men terrified him. His faith was weak; his courage small; joy had departed from his soul, and clouds of sorrow darkened his mind, which vented themselves in tears. That night had been the most painful and distressing one he had ever spent; he saw nothing but death before him, which Esau had sworn concerning him, and he knew that he was not to be trifled with. It seemed as if God himself had given him over unto death, when he commanded him to return out of Mesopotamia. He had recourse by prayer to that God, who had hitherto blessed and protected him, in order to pour out his fears and his distress before him, and to entreat his deliverance. He knew not by what means he would help him. But what befel him during prayer? We know already. A man struggled with him in such a manner as to dislocate his thigh.

Thus the Lord exercises his people by a variety of afflictions; not unfrequently in such a manner as to cause them to think they must despair and perish, and really would do so, did not the Lord sustain them, in a faithful and confident manner, although imperceptible to themselves; nay, to say the truth, they really do perish and despair—that is, with reference to themselves; so that, on their part, they are compelled to exclaim, 'We perish!' and are deprived of the power to believe, and hope; even as Jacob was not only stripped of the ability to defend himself, but also even to flee. Such situations are, indeed, no pastime; as Jacob also found it. But the end of the ways of God is better than their beginning; exaltation follows humiliation, and life follows death.

Thus it proved also in Jacob's case. 'My life is preserved,' said he. He now felt very different. He was like the eagle, who renews his youth, whose feathers grow again, so that he can again elevate himself upon his pinions and soar aloft to hover in the rays of the sun. His confidence in God was quickened, and his whole soul was tranquilized so that he could boldly look around him. Fear had departed, and he was enabled confidently to appear before Esau. He had all, and abounded.

Such a pleasing reverse is promised in numberless passages; ' I will see you again, and your heart shall rejoice, and your joy no man taketh from you ;' ' I will comfort thee as a mother comforteth her child ;' ' I will strengthen thee ; yea, I will help thee; yea, I will uphold thee with the right hand of my righteousness ;' and many more such promises. They are also faithfully fulfilled in all those whom the Lord humbles ; and hence, it is said, ' Humble yourselves under the mighty hand of God, that he may exalt you in due time.' My heart rejoices at thy willingness to help. I will praise the Lord for his mercies towards me. He hath preserved my soul from death, my eyes from tears, and my feet from falling. Bless the Lord, O my soul ! and all that is within me, bless His holy name ! Bless the Lord, and forget not all his benefits !' Thus the same David rejoiced, who had uttered so many complaints. Thus many a child of God is able to rejoice ; and what exultation, and blessing, and praise will there be, when they shall arrive in heaven out of all their tribulation, after having washed their robes and made them white in the blood of the Lamb !

But what praise to the glory of Divine grace is excited, even here below, in those favored souls who can exult with David, and say, ' The Lord hath delivered me from all my fears ;' who possess peace in the Lord in an uniform and permanent manner, although in the world they may have tribulation ; and who have attained the great grace of being able to rejoice in the Lord always, and to exclaim in the spirit of adoption, ' Abba, Father !' O happy souls, who are redeemed from the servile spirit of bondage, delivered from the fear of death, made free by the law of the Spirit of life in Christ Jesus, from the law of sin; and who serve God, not according to the letter, but in the Spirit. These are the glorious results of beholding the glory of God in the face of Jesus Christ, by the Holy Spirit.

If we wish to enter into the full meaning of Jacob's expression, we must remember that he really expressed himself in his language as follows:—" I am preserved, and shall be preserved;" so that he was animated by a vigorous confidence with respect to the future. The Lord had said to him, ' Thou hast had power;' or more correctly speaking, ' Thou wilt be enabled to prevail.' Now, here is the echo of faith : " I am preserved, and shall be preserved ! although new tribulations may befall me, according to the will of God; yet, I shall be preserved, and at length he will deliver me from all evil, and bring me to his glorious kingdom; of this I am assured, for I know in whom I have believed.'

God performs what he promises. He faithfully helped Jacob through everything, although he had to experience many grievous trials; one of the most painful of which was, the supposed death of his favorite son, Joseph, whom he was told a wild beast had devoured, on his being sent out by him; respecting which he doubtless reproached himself bitterly, as having committed a great piece of thoughtlessness, and on whose account he mourned long, until this also cleared itself up in an unexpected and glorious manner. Whether Jacob, under all these circumstances, was able with the same serenity to say, ' I shall be preserved,' I know not.

16*

From his long mourning over Joseph, and his declaration, "that if mischief befell Benjamin by the way, then shall ye bring down my grey hairs with sorrow to the grave,' the contrary may be inferred; as also from his exaggerated statements to his sons, who wished to take Benjamin with them into Egypt. ' Me ye have bereaved of my children,' said he; ' Joseph is not, and Simeon is not, and ye will take Benjamin away; all these things are against me.' And when his sons, on a previous occasion, had committed the shameful murder of the Shechemites, he was again afraid, and said, ' I being few in number, they will gather themselves together against me, and slay me, and I shall be destroyed, and mine house.' Where is now thy faith? it might be asked. But this also tends much to the glory of God, and to prove that he is alone good, and that we without him can do nothing. In the joy of his heart, and in the enjoyment of Divine gifts, the man probably imagines that his mountain stands so strong, that he will never be moved. And why does he suppose so? Because he secretly thinks that he himself has become something, and imagines he is in possession of the faith &c., for which he has so long supplicated. But it may still be the case with him, that like Jacob he looks at himself, and is afraid lest his powerful foes should at length destroy him and his whole house. O how much has God to do with us, in order to bring us into true poverty of spirit, and to keep us in it! We are invariably desirous of becoming something in ourselves—of growing, being strong, and able in ourselves. Hence the Lord is continually obliged to convince us of

our poverty and misery; yet all this would avail nothing, if he did not himself enable some souls to ascribe
to him the kingdom, the power, and the glory; and to
regard themselves in truth and reality as nothing, even
in the possession of abundance of gifts; and at the same
time to believe in reality and with serenity, and to be
satisfied that in Christ dwells all the fulness of the Godhead bodily. It is true indeed, that no one can receive
anything, or retain it, except it be given him from above.

The sun now rose. This splendid spectacle in nature
was also an image of that which had passed in the
soul of the Patriarch. The night had disappeared. A
lovely morning dawned. It rose upon him. The Sun
of Righteousness and the Day-spring from on high, was
at length to arise upon them that sat in darkness and
the shadow of death, to guide their feet into the way of
peace. O may this Sun rise; may it rise upon us with
its healing beams; may it rise upon all who call
themselves Christians—upon the posterity of Israel—
upon the whole world!

And Jacob halted upon his thigh. Every step reminded him of the great mercy of the Lord, and at the
same time of his own nothingness. Every step exalted
and humbled him. And when others heard his name
and saw his lameness, they would also be reminded that
the Lord condescends more graciously to his people,
than it might be supposed. To him be glory for ever.
Amen.

SOLOMON AND SHULAMITE.

SERMONS

ON THE BOOK OF CANTICLES.

SOLOMON AND SHULAMITE.

SERMON I.

SOLOMON'S SONG III. 1—4.

By night on my bed I sought him whom my soul loveth: I sought him, but I found him not. I will rise now, and go about the city; in the streets and in the broad ways, I will seek him whom my soul loveth: I sought him, but I found him not. The watchmen that go about the city found me: to whom I said, Saw ye him whom my soul loveth? It was but a little that I passed from them, but I found him whom my soul loveth: I held him and would not let him go, until I had brought him into my mother's house, and into the chamber of her that conceived me.

THE Bride, the Church of the Lord, or the individual believing Soul, opens to us in the text the treasury of her spiritual experience, and displays to us glimpses of her inward conflicts, to which some amongst us will, doubtless, find a key in their own Christian experience. O how deep and important the truth unfolded to our view in the narration of the Bride! That which binds us to Christ should not only be the sweet savor of his benefits, but, moreover, the painful sense of our poverty and misery. May our meditations this day lead us to a deeper insight into the meaning of this great truth. With continual reference to ourselves, let us consider the Bride in the fourfold state in which she appears to us in the text.

I. How she revels in spiritual abundance.

II. How she loseth what she had, and languishes in banishment.

III. How she is engaged in a fruitless search.

IV. How she findeth, never to lose again.

I.—'By night on my bed I sought him.' Sought whom? 'Him whom my soul loveth—Christ, the fairest of the sons of men; Christ, the heavenly Bridegroom.' Him the complaining soul had had upon her couch. Delightful figure, by which the entire blessedness of her former state is indicated! She had had the Lord upon her couch. To have the Lord upon our couch, what else can it mean, than to dwell with him and in him, to have the most lively consciousness of his blissful presence, to enjoy his favor, to be filled with the most devout and ardent feelings of love and tenderness towards him, and with the purest joy and delight in the contemplation of his person, his acts and words! To have the Lord upon our couch, what is it, but to possess the assurance of his attachment and love, and an inward joyful conviction of our interest in his promises and declarations; to be animated with devout emotions, and with lively impulse to praise and magnify him, to rejoice, and to exult in him.

Let us look back upon the declarations of the Bride in

the former verses of her song. When she exultingly declared, 'The savor of thy ointments is delightful; thy name is as ointment poured forth.' When she ex-claims, 'My beloved is to me as a cluster of camphire in the vineyards of En-gedi. Behold thou art fair, my love; behold thou art fair. As the apple-tree among the trees of the wood, so is my beloved among the sons. I sat down under his shadow with great delight, and his fruit was sweet to my taste. He brought me to the banqueting-house, and his banner over me was love. Stay me with thy flagons, comfort me with apples; for I am sick of love. · My beloved is mine, and I am his; he feedeth among the lilies.' As she thus sang and re-joiced, and when there was melody in her heart, then she hàd him whom her soul loved, upon her couch.

This sweet and delightful state, in which we may be said to have the Lord upon our couch, is generally ex-perienced in the early period of conversion. Under the almighty influence of the Spirit of God, the delusions that had obscured the barrenness of our heart and life, gradually melt away like snow. It rends the veil of self-deception; and, before we are aware, our entire destitution of peace and joy is presented to our view, though we had till then deemed ourselves full and in need of nothing. We feel voids that must be filled up, and spiritual wants that must be satisfied. We find it is not with us as it should be, and we become deeply impressed with the necessity of a change. Words and actions, sentiments and pursuits, which have hitherto appeared correct and good, begin to disturb us; and we feel an inward gnawing, like the worm that dieth not,

17

and the fire that is not quenched. Then we run to and
fro to seek a cure, and how we may still the raging
thirst of the soul. But this world is not Gilead; and
its reliefs, counsels, and consolations are broken cisterns,
that can hold no water. The stronger this feeling becomes the greater our depression and grief, till at length
there is an end of all joy, the sluices of sorrow are
opened, and laughing is turned into bitter weeping.
The Spirit breathes upon the soul; the icy bands of natural pride and impenitence begin to fall asunder, and
the sinner beholds his misery, divested of every covering. Where now shall he look for help? Behold
even here the work of grace; a Hand in the cloud
which guides securely, and never leads astray. He
comes to Jesus, sighs and implores for mercy: and having received an answer in his soul, that sweet season
commences, when, like the Bride, he has the Lord upon
his couch. How delightful his sensations! What a
life compared with the poor miserable existence afforded by the world! Let us call to mind our own experience, when our spiritual affections possessed their
early freshness. We could then, like children, shed
tears of joyful emotion, as often as we perused the
Scriptures, or reflected on the faithfulness of the Lord,
on his word and history. How great was then our joy,
when we heard his name preached, and his people bear
testimony to his faithfulness? With what ardor we
were filled when his praises were sung; with what fervor we prayed, with what necessity, with what desire
and love! How strongly were we then incited to
speak of him, and thought to convert the world at

once, and to proclaim his name from the house tops, and in the streets! Then we gloried in difficulties, that we might overcome them in the strength of the Lord; and we sought for living stones, wherewith speedily to erect a temple to our God. How incomprehensible it appeared to us, that other Christians were so still, so calm and composed; that they did not participate in the fulness of our joy, or join in our triumphal song; that they even uttered sighs and complaints, while we imagined that with sighing and complaining we had for ever done! Do you still recollect this time? Then, in this sense, in which the Bride in the text meant it, we had the Lord upon our couch.

This state was sweet and blessed; but the welfare of our souls required that it should not be perpetual. The Lord in his own time had to lead us forth from this Goshen of spiritual pleasures, from this luxurious pasture of mental enjoyment. For did we not surely begin to be presumptuous, considering ourselves as great saints, and distinguished from others, on account of our blissful serenity of soul? Had we not begun, while rejoicing in our wealth, to be ashamed of the beggar's staff; and had not the sense of need abated, which had compelled us to knock at the door of mercy, and to prostrate ourselves at the rich man's gate, with the poor and destitute? Was it not in reality far more our own piety and fulness of delight, on which we built and rested, and for which we hoped to escape condemnation, than Christ and his merits? Were we not already seeking the foundation of our future bliss *in* ourselves, instead of *without* ourselves, in Christ crucified? And

did we not love the bread with which Christ fed us, and
the wine which he gave us to drink, much more than
himself? We loved and clung to him, it is true—but
with what sort of love? Was it the intense, holy,
stedfast love, which is grounded on the consciousness
that Christ is our Surety, who hath redeemed our souls
from hell, and rescued us from consuming fire? Was
it a love based on the humiliating thought: I am not
worthy that the sun should shine upon me, yet Christ
has descended from heaven for my sake, to save my soul
from hell, and to purchase it with his own life? Was
it that attachment and clinging to him which spring
from the most lively perception of our entire destitution, nothingness, and impotency, and from the conviction that it is on the grace of Christ alone we exist
every moment? Oh no, so far our glance did not extend, neither into the abyss of our own ruin, nor into
the depths of the merits of Christ. We had merely
skimmed the pool of our misery, and the unfathomable
ocean of the Redeemer's love and mercy. Our love to
him could, therefore, be only superficial. Single sins
had, indeed, presented themselves to our view, but not
yet our entire sinfulness; this and that transgression, but
not the entire desolation and corruption of our heart;
one deformity and another, but not the pernicious sap
which pervades us, not the whole image of Belial that
we bear within us. In one word: we had adhered to
Christ more for the sweet savor of his gifts, than from
a sense of our misery, and of His being indispensable
to our salvation. This was a lax and weak band, a love
which every wind of temptation might destroy—not

an ardent glow, strong as death, and unchangeable as hell—which many waters cannot quench.

II.—But that we may attain unto that perfect state, in which we cling to Christ, no longer for the mere pleasure we enjoy in his presence, but because of the misery we experience in ourselves; no longer for the apples and flowers with which he has regaled us, but because he is necessary to our eternal salvation; not for the pleasurable feelings and delightful hours enjoyed in his kingdom, but because apart from him we feel ourselves abandoned to the wrath and fiery indignation of God, and to all the powers of darkness. That our attitude may be that of exclusive dependence upon him; that we may hang upon his neck and say, 'Lord Jesus, do with me what thou wilt, refresh me or not, fill my heart with manna, or let me suffer want—to thee I cling; for where thou art not, I shall perish in my misery; for out of thee all is darkness, death, and hell,'—that this may be our state, the Lord generally proceeds with us, as he did with the Bride. In his own time he changes the sunshine in our souls into the gloom of night, and withdraws from us all consolation. 'By night upon my couch I sought him whom my soul loveth,' says the Bride; 'I sought him but I found him not.' It had become night with her, and she was forced to complain, 'I have lost the Lord.'

It has become night in us, in the sense intended by the Bride, when the consciousness of the blissful presence of the Lord has departed from us, and the soul no longer retains any perception of the felicity enjoyed at

17*

his right hand. It is become night when the flow of holy feeling and emotion is dried up, and our joy in the Lord and all that is his, has expired within us. It is night when the word that we read no longer affects us, when its promises leave the soul cold and insensible; when the sermons we hear afford no enjoyment, and the worship of God, once our most joyous employment, has become a burden; when we are no longer impelled to pour forth our souls in prayer and praise, and when the most sacred engagements do not cause the heart to overflow with holy joy and delightful emotion. Then it is become night! O deplorable state! When the spikenard of our spiritual knowledge has lost its fragrance; when the grapes on the Gospel-vine yield for us no juice, and the flowers no perfume; when our hearts are become barren, and our spiritual tongue cleaves to the roof of our mouth. Then we are full of complaint and lamentation; we are cast down and know neither counsel nor consolation; for the prop on which we had leaned was not the merit of Christ, but our own feelings; and this prop is now broken. The foundation, on which the superstructure of our hopes had been erected, was not the beam of the cross, but the loose ground of our own piety and lively sensations; we had been accustomed to look more to ourselves than to Christ; our confidence had been our love to the Lord, not his love to us. Therefore a cloud no sooner dims the bright glow of our sensations and feelings, than we find ourselves deprived of the consolations of Christ, and are forced to complain, with the Bride: We have lost the Lord.

III.—We will now examine what further occurs in this state of destitution and banishment, when the luxu-riant spring-time of our soul is changed into the chill of winter, and the melody within us has ceased ; when the heart, once so animated, sensitive, and happy, has become a barren sand. We see it in the Bride.. When it had become night in her, she resolved : ' I will arise and seek him whom my soul loveth.' 'Yes, I will! I will !' By this we perceive how little she knows herself. I will arise, will restore myself, will take possession of the paradise I have lost, and of my former blissful state. I will again warm and animate my heart, will again acquire my former joyfulness and my former delight in prayer and praise. Yes, what is there that she will not do ? Well, let her resolve, let her strive. On the path she has entered she will make wonderfully wholesome discoveries. It is a path of sorrow, but its . end is joy and peace.

' I will arise.' Whither will she go ? ' I will go about the city, in the streets, and in the broad ways. I will seek him whom my soul loveth.' In the city ? yes, in the spiritual Jerusalem ; in the kingdom of God ; in the congregation of the faithful ; there she hopes to regain the exquisite felicity she has lost. But alas ! we hear her complain, ' I sought but found him not.' What the Bride here confesses, have we not all here experienced ? When that night overshadowed us, we also imagined we could ourselves rekindle joy in the soul, again render our barren hearts fruitful. We also could exclaim : ' I will ! I will !' as if all had been within our grasp. Then we also arose, and went about the streets of Jerusalem ; tried every means, and hoped to force the waters of spiritual consolation again to flow ; but ah, ' I sought, but found him not.'

We had resource to heart-stirring, beautifully spiritual books, which we allowed to preach to us, in the hope thus to obtain relief, and to re-animate our stagnant feelings. But, alas ! the books seem stale and insipid, and left us as we were, dull and cheerless. We sought, but found not. We hastened to the assemblies of the saints, where the love of Christ was joyfully proclaimed ; where his praises resounded in spiritual songs, and fervent prayers ascended to heaven ; here we expected a joyful spirit would again possess us, that our hearts would melt, and our tongues be loosened. But we sought and found not. While the eloquence of others flowed like living waters, and their prayers were ardent, we were speechless, or uttered empty words ; they spread the wings of devotion, and soared on high ; we too essayed to rise, but we had no wings to spread. We forced ourselves to sing, but the song died upon our lips, unresponded by our hearts. We sought, but found not. We eagerly thronged to whatever was solemn and sublime, hoping that there our icy hearts would melt again ; and there we should again taste that joy, which is eternal, at the right hand of God. But it was and remained night ; and it seemed as if no spring would succeed the winter in our souls. We sought, but found not. We wearied ourselves in the streets of Jerusalem, and fatigued our friends with our complaints ; we resorted to every expedient to refresh and invigorate our hearts ; but we had still to complain with the Bride :

'I sought, but found him not.' The Bride meets with the watchmen who go about the city. The watchmen —who are they? We, the ambassadors for Christ, whose business it is to go about Jerusalem; to watch for the safety of the city; to arouse those found slumbering in burning houses, and on the edge of precipices; to conduct those walking in their sleep from the dangerous rocks on which they climb; to warn those who stray from the path of life, and comfort those who sit solitary and weep; to encourage those who he breathless in the streets unable to proceed. Yes, the watchmen are the Stewards over God's mysteries. To them the Bride came, and addressed the inquiry: 'Saw ye him whom my soul loveth?'. Amongst them she expected certainly to find what she sought; but even this last hope deceived her. Here too she was constrained to exclaim: 'I sought; but found him not.' Exhortation, counsel, and instruction enough; but no life, no joy, no interest in the Lord and his cause, nothing of that which she desired. She had now wearied herself in the streets of Jerusalem, had tried every thing; but still she remains, and complains, 'I sought, but found him not.'

IV.—It would now seem as if the Bride were for ever cut off from all salvation; and yet her salvation was never so near as at this moment. She had now reached the point of connection and union with Christ, which is eternal. She had made great efforts to rekindle her love for Christ, his kingdom, and his cause, but all in vain; and even amongst the watchmen who go about the city, she had not recovered what she had lost.

Lifeless as she had come to them, had she again departed. And as she proceeded a little onward, there—
.Well, what happened there? There, methinks she
first paused, communicating with her disconsolate heart,
and felt, for the first time in her life, with the full clearness and force of truth, the worthlessness of man and all
his acts, and that sin hath sunk him into the most abject
helplessness. Nay, that so deplorable is his state, and
he is so inwardly dead, that, of himself, he is incapable
of gratitude towards the greatest of all benefactors, the
most faithful of all friends; that he cannot even open
his mouth in praise and thankfulness to him, who, beyond all in heaven and on earth, is worthy to receive
glory and honor, thanksgiving and praise; that of himself he is unable to rejoice in the greatest blessings, or
elevate his heart in prayer to God; that he cannot excite in himself any desire after the Lord and his benefits; and that even the best adapted means are insufficient to dissolve his rocky heart in devotion, love, and
holy joy. This she had never dreamt! Indeed how
could it have occurred to her, that human nature was
so debased? But now experience had opened her eyes
to behold, for the first time, its complete corruption; to
perceive, that the natural life was in reality death, and
not life, now for the first time she felt how deep her
fall, how weak and barren her life and will, how great
her ruin, and need of help. Hitherto she had desired
from her Bridegroom nothing but kindness, pleasure,
and refreshment: now she requires a surety to appear
for her, a mediator to undertake for her, an intercessor
to plead for her before the judgment seat, a renovator

to mould her into something on which the eye of God might rest with delight. All this she found in him, who had till now been nothing more to her than a beloved friend, that had cheered her life and rejoiced her heart; but now how infinitely precious had he become. When she had passed on a little, she exclaims; 'I found him whom my soul loveth!'

Was it not the same with us? At first we, too, attached ourselves to the Lord, more for the delight we had in him and in his words, than because without him we felt ourselves to be eternally lost. But this was a slender attachment, a feeble love; transient as the pleasurable emotions which called them forth. When they vanished, and the table at which we had been regaled, was removed, then, alas! we fell away from Christ, and could deny him ten times in a breath, and in various ways. But when enlightened by the Spirit, we knew ourselves as lost, as ruined creatures, and were enabled to discover in Christ a Savior, whose hand alone could snatch us from eternal flames, our attachment to and our connection with him assumed a new and very different character.

I hold him, the Bride joyfully exclaims, and will not let him go. And why will she not let him go? Because he fills her heart with joy, and is the source of many delights. The Bride, if in our midst, would reply; Though he left me to languish, and suffered me not to taste of his loveliness, I hold him, and will not let him go, because I know that he alone can save me from eternal death. 'I hold him, and will not let him go.' Why not? Because he sweetens her life, and

richly provides for all her necessities?   Oh no; oh no,
she would reply; though he gave me gall to drink in
this life, I know that he alone can conduct me safely
through the gloomy portals of eternity, and the fiery
scrutiny of the last judgment: therefore I hold him,
and will not let him go.   'I hold him, and will not let
him go.'   And why not?   Because he can help her to
attain that righteousness which is approved before God.
Help, the Bride would exclaim : I cannot furnish any
thing to adorn myself for the great wedding ? He must,
and he alone can, clothe me in the garments of salvation, in which to appear before God.   Therefore I hold
him, and will not let him go, but surrender myself entirely into his hands. ' I hold him, and will not let him
go,' she exultingly exclaims—or rather the Spirit within her—'till I have brought him into my mother's
house.'   What are we, then, to understand by her
mother's house ?   Paul says, (Gal. iv. 26,) ' But Jerusalem which is above is free, which is the mother of us
all."   There she will bring her Surety, and there be
brought by him.   Now, beloved, we behold a soul by
the grace and guidance of the Lord, united to Christ;
not as formerly, by a sense of the abundance of joy
which is derived from him, but by a feeling of its poverty and great misery ; not by the experience, ' It is good
to be here,' but by the thorough conviction that without him hell, death, and ruin are its portion.   It recognizes in him now, not merely a Comforter, but a Savior ; and, conscious of its own frailty, it no longer
hopes for eternal life as the reward of love to the Lord,
or leans on its pious emotions : but it rests exclusively

on the merits of Christ; and it can say with Asaph, in Psalm lxxiii., 'Whom have I in heaven but thee? and there is none upon the earth that I desire beside thee. My flesh and my heart faileth; but God is the strength of my heart, and my portion for ever.' May the Lord thus guide us, one and all; and may the consciousness of our worthlessness form the chain which binds us to him; and his merit and love to sinners be the rock on which our peace is founded.

18

SERMON II.

SOLOMON'S SONG, II. 14.

O my dove, that art in the clefts of the rock, in the secret places of the stairs, let me see thy countenance, let me hear thy voice; for sweet is thy voice, and thy countenance is comely.

WHOSE voice is it we have just heard? It is the voice of the fairest of the children of men; the heavenly Bridegroom speaks to Shulamite, his dearly purchased church—or to individual souls affianced and wedded to Him in faith. Sweeter than milk and honey are the words which flow from his lips; and when the Bride afterwards so joyously exclaims, ' Thy lips, O my spouse drop as the honeycomb: honey and milk are under thy tongue;' she does so, undoubtedly, in the blissful recollection of this address of her Bridegroom, and of the soul-refreshing words: ' My dove in the clefts of the rocks, in the secret places of the stairs, let me see thy countenance, let me hear thy voice; for sweet is thy voice, and thy countenance is comely.'

We will now consider the words more closely: and may the Lord abundantly refresh us from this fountain of living waters!

I. Let us contemplate the dove in the clefts of the rocks.

II. Then, consider what the Bridegroom intends by this address to her; ' Let me see thy countenance, let me hear thy voice.'

I.—' My dove.'—Thus the Lord addresses the elect. He calls them frequently by this tender epithet. In the fifth chapter he says, ' Open to me, my sister, my dove :' and in another place, ' My dove, my undefiled, is but one.' But why are they addressed as doves? Is it on account of the splendid plumage, the righteousness of Christ, in which they are arrayed? As it is said, Psalm lxviii., ' Though ye have lain among the pots, yet shall ye be as the wings of a dove covered with silver, and her feathers as yellow gold.' Or is it because of the gentle spirit of Jesus which is in them, and which once displayed itself visibly under the form of a dove? Or are they called doves, because they rise above the world ; as Moses declares : ' and thou shalt be above only, and thou shalt not be beneath ?' Doubtless all this appertains to the character. But if we take a deeper and more enlarged view of the figure, we shall find points of resemblance, between a soul converted to the Lord, and a dove, more numerous, and perhaps more attractive and striking.

If the lamb be excepted, there is no creature more defenceless than the dove. She has neither tooth nor claw, neither hoof nor sting, only a pair of wings for flight; in flight lies her entire strength and triumph. Thus, we confess it, whether it be to our honor or shame, thus it is with us, whom grace has transformed into the doves of Christ. Those who are out of Christ,

are all stronger.   What heroes do we not find amongst
them! who think themselves equal to every encounter;
who know nothing of fear and caution; whom no
enemy can make tremble, no danger appals; and who
would disdain to look for help in circumstances ever so
perilous.· They think to vanquish empires by the
strength of their arm; to seize the promises as a prey;
with the right hand of their own righteousness to stop
the lion's mouth; to extinguish the fires of the last
judgment with self-acquired virtues; and to escape the
edge of the sword by their own wisdom and dexterity.
Of all this, like dreamers, they think themselves capable, through the power of their own might.   Yea, what
cowardly fugitives are we, when contrasted with those
giants in virtue, who think to scatter their enemies like
chaff; that sin, the world, and the devil, with every
other bitter foe, shall fall before them; whilst we pre-
pare for instant flight, if we but hear the distant roar·of
the approaching lion.   We venture on no contest
alone; but as soon as the trumpet of conflict sounds,
seeks protection behind the shield of our champion.
They display a more heroic spirit; and, proudly scorn-
ing all support, rush, as if invulnerable, into the hottest
fire of temptation; and, though vanquished, exult in
the glory of falling on the scene of conflict, the field of
honor.   Such honor we disclaim.   We are not such
Anakim, such giants and lions.   St. Paul, indeed,
speaks of breastplates and armor; of the helmet, the
shield, and the sword, with which we are equipped;
and, judging from this description, we might be taken
for wonderful heroes.   But such is not his meaning.

As a dove escaped from the hawk, and safe in the shelter of her covert, may be said to be armed against her foe, and to be covered with helmet and shield; in the same sense are we renowned in many parts of Scripture as formidable, as cased in armor, and terrible as an army. But like the dove, our entire strength and invincibility consists in flight, and in taking refuge; for we are defenceless in and by ourselves, and it has happened to us as it once happened to Saul—the Philistines have stripped us of our armor, and have deposited it in the house of Ashtaroth. Do Satanic temptations assail us? We hasten to Him who will be our house and our refuge, and there we are found secure. Do we hear the devil roar? We venture not to encounter him, well knowing it would be rushing immediately into his jaws. We cling to the Savior, and a wall of fire compasses us around. If the lusts of the flesh revive and stir within us—unlike those who strive to conquer them by firm resolves, and other self-devised expedients—we quickly fly to him who is our shield. And scarcely have we beheld his bleeding wounds, scarcely stammered forth a single ' Lord Jesus,' when the victory is ours; while they, with all their panoply of self-will and self-exertion, sink deep into the mire. This is our method, and it is that of the dove. We by no means enter into any conflict; we seek our salvation solely in flight. Jesus is our armor: the shield that protects us; the helmet that screens us; the sword that defends, and the fortress that encircles us.

Doves, it is well known, love their accustomed dwelling-place. And would we ascertain whether we belong to the spiritual swarm of doves, we must minutely examine how we feel in the world, whether pleasure or pain; for by this we may know it. If we are the doves of Christ, born of him, we feel pain, anxiety, and fear, wherever he is not; and as this must ever be the case, it is impossible to experience the delights and comforts of home in worldly society, or in worldly pursuits; on the contrary, we are uneasy and straitened, the heart is oppressed, and lifts its wings to seek a purer atmosphere. As a child among strangers is alarmed, and ceases not to inquire for its mother; and as the soul of an exile swells with inexpressible longings after the land which gave him birth; so feel the doves of Christ in the air of this world. Nay, in it they cannot live nor endure to the end; they must continually ask for their mother, and are no where so happy as in the air which encircles the mountains of Jerusalem. 'In the world ye shall have tribulation,' says Christ; this is one of the most infallible marks of a state of grace.

Whilst we are speaking of doves, some one amongst you may perhaps be reminded of the ancient well known, and so called carrier pigeon, and inquire whether there are no points of resemblance between spiritual doves, and them? Undoubtedly there are. They both are able to return to their homes, wherever placed. They have a free passage; and are ever willing to carry with them the burdens and messages of strangers.

When the fiery serpents came upon idolatrous Israel, the people themselves venture not before the Lord with their complaints, but applied to Moses to intercede for them; and he flew up to the house of the Lord, and poured the distress of Israel into the ears of an all merciful God; thus Moses became the carrier dove of his people. So David flew for Solomon, Lot for Zoar, Daniel for Jerusalem, and Job for his children—ascended on the wings of prayer, and brought the suit of those for whom they went forth before the Father's throne. And when Jeroboam besought the man of God to pray that his withered hand might be restored; and Darius entreated the Jews to pray for the King's life; and Simon requested the Apostles to pray, that none of the things which he had threatened might come upon him; —then the man of God, the Jews, and the Apostles were employed as carrier doves, to bring the affairs of those, who have themselves no wings, into the Father's house. O all ye winged souls, who know the way above, and have free ingress and egress through the blood of Christ; disdain not ye likewise, to be the flying post between heaven and earth, and 'willing interposers between your brethren, who have as yet neither wings nor voice, and God. Carry not only your own burdens before the throne of grace, but likewise those of strangers. To be a dove of Christ; to have unrestrained access to Him, as to our house; to receive from his hand daily and hourly supplies of grace and mercy, and to drink of the pure fountains of Israel—truly this is a happy state! O that God would form all our souls in this dovelike manner, to this dovelike state.

But to return to our text. ' My dove,' says the Lord. Where is this dove now to be found? where is her place? Ezekiel once speaks of doves of the mountains,

all of them mourning for their iniquity. Shall we meet
our dove there? No; once, it is true, she may have
had her seat amongst them, mourning and sighing with
them, in ashes; but now she has soared upwards from
this gloomy region and vale of tears, and dwells elsewhere. Isaiah beholds from a great distance a whole
swarm of doves flying as a cloud. Is ours perhaps
amongst them? No, our dove has already reach--
ed the windows, towards which they are only flying. Noah's first dove, as you know, fluttered rest-
lessly over the surface of the waters, and found
no resting place. So flutter many. Does our dove resemble Noah's? Not at all: our dove has found rest
for the sole of her foot, and the olive tree on whose
crown to alight. She is in the clefts of the rock. ' My
dove is in the clefts of the rock, in the secret places of
the stairs,' says the Lord. Now behold this weak and
defenceless bird, seated proudly and securely in her
rock, like a king in his castle, or a chieftain in his camp,
bidding defiance to the whole world. No fowler can
reach, no hawk penetrate her dwelling; no serpent cast
its venom so high; and though the beasts of prey that
roam the valley, howl amongst themselves, the dove in
her fortress can laugh and look calmly down upon the
tumult. Clouds roll their thunders over them: but she
has no fear. Lightnings flash fiercely around; but the
rock is not melted in this fire. Mountains sink before
the storm, and mighty forests are laid waste; but the
foundations of her house stand fast.

The dove then dwells in the clefts of the rocks. If
we now abandon the figure, and judge the subject spirit-

ually, the rock will be Christ, the rock of salvation, and the clefts his bleeding wounds, in which rests, like a dove, every believing and accepted soul. Of a truth it has found a safe retreat. Not so you, who are firmly nested in the dry brambles of your own righteousness. Behold the branches will be burned in the fire of the judgment, and oh! the poor bird with them. Not ye, who depend upon your own piety, and expect salvation from it. Oh! believe it, that in the day of judgment this will be counted as stubble, which is cast into the oven, but not as a ground of your redemption. But our dove has found a Zoar, not in herself; for there she could only discover what merited condemnation; nor in her own works and feelings; of these she could only exclaim, Unclean! unclean! She was not so foolish as to dream of gathering grapes on the shores of the Dead Sea. She found her rest, and the certainty of her salvation and future bliss, not in herself, but in the wounds of Christ, in his bleeding merits and atoning death. Her mind was so staid and governed that she knew herself just before God, not on account of the new life that had sprung up within her, but only on account of the blood-shedding of her surety. And this is the foundation which is firm and abiding, when every thing else sinks and passes away.

Of him, whose salvation is firmly settled on the perfect satisfaction rendered by his Surety, whose hopes centre in the merits of the true Paschal Lamb, and who esteems himself secure in Christ alone—of him, it may well be said: ' Behold a dove in the clefts of a high rock, and in the secret places of the stairs !' No prince was ever so securely entrenched behind his fortifications, his ramparts and walls, as this dove. Moses is a skilful archer, and sends out curses; but here he may leave his skill; no ban can disturb, no curse affect, this dove. For her silence of night reigns on Sinai and Ebal, and the wild flames of fire are quenched in the blood of the Redeemer. The subtilty of Satan is foiled; he may indeed go about the rock, and roar, but he cannot seize the dove, without swallowing the rock itself, in which she dwells. Should even her love decline, and her faith glimmer as an expiring light; should her zeal cool, and her heart become steril, as a barren sand; yet is she safe, for, God be thanked! her faith, her zeal, her love, are not her resting place; her stronghold and her fortress are alone the blessed wounds of Christ. In this frame she is ever fair in the sight of God; and though miserable herself, she shines as a crown of gold in the hand of the Lord. And supposing the Eternal would consume her, as a devouring flame; in this palace she is stronger than the anger of God, and conquers the Eternal in his wrath. I therefore call upon you all, in the words of Jeremiah, ' O ye that dwell in Moab, leave the cities, and dwell in the rock, and be like the dove that maketh her nest in the sides of the hole's mouth.'

II.—We have now contemplated the dove in her secure retreat, after she has renounced all self-dependence, and, despairing of herself, has taken shelter in the clefts of the rock, the rock of Christ's merits. Let us now listen to the voice of the Bridegroom. ' My dove,'

he cries, ' my dove in the clefts of the rock, in the secret places of the stairs, let me see thy countenance, let
me hear thy voice; for sweet is thy voice, and thy
countenance is lovely.' What does the Lord mean by
this address; how is he to be understood; and what
secret motive may have prompted it ? To me it appears thus :—

The Lord will see the countenance of his dove and
hear her voice, because her voice is sweet, and her
countenance is comely. By her countenance is intended the golden plumage, the imputed righteousness of
of Christ, in which she is adorned; the new life in
God, the new creature within her, the man of light for
whom the world is become too narrow; the faith with
which she is filled, the peace and tranquillity which take
possession of her pardoned soul; it is her illumination,
her holy longing and desires, and her inward, constant,
spontaneous resistance to all darkness and sin—all these
belong to the countenance of the dove. Her voice is
the incense of prayer and supplication, of praise and
adoration, kindled by the Spirit's sacred fire. This is
the voice the Lord wishes to hear, and this is the countenance he desires to behold. Do you wonder that he
should desire this ?. Is it not said (Psalm civ. 31.)
' The Lord shall rejoice in his works ?' He is himself
the perfection of beauty, and his pleasure is to behold
himself, and all that has proceeded from him. The
Seraphim around his throne are his delight, because he
sees in them, as in a mirror, his own glorious image.
But he rejoices still more to view it in the dark ground
of the sinner's soul.

The morning stars proclaim his praise, even in their silence; and they display with astonishing lustre the purity of him who made them.   But of all his works none so loudly declare his praise, as the work of grace in the sinner's heart.   With inexpressible glory his power and love are there exhibited.   Imagine, a sinner worthy only of condemnation, becoming at once holy; as David in the same breath declares: I am poor and needy, I am holy; a servant of the wicked one transformed into a dear child of God: a creature of darkness becomes light, like the sun, because its light is come; dead wood begins to put forth and bud; and in miry clay begins to be formed the image of the Godhead.   What a manifestation of the glory of the Lord! How grand, how amazing an exhibition of the glory of his name, of his infinite power and inscrutable mercy!

And shall the Lord not find pleasure in the work of his hand?   He desires to see this work, and rejoice to contemplate himself in it.   'Shew me thy countenance and let me hear thy voice; for thy voice is sweet, and thy countenance is comely."   But why 'shew me thy countenance?' why 'let me hear thy voice?'   What does the Bridegroom mean?   Is not the Bride always looking towards him?   Does she not live and move in him?   Does he not behold her every moment?   Why then this call to shew her countenance?   And does he not hear her voice, in the inmost recesses of her soul?   This voice is never silent to his ear.   This is indeed all true. Yet, sometimes it pleases the Lord to require a more prominent display of what his grace has wrought in the secret sanctuary of the soul: partly, that those in whom his work is carried on may attain to clearer perceptions of it, and be incited to more elevated devotion ; partly to furnish a glorious spectacle to angels, and to the world, and to magnify his holy name in their eyes. With this view he leads his people from under the grateful shadow of the palm-trees of Elim, again into the wilderness ; and calls them forth from tranquility and calm contemplation, into the tumult of life, into various perplexities, into night and gloom, where the light which his grace has transfused into them has opportunity to prove its existence, and to shine forth conspicuously. The severe trial which he suspended over Abraham, and the command, ' Go, and sacrifice thy son whom thou lovest'—what was it but the same call, though disguised, ' My dove, shew me thy countenance, and let me hear thy voice.' And, behold, the voice of this dove was sweet, and her countenance comely ! The conflict with Jacob—for what purpose did it take place ? That it might evince, how powerful the strength of the Lord is in our weakness ; and what courage, what invincibility, he can infuse into a dismayed and fearful heart ; and the countenance of this dove also was most comely in its appearance. Therefore know, all ye spiritual doves ; if Jesus lead you in a similar way, if thick darkness encompass, or the fires of temptation rage around ; if he rouse you from your security, and causes Laban to assail you from behind, and Esau from before ; he only seeks in this way an opportunity, partly himself, to behold the work of grace within you, and partly to discover it to yourself and others ; and in this gloomy dispensation the call goes forth to you, ' My dove in the

clefts of the rock, in the secret places of the stairs, let
me see thy countenance, let me hear thy voice; for
sweet is thy voice, and thy countenance is comely.'

What we have now said is true, but whether it be
also applicable to our dove in the Canticles is another
question.   I believe it is not. . In my opinion it is not
the intention of the Lord, in this instance, to call forth
the soul from her tranquil and contemplative state, and
to involve her in perplexities, in order that her graces
may appear in a stronger light.   No, I think I can perceive a motive yet infinitely more lovely and tender in
this call; ' Shew me thy countenance, let me hear thy
voice.'

The soul, whom Jesus here calls his dove, has ac-
quired an insight into herself, and her ruined state—and
into the depth of that fearful abyss on the edge of which
she had so long unconsciously slumbered; she has
caught a distant glimpse of the judgment-throne, and
the Lord, as a consuming fire seated upon it, with her
sentence of death upon his lips: then anguish and horror took hold upon her, as an armed man; then she fal-
tered from place to place to find a refuge, a secure retreat from his vengeance.   She sought but found none;
the billows of anguish mounted high, and rolled tumultuously over her—then the Savior appeared to her with
the cheerful declaration, ' I, even I am He that blotteth
out thy transgressions, for mine own sake, and will not
remember thy sins.'   She no sooner heard these glad
tidings, than she rose and embraced him; she cast herself upon Him as her only hope; and in his merits, in
his wounds, she found the long-sought refuge and place

of rest. Now she is in the clefts of the rock, rejoicing as a brand just plucked from the burning. But her joy is not unmixed, her state of grace not yet perfect; many things still separate between her and the Lord. Her soul is yet oppressed with difficulties that render it impossible freely to exult in the grace she has received. Sometimes the sense of her unworthiness weighs like a mountain on her heart, and she is ashamed to lift up her eyes; she cannot conceive, that, for her sake, the Savior should submit to such labor and trouble. The wounds, that constitute her safety, become her pain. Sometimes the fear of again falling into sin, and of losing what she has gained, afflicts her; and she strives, with fear and trembling, if by any means she might arm and defend herself from the roaring lion who threatens her destruction. She cannot believe that he who delivered her should still care for her—feeling deeply her unworthiness she considers this would be requiring too much; it is enough, more than enough, that he so mercifully snatched her from the fire. She is as yet entirely destitute of filial confidence in Jesus; she lies prostrate at his feet, and would pour forth her gratitude, but the thought obtrudes itself: " Ah! what value can the King, surrounded by his seraphim, place on my poor thanks?" She would pray, but awe restrains her tongue, and she imagines so much has already been done for her, she ought not to desire more. Such is her state; great fear yet blended with her joy, great pressure of heart; her intercourse with the Savior is not yet that filial, cordial, unrestrained communion, which is so full of great benefits and of rich blessings.

The Lord well saw the state of his poor dove's heart;.

and he saw it partly with delight, and partly with sincere compassion. He approached her, and addressed her tenderly, in order to gain her confidence, ' My dove, why art thou cast down ? Art thou apprehensive, that I having extended my arm for thy deliverance, thou hast no farther interest in me, and that my mercy is exhausted ? Thou knowest not how my heart is affected towards thee. I have indeed redeemed thee ; but thinkest thou that it has been like one redeeming a creature of indifference, and then going on his way ? No, I also love thee—thou pleasest me : shew me thy countenance—thy countenance is comely unto me, I have pleasure therein : be not silent before me, let me hear thy voice, it is sweet to me ; thou art my delight ; and it is perhaps of higher importance to me, than even to thee, that thou shouldst be kept from the enemy, and that the work begun in thee should be perfected to thy profit, and to my honor and glory."

And it was not perhaps until the dove comprehended the force of this endearing declaration, that she was able fully to rejoice. Every oppression, every burden was at once removed from her soul. Her heart was now free, her courage glowed, and her relation to Jesus had assumed an entirely new character. It had become a blissful, familiar intercourse of giving and receiving ; of ingenuous, childlike application and desire, and of unceasing supply ; and, in the place of fear and trembling, had succeeded the most joyful assurance ; for she now knew, not only that Christ was hers, but that she was his. What a blissful state ! in which whatever had intervened between us and the life-spring of our spiritual joy, has disappeared ; in which every doubt or

difficulty that had prevented an entire surrender and
devotion of ourselves to the best of all masters, is abol-
ished; and in which every impediment to an unrestrained supply of grace from his fulness is removed. O ye
redeemed of the Lord, who have, by Divine grace
found the only secure hiding place, whose souls have
fled to the rock which was founded by God before the
foundation of the world; but who have not, like our
dove, attained to a child-like, confidential, and ingenuous intercourse with your Surety ; who have embraced
him as a Redeemer, but not yet as a friend, not yet as
a brother, and the benignant guide of your life, who is
willing to dwell with you under one roof, to carry you
in his bosom, and who entirely *lives* for his own, as
once he *died* for them—may you soon obtain from the
Lord of Lords, in this or in any other manner, the
blessed assurance that he is not merely pleasing in
your sight, but that you are likewise well pleasing in
his ; that your countenance is comely to him, and your
voice sweet, much sweeter than ever his voice to you;
that you may not continue oppressed and fearful, and
appear as brands scarcely plucked from the burning ;
but that you may enjoy the blessed state of the Apostle
John, and repose upon his bosom as free and beloved
children, in the full experience of what is said by David,
(Psalms xxxvi. 7—8,) .' How excellent is thy loving
kindness, O God ! therefore the children of men put
their trust under the shadow of thy wings. They
shall be abundantly satisfied with the fatness of thy
house, and thou shalt make them drink of the river of
thy pleasures.' Amen.

19*

SERMON III.

SOLOMON'S SONG I. 5—6.

*I am black, but comely, O ye daughters of Jerusalem ; as the
tents of Kedar, as the curtains of Solomon.   Look not upon
me, because I am black, because the sun hath looked upon me ;
my mother's children were angry with me, they made me the
keeper of the vineyards ; but my own vineyard have I not
kept.*

THE words of the text are those of Shulamite, a redeemed soul ; and they contain a remarkable testimony
of herself.   She here describes her inward and outward
state, in a well conceived picture ; and she gives us at
the same time a passing sketch from the history of her
inward life.   Let me beg your attention, while en-
deavoring to investigate the import of her words.   We
will consider :

   I. Shulamite's blackness : ' I am black—the sun has
      looked upon me.'

  II. Her comeliness and beauty : ' I am comely as the
      tents of Kedar, as the curtains of Solomon.'
      And lastly, reflect upon,

 III. The experience which she mentions : ' my
      mother's children were angry with me ; they
      made me keeper of the vineyards ; but my own
      vineyard have I not kept.

I.—' I am black!' Singular confession! The Bride
of the Most Lovely, black! In the kingdom of Christ,
how counter every thing runs to reason, and our natural
conceptions! For example: one would imagine the
natural order to be, first, holiness, and then pardon.
But the law of this kingdom reverses the matter, and
declares, Pardon first, and then sanctification. Reason
thinks virtue to be the way to peace ; but the Divine
rule makes peace with God precede, and virtue follow
as the fruit of peace, and not peace as the fruit of virtue. Human wisdom supposes a man must become
upright before he can attain the rights of citizenship in
the kingdom of heaven ; but the wisdom of God ap-
points the kingdom to sinners, and numbers integrity of
life amongst the things to be enjoyed within its bounda-
ries—not without them. Reason cannot think otherwise, than that a child of God must be pure and imma-
culate ; and behold, here steps forth such a child of
God, a soul entirely devoted to the Lord, and declares
without the smallest reserve: ' I am black, O ye
daughters of Jerusalem.' Black both inwardly and
outwardly. Whence then thy blackness, thou fairest
among women ? ' The sun has looked upon me.' The
sun ! what sun ? Surely not the Sun of righteousness,
that bringeth healing in his wings, and is the fountain
of all light ? Yes, the very same. In his vicinity, in
the blaze of his light, the Shulamite has become black.

Whence does she come, the heavenly dove ? Can it
be from the world, has she there soiled her plumage ;
or from the paths of sin, or the fires of temptation ?
By no means ; she is come straightway from the King's

chamber; where she has rejoiced in him, and refreshed
herself with the fulness of his grace.   And she no sooner leaves this sacred place, than she discovers that she
is black.   Whence then her blackness ?   She is black
from the rays of that Sun, in whose beams she has been
reposing ; for her king—even Christ, with whom she
had been—he is the sun.   We are all by nature black;
to the very core the complexion of our heart, our life
and being, is black.   But who is sensible of this ?   We
perceive not our blackness and sinfulness, until exposed
to the radiance of the Eternal Sun ; until the effulgent
glory of God's presence renders our darkness apparent,
and the light of his Spirit penetrating the gloom, discovers to us the dark abyss of our nature; then we
exclaim: 'I am black, O ye daughters of Jerusalem ;
the sun has looked upon me.'   How was it with Isaiah,
when he found himself suddenly near this sun, and saw
the Lord sitting upon his exalted throne ?   He was all
at once so black, and found himself so unholy and so
miserable, that he began to tremble at himself, and before God, and anxiously exclaimed, ' Woe is me! I am
undone ; because I am a man of unclean lips.'   What
happened to Simon Peter, when he became aware that
the Day Spring from on high was with him in his
boat ?   As if struck by lightning, he fell at Jesus' feet,
saying : 'Depart from me; for I am a sinful man,
O Lord !'—that is, in other words, 'I am black, O
ye daughters of Jerusalem; the sun has looked
upon me.   And when the Lord looked up at the
publican Zaccheus in the sycamore tree, what was the
first impression which this look produced ?   The pub-

lican became a sinner, became black in his own eyes,
black as an Ethiopian, and began to make confession :
' If I have taken any thing from any man by false ac-
cusation, I return him four fold.'   Thus it is still : when
the Lord condescends to draw near to us, the first effect
of his presence is, that all our imagined lustre is dis-
pelled like the mist, and our darkness becomes palpa-
ble.   The sun makes us black.   When the Lord rends
the heavens, and comes down to commune with a child
of man, and to establish his covenant with him, the immediate effect is, that he feels himself black, and knows
his misery.   And be assured that he who has not experienced the searching power of that Sun, has never yet
come in contact with the Sun itself ; he is still without ;
not even having taken the preliminary steps towards
the ratification of the covenant.

'I am black,' says the Bride.   From whence does
this confession proceed ?   Is it the excessive fervor of
a first repentance, as a newly awakened sinner ?   By no
means.   It issues from her secret intercourse with the
Lord, from a state of grace, and from the chamber of
her King ; as one of the redeemed, as a member of the
kingdom.   And she is still black ?   Yes—that appears
strange to many.   But is it not strange to him who has
been planted in the same soil with the Bride, and who
has been led in the same way of salvation ; he knows
well the impossibility of living in the communion of the
great Sun of Righteousness, without daily discovering
in himself, by means of the bright rays, new and deeper
shades of darkness ; that by means of communion with
Christ, one becomes daily blacker, and the state of the
soul, as it is by nature, appears worse every day.   Those

who so easily and rapidly pass over into a state of glorying, on account of their progress in holiness, cause us
at least to suspect that they do not sufficiently walk in
the light of Jacob, nor hold close communion with the
Lord himself. It arises from the nature of the intercourse itself, and is confirmed by the experience of all
the saints, that the more unreserved our confidence is
in the Lord, and the closer our intercourse with Him,
the more comprehensive will be our perception of the
depth of our own ruin. Every fresh insight into the
glory of Immanuel becomes a torch, to display, in a
clearer light the greatness of our depravity. Every
new discovery of the purity of his nature and his will,
strengthens the consciousness of our own impurity.
Every new communication of his grace will be a coal
of fire upon our head, and will deepen and quicken the
feeling of our own unworthiness; and every new experience of his love and faithfulness will make us more
painfully sensible of the absence of those qualities in
ourselves, and of the coldness of our hearts. Thus, in
the light of his countenance, we shall daily discover
deformities and stains, which we have hitherto overlooked; daily find occasions to humble ourselves at his
feet, and devoutly to rejoice that our wedding garment
has long been woven and finished for us; and that the
blood and righteousness of Christ are abundantly sufficient to cover us before the judgment-seat of God. Yes,
only be and walk with Christ, and have fellowship with
Him, and I will warrant you that to the end of your
days the Shulamite's confession will be yours. 'I am
black, O ye daughters of Jerusalem; the sun has looked upon me.'

'I am black.' Black is the Shulamite in her own, and black in the eyes of the world. ' Look not upon me, because I am black.' Her Sun has deprived her of her natural complexion, and has made her dark. What does the regenerated soul still continue to bear about her of all the world calls beautiful and delightful ? It has all faded like grass in the heat of the Sun that shone upon her. She is no longer seen in the assemblies of her former associates; she has forsaken the counsel of the children of this world, in which she once so joyfully participated; she no longer relishes their frivolous jests, and can contribute nothing to their diversions. She no longer attaches importance to appearances and dazzling show. Worldly fashions, and worldly conviviality, have lost their charm, and worldly views and opinions their hold and their reality. The doctrine of insufficiency which the Shulamite professes, which strips man of every thing, and renders him destitute; the air of conscious sinfulness she bears about with her: the gravity she maintains; the sharp condemnation of unbelief and disregard of the truth ever on her lips; the eternal singing, praying, and Bible-reading, with which she spends hours, and even days; oh how odious and disgustful they are to the world, and how liberally derision and abuse are showered down upon her. She is slandered, decried, ridiculed; and with good reason may she exclaim, 'I am black, O ye daughters of Jerusalem'—black in the estimation of the world : but she adds, ' The Sun has looked upon me"—in this she rejoices, and lets the world rage. And were she also black through crosses, persecutions, and

adversity; black as Job found himself when he said,
' My skin is black upon me ;' even then she would not
waver, but would remain unshaken in her confidence
that this blackness proceeded likewise from her Bridegroom, from her Sun.

'I am black.' We have already seen the more obvious and general meaning of the Bride in these words.
But perhaps this confession may likewise have its origin
in a peculiar state of soul. The Christian experiences,
in his communion with the Lord, days and hours in
which, so to speak, and to all appearance he ceases to
be a dark moon, and breaks forth and shines with all
the radiance of the rising sun ; in which with holy
transport he soars as on the wings of a young eagle,
and would even seek for the highest walls, in order to
leap over them with his God. O happy state ! How
gladly would he then see himself surrounded by Anti-
christ, and all the powers of darkness, that he might
testify, to their face, of Christ, and of the efficacy of
his blood, and with him trample them under his feet ;
how joyfully would he then proclaim aloud from the
house-tops, and in the streets, that Christ is Lord, to
the glory of the Father ! How sweetly the heart
is then invigorated to the fulfillment of every command !
With what intense love, with what ardent devotion,
the soul is then inflamed. Faith is changed into sight ;
we not merely speak, but we prophesy and sing psalms ;
and the mouth becomes an inexhaustible spring of evangelical wisdom and consolation. We are ready to say
with David, ' Lord, thou hast made my mountain to
stand fast ; I shall never be moved :" and we already

triumphantly exclaim, " the eternal hills are our possession." But in the midst of all this exultation, our glory becomes suddenly obscured. The daughter of Zion,
that had been exalted to heaven, is cast down to the
earth again, and her lustre has passed away like a
shadow. No sensible supplies of grace are experienced,
no blissful emotions are felt, no alacrity of spirit elevates
the soul. Prophesying has come to an end; our praises
are languid; the law causes us again to labor and to
be heavy laden: and, like a tree deprived of its leaves
in autumn, all the splendor in which we had for a time
been arrayed, to the joy and astonishment of our acquaintance has been stripped off, and not a vestige of
its beauty remains. Then, again, we are black; and
the daughters of Zion behold it, and compare our blackness and dimness with our former state of life. Those
who are but partially enlightened, who are not yet able
to estimate these dealings of the Lord, will view it as a
melancholy relapse into our former state of nature—as
a sudden separation from the Lord, and from his love.
But Shulamite may say to them with confidence, ' Look
not upon me because I am black: the Sun has looked
upon me.' Do not judge me by the present darkness
of my appearance; be not deceived by the sudden barrenness, stupidity, and exhaustion, which have come
upon me; as though they were a sign that the union
between me and my Sun had been dissolved. It is not
the absence of the Sun, but his nearness and the fervid-
ness of his beams, that has tinged me with so dark a
shade, and rendered me so sterile and devoid of brightness. My Bridegroom has himself withdrawn from
20

me that excess of spiritual excitement in which I revelled, that I might not be high-minded, but fear; that I might not forget my former state of sin and misery, and might learn to trust Him for his word alone, without seeing or tasting : therefore look not upon me, because I am black ; and do not start and be confounded : believe me the sun has looked upon me, and our union is as firm as ever.'

There is one other way in which the Lord sometimes makes his people black. To promote their salvation, and their humility, he suffers the leprosy of sin still lurking in their breast, to break forth and to display itself outwardly, that they may not remain ignorant of its existence. On this point much might be said ; but as there may be some amongst you who cannot yet bear it, and who might be led by it into lamentable errors, we will pass it over in silence, and turn from the contemplation of the Shulamite's blackness, to admire her comeliness.

II.—' I am black,' says the Bride ' but comely.' Black and comely at the same time ? How contradictory ! And yet the Shulamite may say with truth, The blacker I am in my own eyes, the fairer I am before Him. His love to us is in proportion to our self-knowledge, and to the consciousness of our sinfulness. Do we seriously complain to him of the burden of one sin, he welcomes our approach. Do we sigh before him, confessing that our transgressions are more in number than the sands upon the sea-shore, he views us with increased satisfaction. But do we reject all that we have and

are, as vile and accursed, and appear before him stripped of all self-righteousness, then we are most pleasing
in his sight.   There is but one complaint he cannot
bear—the complaint, that our sins are too great to be
forgiven—for that is the suggestion of Satan, who seeks
to close against us the fountain of Christ's blood, and
to derogate from its merits.   He delights in the pardon
of aggravated sins, and finds most pleasure in the cure
of the severest wounds, and in the removal of the greatest afflictions; for thus his love and mercy are most
conspicuously manifested, and the renewed soul becomes more closely, gratefully, and devotedly united to
him.   If the cry ascend to him, from a thorough conviction of our misery, that we are nothing, and can do
nothing; oh, how willingly does he hear it! His hands
are then unbound, the work is his alone—he has room
to display his wonders, and opportunity to shew who
he is, and of what he is capable.   For this reason, the
blacker we are in our estimation, the fairer we are before Him.

'I am black, but comely.'   In what sense then, is
she comely ?   Comely and beautiful, as the curtains of
Solomon.   Solomon's curtains may have been costly
and magnificent; but there is one curtain that surpasses every other in splendor and beauty.   It was not fashioned by the hand of man, nor can it be imitated by
man.   It is the work of the Eternal King, who wrought
it with many cries and tears.   This curtain is the only
one that is pure in the sight of Him before whom the
heavens are not clean, and who chargeth his angels
with folly.   In it he perceives no stain; and so won-

derful is its efficacy, that if it were possible for Satan to wrap himself in it, even his blackness would be concealed from the searching eye of Omnipotence. It was in this covering, that David, Mary Magdalene, the thief, and every other sinner, received the blessing of the Father, and have been raised above the stars in the firmament. And Abraham pleased God, for no other reason than because he was clothed with this golden mantle. What is this wonderful covering? It is the robe of salvation—the righteousness of our Surety, which is imputed to faith by grace. For if we are in Christ, sin has no more dominion over us, as the Spirit testifies. We are accounted as righteous before God, for Jesus' sake, as fully as though we really were so, because he was so for us—the curse and condemnation are removed, for they have been sustained by us in the person of our Surety and Substitute. And this garment of imputed righteousness is not circumscribed, nor inadequate to cover all our sins; neither is it of so thin and loose a texture, as not to conceal from the glance of the Almighty every stain and spot upon us. Praise and thanks to God! This garment will suffice in the day of judgement, and will as surely bring us to Jerusalem, as if Solomon himself were entering the city in it. Put on, then, this garment, and the blessing of the Father will descend upon you; and it shall be said of you also, 'Cursed is he that curseth thee! Blessed is he that blesseth thee!' Yes, the Shulamite is fair and comely—comely as the curtains of Solomon. She is arrayed in the golden vestments of the king himself—in Solomon's princely apparel, in his robe of righteousness.

But within also, the king's daughter, as David says, is all glorious, notwithstanding her blackness; and she is not only comely, as the curtains of Solomon, but also as she herself here tells us, as the tents of Kedar. The Kedarites were a pastoral people, living in the deserts of Arabia; and having no abiding place, they roved from pasture to pasture. They dwelt in light huts, or tents, some of which were made of black goat-skins, and others were made black by the scorching heat of the sun. Such are the Kedarites to whom the Shulamite compares herself. In the first place, because of her blackness; then, with reference to her position in the rays of the majestic Sun, and to her walk in the light of Jacob, and in the sight of the Lord. But by it her thoughts are chiefly directed to the idea of ' Christ in us;' whilst, in the curtains of Solomon, her eye contemplates, moreover, ' Christ for us.'

Shulamite, a Kedar-tent, black in herself, worthless and unsightly, and burnt by the sun—deformed in her own eyes, in those of the world, and beset with misery; but fair, and lovely, and highly exalted—the dwelling of the great Shepherd, the glorious Morning Star, to which he has free ingress and engress—the place of his rest, the theatre of his miracles, where all his wonderful works are made manifest. Christ has taken possession of her, and extends that possession continually. The new man within her also sighs, longs, and struggles upwards—having fallen out with sin, and hating and abhorring it in every form—weeping and mourning over the weakness and corruption of the flesh, feeling himself forlorn, a stranger in the world, and finding no

20*

pleasure in its ways ; but loving, praising, singing, and praying—behold this is the work of the Lord, fashioned in his own likeness, and without weariness. The Lord is ever busied within her, by his Spirit, strengthening and maturing this new creation—in mortifying, weakening, and destroying the old Adam. It is Christ, who inwardly chastens the Shulamite and consoles her ; who cheers and strengthens her ; who visits her with wholesome affliction, and imparts to her delightful peace, exactly as the case requires. May she not therefore pronounce herself a comely tabernacle, a habitation of the Lord, a tent which her Bridegroom delights to visit ? Thus she stands there with the door wide open, imploring and sighing ; and it may with truth be said of her, ' Behold a tabernacle of the Lord among men ! O, Israel, where is there a people so glorious, to whom their gods are so near, as is the Lord our God and Savior to thee.'

' I am comely as the tents of Kedar :' this comeliness consists, lastly, in her no longer following her own inclinations ; but as the tents of Kedar are borne by the shepherds, so is she borne by her King, removed and placed wherever it may please Him and His love. She is no longer her own, but her faithful Lord and Savior's, both soul and body, in life and in death. She knows herself to be in his hands, in his bosom ; and she willingly surrenders herself to his guidance, whether he may please to lead her into green pastures, or assign her a place in the desert. And like as the Kedarites wander with their tents, and pitch them sometimes in one place, and sometimes in another ; she also is aware that she is a stranger in the world, and rejoices in the knowledge that she has here no abiding city, but seeks, with earnest longing, that which is to come, and contemplates the time with joyful hope, when her King shall entirely destroy her earthly tabernacle, and assigns her one all-glorious and beautiful. Yes, thou art black thou bride of the Lord ; but we will not look upon thee because thou art black, for the Sun has made thee so. Thou art likewise fair and comely ; comely as the curtains of Solomon, and as the tents of Kedar.

III.—Let us now attend to what the Bride has further to relate : ' My mother's children,' she says, ' were angry with me ; they made me keeper of the vineyards ; but my own vineyard have I not kept.' By her mother's children, she means the children of the kingdom, who journeyed with her on the same road, and participated with her in the same spiritual privileges ; but whose walk in the light of Jacob had been of too short duration, and their experience in Divine things too limited, for them to conceive that a life in God could be a concealed one, full of godly activity, but devoid of all exterior splendor. A child of God in a state of dejection was to them as yet an incomprehensible mystery. Now it appears to me, that it may have been precisely such a state of apparent dejection and barrenness, in which they discovered the Shulamite to be. She, whom they had known as so highly a gifted, joyful witness to the truth ; whose distinguished and effective course apparently resembled that of a prophetess ; who had been as a light shining in a dark

place, inexhaustibly rich in sententious wisdom, in
awakening addresses, in feeling effusions and fervent
prayers ; who understood how to make all hearts overflow with living waters, to melt them into sacred emotions, and to hurry them from one fragrant eminence to
another ;—she, who had only lived for the brethren and
their communion ; who had hastened from assembly to
assembly, there to pour forth her treasures ; who had
devoted all her energies to the kingdom of God, and
from morning to evening, with the most flaming zeal,
had thought of nothing but converting, edifying,
strengthening, rousing, and comforting the brethren ;
and in the performance of all which she had been so
conspicuous ;—behold, how suddenly she is overcome !
This overflowing spring, how suddenly is it exhausted ;
this rose, so recently blooming and redolent, how
quickly has it lost its beauty and its fragrance.   Behold, the Shulamite's fire is extinguished, her zeal cool-
ed, her sensibility dried up ; her evangelizing spirit,
how dead ; her mouth closed ; her carriage, how constrained, reserved, and unsocial ! The sisters see it with
sorrow ; they are heartily grieved to have no further
communion with their friend.   Yes, they even behold it
with indignation, for in this transformation they perceive nothing less than an entire relapse into a state of
nature.   Alas ! to her own sisters she has become, not
only a riddle but a vexation.   Yet so far from having
fallen away, or from having departed from the school of
her Lord and Master, she has been elevated by him to
a higher class in this school, where she shall learn to
believe without seeing or tasting, and with Asaph to

desire nothing in the world but God : that though heart
and flesh may fail, yet to rejoice and be in perfect
peace—not as arising from any subordinate communi-
cations from the Lord, but because he is himself the
strength of her heart, and her eternal portion.   With
these things her sisters were not then acquainted.
Their inward light was too faint for them to perceive
in the change that had passed on Shulamite, in her external sterility and blackness, the pure benevolent dis-
ciple of the Lord, the guidance of the most faithful of
all shepherds.   They imagined it to proceed from very
different causes, and Shulamite could not please them :
' My mother's children were angry with me.'

And what would they now in their folly do with her ?
They would make her keeper of their vineyards ; that
is, they would attract her back to the scene of use-
fulness, activity, and tumult, in which they so greatly
delighted : in their kind but blind zeal, they would
have her re-assume their favorite form and aspect of
Christian life, and thus interfere, uncalled, in the work
of the Lord : and behold they succeeded, at least for a
short time.   The Shulamite yielded, and the Lord permitted it.   ' They made me the keeper of the vineyards.'

The experience of the Shulamite has, in various
ways, been that of many.   Do you inquire how ?
Listen : Is a man a Christian, has he bid adieu to the
world, and does he live to God ?   Is he enlightened,
rich in experience, and by the brethren accounted faithful, sincere, active, and qualified ; they at once begin to
calculate how he may be made useful.   He is asked to

preach in one place, in another to direct some society ; business and labor are heaped upon him, and he is expected to undertake whatever is offered to his management. He submits ; though it may often be more from a carnal than a sanctified spirit : for how can he refuse the brethren, particularly as their requests are confined to sacred things. His occupation begins and ends but with the day ; he is so active, so clever, does every thing so well, that he is praised and encouraged from all sides, till it becomes his delight. Thus he is incessantly engaged in the work of the Lord. He preaches, exhorts, expounds the Scriptures to the brethren, prays with them, relates to them the passing events of the kingdom of God, superintends their societies, and does a thousand other things. That all this is good and praiseworthy in itself, who will deny ? Yet, before he is aware, his own heart, with its wants, has been lost sight of ; his secret, healthful intercourse with the Lord is interrupted, and the desire for it gradually extinguished ; as if the soul had been satiated with this external employment : but when God in his mercy restores light to the mind of the believer, he is constrained to join in the complaint of the Shulamite : 'They made me keeper of the vineyards ; but my own vineyard have I not kept.'

But it is asked, was it in this way that Shulamite likewise forgot her vineyard ? I answer No. She found herself in very different circumstances ; and I will endeavor to describe them. The sun has burnt us, when we have lost the sensible tokens of God's grace, and feel ourselves deprived of the consolation, peace, and hope which had been our confidence and rejoicing, and cast into a barren land. What the love of God designs by such seemingly hard dealings with his faithful people, is well known. Our associates mark the change; they are displeased that our glory has passed away, that our beauty is so faded. They are angry with us, and even apprehensive that we have fallen from grace. Our mortification is deep, we cannot bear the suspicion; and consequently, strain every nerve to re-instate ourselves in our former condition. We again put ourselves forward, but the Lord has not called; we again attempt to prophesy, but the Spirit is not with us; we seek again to appear as one of the anointed, but our oil is consumed; we wish to warm others, but our own fire is extinguished. In short, instead of bowing before the Lord, and awaiting, in prayerful submission, the return of his pentecostal breathing, we try to sail with an adverse wind; we try the oars of our natural strength, and resolve to supply the deficiency of Divine inspiration from our own resources; to take again upon our own shoulders the work which Christ reserves for himself alone; and, instead of drawing water from the Rock that follows us, to force it from the barren sandy waste of our own nature. Our state is lamentable; we are separated from the Lord, and have strayed into, and lost ourselves in, a maze of presumptuous self-will and self-prescribed performances. And if the Lord again open our eyes, we must judge ourselves, and complain, in the language of the Bride, 'They have made me keeper of the vineyards; but my own vineyard have I not kept.' Instead of abiding in union with the Lord, enjoying his favor, and participating in the abundant fulness of his vineyard;—instead of remaining at the Fountain of life, and surrendering myself like a child to the guidance of Jesus, I have lost myself in the dark wilderness of self-prescribed duties, estranged from God.

Let us here conclude. My brethren, when after the Babylonish captivity the city of Jerusalem had been rebuilt, Nehemiah gave this command; 'Let not the gates of Jerusalem be opened, until the sun is hot!' This command is spiritually in force to this day. Jerusalem is opened to no one, till the Eternal Sun of the universe has shed his heat upon him; till he has become black in his own eyes. Oh that each one amongst us, who now accounts himself fair and beautiful, may soon, from a deep and thorough conviction of his misery, be able to declare with Shulamite, 'I am black, O ye daughters of Jerusalem! Not that he should then attempt to purify himself: the Ethiopian cannot change his skin, or the leopard his spots; but may he experience the royal purifying power of Him who clothes all his children in white robes. May the Eternal King be with us all; may He encircles us in his golden mantle, and make us comely as the tents of Kedar. Amen.

SERMON IV.

SOLOMON'S SONG VIII. 6—7.

Set me as a seal upon thy heart, as a seal upon thine arm : for love is strong as death ; jealousy is cruel as the grave: the coals thereof are coals of fire, which hath a most vehement flame. Many waters cannot quench love, neither can the floods drown it.

THE words we are about to consider, are not those of the Bridegroom, Christ ; but of the Bride, the awakened believing soul. She begs her heavenly Friend to preserve her still in his love ; and at the same time relates, in few but in expressive terms, the nature of Christ's love.

Let us then consider, in reference to the text, the love of Christ to sinners. Let us contemplate it :—

I. As a great and free love.
II. As a strong love.
III. As a jealous love.
IV. As a faithful love.

I.—' Set me as a seal upon thine heart, as a seal upon thine arm.' These aspirations of the Shulamite appear, indeed, to be lofty ; but in what do they exceed, in extent or magnitude, what the Savior continually does for sinners without their solicitation ? He sets them as a seal upon his heart, as a seal upon his arm,

21

The Savior's heart is the inexhaustible source of all
love.   If but the smallest drop from this fountain enters
the human heart, it immediately dilates and overflows
with love.   Witness its surprising effects on Abraham ;
the love of God in him absorbed the love of nature,
and stretched his arm to offer his beloved, his only son,
a sacrifice to the Lord.   What a noble display of it in
David !—when with a love contrary to nature, and elevated high as the heavens above it, he wept the death
of Saul, his mortal enemy, and broke out in bitter lamentations, that the shield of the mighty had been cast
vilely away, as though he had not been anointed.
Behold it in Moses !—when in the desert he cried unto
the Lord : ' Oh this people have sinned a great sin ; yet
now, if thou wilt forgive their sin—if not, blot me, I
pray thee, out of thy book which thou hast written.'
What amazing love !   Hear the prayer of Stephen !—
stoned by his enemies, and prostrated on the earth, with
his last breath, he cries to heaven : ' Lord, lay not this
sin to their charge.'   Behold a Paul !—renouncing
joyfully all the advantages and pleasures which the
world has to offer, suffering ignominy and persecution,
scourging and stoning, imprisonment and chains, and
not even counting his life dear unto himself, that he
might bring the Balm of Gilead to his brethren, who
were sitting in the shadow of death.   The love of these
men was astonishingly great !   Who can utter all the
purity and faithfulness, the height, length, breadth, and
depth of such love ?   And yet it was but a small drop
from that ocean of love which flows in the heart of
Christ.

    But who can declare the love of Jesus ? · By what

standard shall it be estimated, in what language can it be expressed ?   There is nothing with which it can be compared ; the boldest imagination cannot grasp it.   It is a depth, into which angelic spirits look adoringly down, but cannot fathom ; an height, to which the thoughts of a seraphim cannot attain.   As he himself has been loved by the Father from all eternity, in the same measure and degree does he love all who are the objects of his regard.   No mind can comprehend, no imagination conceive, the love of Christ ; it surpasses all knowledge and all thought.   And his power, like his love, is boundless, unsearchable, incomprehensible. Obedient to his will, the waves of the Red Sea mount- ed into a heap like a wall of crystal ; at his command the solid rock became a fountain of waters ; the impreg- nable walls of Jericho fell down at the sound of a trumpet, and the sun stood still in the firmament ; with a word he restored life to corruption, and called the dead out of their graves : and this was but a small dis- play of his power, a trifle for his gigantic arm.   Did he he not call a world into existence out of nothing, and command that to be which was not, and it stood forth ? Did not his arm plant Orion in the heavens, and group the Plæiades ?   And yet we have seen but a shadow of his power !   He can create and do his pleasure ; as the Scriptures declare, ' All power is given him, in hea- ven and on earth.'   Oh who can measure the power of his arm ?   His arm is like his heart, his power like his love.   We have attempted a faint description of them, but the thunder of his power who can understand ?

And who are the recipients of this love, and for whom is this mighty power revealed ?   In general it is similarity of taste or disposition that attracts men to each other, and forms the bond of union between them. But the love of Jesus is guided by other rules. It was not the angels and cherubim, who were the exclusive objects of his love: ' He took not on him the nature of angels,' says St. Paul; it was not the just, the virtuous, the noble, the wise, the mighty, and the great, after the flesh, that he sought to bear them on his heart; for his love is the love of sinners, and his arm is stretched forth to the miserable. It was for us, the children of death, that the bowels of his mercy yearned from all eternity, and for whom his heart burned with infinite tenderness. How wondrous that love, which could impel the Sovereign of the universe to lay aside his glory, and in the form of sinful flesh to descend into this dark valley of tears! A love which prompted him to assume our griefs, the whole weight and curse of our iniquities! A love, which moved Him to become the most despised and vile amongst the children of men, to humble himself even unto death, and to shed his blood upon the cross! What an amazing love! And yet it was a love for sinners, and for sinners only. It was not for angels, but for thee and me, my dear brethren, that he submitted to be thus straightened. The poor sinner is the object of his love, the curse-stricken earth the theatre of its display, and the deadened heart the subject on which it operates. And wherever he has revealed himself in the world, he has revealed himself as one compassionating the miserable, reclaiming the wanderer, and as the sinner's friend. Such is the heart of Jesus : and his arm, his power, is wielded by this heart, by this love of sinners. He has ever acted and governed in the world, as if he possessed his power solely for the deliverance, the salvation of sinners. For them he vanquished hell, and trampled Satan under his feet. For them he conquered death, and burst the bands of the grave; and all that he has done, or is daily performing, is designed to accomplish the salvation of sinners. What do we need more? His heart is for us; his power is for us. He lives not for himself, he lives for sinners. In this we rejoice!

But there is one peculiarity in his love, at the thought of which we should humble ourselves in the dust, and devoutly adore. In what manner, under what conditions, and at what period, do you imagine it to be, that he receives the sinner to his love? Some of you, perhaps, may be ready to reply; When the sinner begins to think about a reformation, then Jesus also begins to love. But I say, No; He loves him before. But, perhaps, it commences when the sinner sincerely begins to inquire after and seek the way of life? No!—long before these sincere desires arise in the sinner, he has been loved by Him who both imparts the will and perfects the good within him. Behold the Lord sets the sinner as a seal upon his heart, as a seal upon his arm! and this is something unspeakably great! What is a seal? It is the clear, perfect impression of a figure engraven upon a seal, or signet ring. When therefore it is said, that the Lord Jesus sets the sinner as a seal upon his heart, it can only mean, that he takes a true and perfect impression of the sinner. He takes his true figure as a ruined, lost creature, with all the marks of sin broadly and clearly impressed upon him; and when it is further said, he sets him as a seal upon his arm, it

means, that, before any good is in the sinner, the arm of
the Lord is promised, and extended for his relief; that
for his salvation, the power and love of Jesus are united.
And thus it really is! ˙ Yes, believe it, before a spark
of the new life had been kindled within you, before the
smallest change had taken place, you were already received to the love of Jesus ; for how had you otherwise
become converted and believing, had not the sustaining
love of Him who is the ʹauthor and finisher of faith,
been previously imparted to you ?   For that you have
not converted yourself, you are perfectly convinced.
Every one, who has undergone this change, confesses
with. deep humiliation : I have not chosen thee, but
thou hast chosen me. . When you were still in your iniquities, and entertained not the most distant thought of
submitting your heart to God, even then the Savior's
love had sought you out.   He had placed you as a seal
upon his heart—that is, you had become the object of
his merciful love ; your image, with all the stains of
sin upon it, was impressed upon his heart; and when
you really were converted to the Lord, then his arm
executed in you the eternal counsels of his love.   Yes,
on every one who is born again, the words of our Lord
are fulfilled : ʹI have loved thee—not from the moment
of thy conversion—but I have loved thee with an everlasting love; therefore˙ with loving kindness have I
drawn thee.'   In thine iniquities have I loved thee ; · as a
sinner wert thou engraven on my heart.   I set thee as
a seal upon my heart, as a seal upon my arm ; before˙
thou calledst, I heard and answered thee.   Behold this
is the great, the free love of our Surety !

II.—And in the same degree that this love is great, free, and unconditional, it is likewise strong and powerful. But how strong? 'Strong, says the Shulamite, as death. What a striking similitude! Yes, strong as death—we have ourselves experienced it. Who can withstand death? With invincible power he wields his sceptre over all flesh—the strongest he casts to the earth, the most mighty become his prey.

And who can resist the love of Christ, when it goes forth towards the sinner, and casts its net around him? A Saul tried, but found it vain to kick against the pricks; the Samaritan woman was not long able to strive against, and to evade it; and Nathaniel, in spite of his conviction that nothing good could come out of Nazareth, was soon obliged to confess: ' Rabbi, Thou art the son of God; Thou art the King of Israel!' The jailer likewise, with his heart subdued, fell down, and anxiously sighed: ' What must I do to be saved?' And the heathen centurion was constrained to exclaim: ' Truly this was the son of God.' Yes, strong as death is the love that seeks sinners, who can resist it! It pursues the sinner, who is its object, through all his devious courses; it follows him into the stillness of the closet, into the bustle of the world, in the midst of dissipation, and on the seat of the scorner; it presses upon him in every way, till his heart is vanquished, and he is rescued from the paths of death. How long, my brethren, did we not strive against its assaults, and seek to escape the net; how long did not we close our ears against its call, and, as it were, struggle not to be overcome. But behold, has it not been too strong for us? Has it not at last subdued and made us captive? Yes,

God be praised! it has also broken our hard and obdu-
rate hearts, and notwithstanding our resistance, has
forced us into the bonds of the covenant! God be
thanked for ever, we have ourselves experienced, that
his love is strong as death! Who can resist it?

Love is strong as death. Does not death separate
man from this world and its concerns? Does it not
snatch him away from all that is earthly and transitory?
And behold, the love of Christ does the same. No
sooner is its influence felt upon the soul—no sooner are
we participatingly assured of its possession, and able to
say with Paul: I also have obtained mercy—than we
bid the world farewell; its pleasures become embittered,
its waters turbid and vapid; for we now drink from
other fountains; and in places where we were formerly
at home, we now feel ourselves strangers, uneasy and
oppressed. Oh, how wonderful the change which
passes on the heart, as soon as it hears the Lord call it
by name, and the words, 'Thou art mine!' vibrate
within it. Then a Magdalene quickly casts away her
follies, and becomes the handmaid of the Lord. Then
a Paul esteems all that he had accounted gain, as loss
and dung, and is Christ's alone. Then we willingly
abandon honor and pleasure, fame, applause, and whatever else the world has to offer, and follow Christ. Yes,
the love of Jesus is strong as death. Wherever it is
unfolded, felt and experienced, it separates the man,
heart and soul, from the world and its trifles. Then
Abraham can no longer dwell in Ur, Lot in Sodom, nor
Moses at the court of Egypt. The heart pants, and
struggles to be liberated; we weigh the anchor and
launch from the shore of this world. The love of Jesus

is strong as death. With the destructive energy of death, and as the fire of lightning, it assails the old man within us. Where the love of Jesus is perceived, and his grace experienced, there also is a constant inward dying, an incessant consuming; there the old Adam lies in the flames that will burn him to ashes. Oh, it is hard to confess, that our sins have caused the Lord of Glory to shed his blood upon the cross—that our sins have occasioned all his humiliation and suffering! How inconceivably mortifying is the conviction, that we must be received to his arms and to his love, as the vilest of sinners! it degrades us in the dust of self-abasement, and overwhelms us with shame and disgrace; while it renders a life after the flesh distasteful and disgusting. With the consciousness: I have obtained mercy; pride cannot rear its head; avarice cannot thrive; lust cannot spring up; that is impossible; for where the love of Christ takes possession of the soul, there it is as death, destructive as the fire of brimstone, and pestilence, to the old man.

III.—And behold, to the strength of death, the love of Christ to sinners unites the firmness of hell.* Its fervor, says the Shulamite, is unchanging as the grave; and our hearts should gratefully respond—' God be praised !' The Shulamite speaks with force and power, but with truth and beauty. It is as she has said. The love of Jesus to the elect is a zealous, ardent, yea, and a jealous

* This is a literal rendering of the author's words, who has of course followed the idea conveyed by Luther's translating the word נשׂף by ' firm,' which is, perhaps, more correct than ' cruel,' as the English version has it.—ED-

love. It encircles its object with a firmness so immoveable
and undeviating, that the idea of surrender on its part, is
as little to be entertained as that of a surrender of the
lost on the part of hell.   Though on earth Satan must
renounce his prey. at the bidding of the Lion of the
tribe of Judah ; but if he have dragged it down into the
bottomless pit, the gates are closed, and none shall open
them.   Hell asserts its rights and its possessions.   No
sighs, no grief, can move it ; no tears, or lamentations
of the damned ; it holds them in its gloomy caverns
with stern, inexorable cruelty, and the smoke of their
torments ascends for ever and ever.   And such is the
constancy of the love of Christ.   The Lord Jesus keeps
what he has.   ' My sheep are mine' he says, ' and none
shall pluck them out of my hand .'   Should the devil,
the accuser, appear, and claim the sinner as his own ;
should he heap every deadly sin upon his head ; should
Moses arise, and call upon the Lord to condemn the
despiser of his laws ; should even the angels of God
cry together, Away with him ! the thief is not fit for
Paradise !—what could it avail ?   For if he has once
taken the sinner to his heart, his love is firm as
hell.   And whether it were Satan, Moses, or the
angels, his answer would be, : ' Away with you all.'
I will have mercy on whom I will have mercy.   His
love is an unyielding love : it never relinquishes what
it has once adopted.   It turned the lost son from the
husks of the swine-troughs, from the seat of the scorner and the profane.   It followed Solomon into the tem-
ples of Satan, into the assemblies of heathen women,
and the dwellings of lewdness : yes, it pursued him
even to the altars of strange gods, and rested not till it

had reclaimed him. Such is the love of Christ! and it declares to Satan, ' I am stronger than thou art.' What it has it has, and never abandons. And if Satan assail the Bride, a conflict immediately ensues; which ceases not till the dragon is discomforted. Yes, the love of Christ for his people is firm and unrelenting as hell. ' I am persuaded,' says St. Paul, ' that neither death, nor life, nor angels, nor principalities, nor powers ; nor things present, nor things to come; nor height, nor depth, nor any other creature, shall be able to separate us from the love of God, which is in Christ Jesus our Lord.'

Once more.—The fervor of his love is firm as hell, and is mingled with a holy jealousy. Where is there a soul with whom he has deigned to hold converse, that has not experienced how jealous is his love ? He will possess his people exclusively, not divided with ano- ther; he will not suffer his followers to adhere to Belial, and coquette with the world: therefore his efforts are incessant, and endlessly varied, till his Bride has cordially renounced the world, and is entirely his own. What has been our own experience, my bre- thren, when we have turned back into the world; when, fascinated by its charms, we have forgotten Him, or have attempted to associate Him with Belial ; when our speech and our actions have faithlessly de- clared with Simon, ' I know not this man;' when clos- ing our eyes and our hearts against him, we have again demeaned ourselves as men of this world ? What were our sensations when reflection returned ? Did not a day of sorrow and anguish, a day of storm and tempest, of darkness and gloom, break in upon the soul? Our peace and joy had departed; we felt as though we had rejected his grace; and we began anxiously to inquire how we might appease the Lord! He seemed to have turned from us in anger, and our souls endured the torments of hell. Behold in this his jealousy and his displeasure! But, blessed be God, it is only the anger of love. His tenderness is wounded because we have left him, and because he has for a time been deprived of the joy of possessing us wholly and undivided. This pains and afflicts him. It provokes his love, and therefore his jealousy is kindled, and he plunges us down into hell. Into hell! Yes, the Lord sometimes conducts even his people into hell; but, God be praised, he does not leave them there.

IV.—Strong as death is the love of Jesus. His jealousy is firm as hell; the coals thereof are coals of fire, which hath a most vehement flame. Many waters cannot quench it, neither can the floods drown it. By these words Shulamite describes the faithfulness of Christ, as opposed to our unfaithfulness. How different is it with our love towards each other, even when it is most sincere and pure; contrasted with the love of Christ, it is but as the glimmering of a torch, which but few waters would suffice to quench. The slightest degree of coldness or unrequited affection, the slightest offence or inconstancy on the part of those we love, is sufficient to estrange our hearts, and quench our love. Such floods it cannot survive. And how is it with our love to the Lord? Alas! if he do not continually quicken it, by fresh and sensible supplies of his grace, it is soon reduced to the faintest glimmer. The streams of worldly temptation, or the waters of conflict and trial, need only beat against it; the Lord need only for a moment hide himself, and withdraw from us the sweet consciousness of his presence, when our hearts begin to cool, and the melody of our soul to cease. Our love is fickle; it may cool and expire; we are faithless and inconstant. But Jesus is faithful; his love to his people is immoveable; the coals thereof are coals of fire; no streams, however violent, no floods, however turbulent, can extinguish, or even damp his love to sinners. Not the floods of our iniquities? No, not even these. How great was that flood of sin and transgression which David poured upon the love of his Surety! But, behold! his love burnt on, and maintained the superiority. He did not forsake the murderer and the adulterer, but kindly extended to him his arm, on which he had placed him as a seal, and mercifully assisted him out of the miry pit, and placed his feet again upon the rock; and David remained, what he previously had been, the man after God's own heart. The unfaithfulness of Simon passed as a flood over the love of Jesus! Another would have said, Now our friendship is at an end; with you I will have no further intercourse. But the love of Jesus is not a glimmering taper, that the first wind can extinguish. The coals thereof are coals of fire, which, though floods of inconstancy, coldness, and ingratitude pass over it, continues triumphantly to burn, and break through every assault. The look of wounded affection which he cast on Simon, from the Judgment Hall, after he had denied him, still continues to excite our admiration and wonder; there was a magnanimity, a divinity

22

in it, which we can neither grasp nor comprehend. His love stands fast. ' The mountains shall depart, and the hills be removed ; but my kindness shall not depart from thee, neither shall the covenant of my peace be removed, saith the Lord, that hath mercy on thee.' ' My sheep shall never perish, neither shall any man pluck them out of my hand. My Father which gave them me is greater than all; and no man is able to pluck them out of my Father's hand.'

But may not a man go on comfortably in his sins, if he knows he should not on that account lose the favor of God ? Oh, how often are we obliged' to listen to this miserable and foolish objection ! A little reflection might teach, that the love of sin, and the thought of sinning that grace might abound, are incompatible with the life of one who is born again; they are utterly impossible. If you entertain a propensity to sin that grace may abound, you are not Christians; your new birth is a pretence ; you belong to those who are without, and have not yet obtained the smallest interest in Christ. Let this sink deep into your hearts, and judge yourselves by it. But we rejoice, and praise God that our hope of salvation is founded on such a rock as the love of Jesus. Did our hope rest on our love to Him, it would weaken and die if ever our love dwindled and expired : were it based upon our faith, we should be obliged to abandon it, if our faith became obscured : still less can it be grounded on our sensations and devotional feelings, for then we should sink into despair, whenever our hearts became cold and barren. No ; our hope is founded on the love of Jesus to us ; and here it has found a secure anchorage. It is based on the love which is strong as death and firm as the grave; whose coals are coals of fire, which many waters cannot quench. It is founded on the love which pursues the sinner through all his deviations and wanderings, which loves him, though overshadowed by many inconsistencies; and which stands unshaken, though ours may waver and decline. His love to us is our resting-place, our sure foundation; it is the prop by which we rise when we have fallen; the staff which sustains us on our pilgrimage through this valley of tears. It is the source of our joy, the spring of our courage, and the fire by which we are refined; it is our sanctification and our life. But who can number all the blessings that are treasured up for us in the love of Jesus? Then take thy harp, O Israel! Believe and rejoice; for thou art encircled by the arms of Everlasting Love.

SERMON V.

ṠOLOMON'S SONG I. 7, 8.

Tell me, O *thou whom my soul loveth, where thou feedest, where thou makest thy flock to rest at noon : for why should I be as one that turneth aside by the flocks of thy companions ? If thou know not, O thou fairest among women, go thy way forth by the footsteps of the flock, and feed thy kids beside the shepherds' tents.*

THERE is scarcely any state of spiritual life that is not here and there described in the Song of Solomon, at least in the way of allusion. This little book is a true mirror of the heart of every child of God. The impure world, indeed, discovers in it only its own vile likeness. But is the stream to blame, that, when a Moor surveys himself in the pure and limped waters, an ugly black countenance is presented to his view ? The fault lies not in the mirror, but in the face of the Moor ; and were he on that account to censure the innocent stream, or, in imitation or a certain raging conqueror, to beat it with rods, would it not be absurd and unjust ? Yet such is the procedure of unbelievers with the Song of Songs. But, let us not be turned aside thereby from this stream which flows from the rock of Zion, or suffer our pleasure therein to be corrupted. We drink water from it which springs up to everlasting life.

The text contains a conversation between Christ, the heavenly Bridegroom, and his Bride, the Church or the soul of an individual believer. The sentiment breathed by the Shulamite, is that of longing for the coming of the Lord, and ardent desire · to be near him. But the answer of Christ calms the longing soul, points out to it the way, and imparts wholesome advice. Many a soul amongst us is in the same state with Shulamite; many require the same refreshment. Let us therefore consider the words more fully, and reflect,

    I. On Shulamite's state.
    II. On her address to the Lord.
    III. On her question.
    IV. On Christ's counter-question.
    V. On His advice.

I.—We are already acquainted with the state of Shulamite's soul. · She has herself, in the preceding words disburthened her heart, and discovered to us its inward aspect. 'I am black,' she complains, 'O ye daughters of Jerusalem. Look not upon me because I am black, because the sun hath looked upon me.' In the text she describes her appearance as that of noon-day —that is, she is exposed to the noon-day heat, when the sun has attained his greatest altitude, and shoots his scorching rays perpendicularly on the head. 'Tell me,' she exclaims, 'where thou feedest, where thou makest thy flocks to rest at noon?' The raptures of morning are past! For it is the morning in the soul, when it resembles a garden of spices, and the Spirit, like the south wind, blowing freshly through it, causes our fragranee to flow abroad; and we hear its sound, and percieve its influence. It is morning when the King himself draws near, and our spikenard sends forth its per-

fume; when our inward spiritual life assumes sensibility
and feeling, and floods the soul like a fruitful vivifying
water; when the presence of the Lord is powerfully experienced, the comfort of assurance blissfully enjoyed,
the love of Christ ardently felt, and the powers of the
world to come tasted in copious draughts.   How delightful is morning! How pleasant the air!. How mild
and exhilarating the warmth of the sun! Then the val-
leys are filled with balsamic odours, and the plains are
moistened by the early dew; then the vines breathe
forth their fragrance, and the turtle is heard in the grove.
It was morning in the life of Shulamite, when she exclaimed : ' Let him kiss me with the kisses of his mouth:
for thy love is better than wine.   Thy name is an ointment poured forth; therefore the virgins love thee.
Draw me, we will run after thee: the king brought me
into his chambers; we will be glad and rejoice in thee.'
Yes, then the light of morning shone upon her head.
What a happy state! To soar above the earth, like a
young eagle; to be placed beyond the fear of death
and hell; to be able joyfully to embrace all the brethren in Christ; to have a heart expansive as the ocean;
to be also dear to all the brethren, and overflowing
with streams of living water!

But the light in which we now meet the beloved
Shulamite, is not that of morning; alas! all with her is
changed. Her very appearance betrays it. Where is
now the dear sunshine, that once animated her countenance; and the eye, sparkling with joy, the lip breathing eloquence, 'the lofty enthusiasm, the intense love of
her espousals, and her glowing testimony? What became of it all? Alas! they seem to have died away.

She resembles a flower that has lost both its scent and its enamel. Shulamite is afflicted and cast down. What then has happened to her ? Has she perhaps sustained a serious fall ? Not exactly so. Then she is assailed by doubts, and asks with John, ' Art thou he that should come ?' Not so. Then she has encountered severe temptations, and conflicts with Satan ? No that is not the case. She says, it is noon in her soul. She reminds us of a hot, sultry, summer's-day ; all nature droops ; the flowers hang down their head ; the grass is faded and dry ; the beasts pant for breath, the birds are silent in the trees ; dark clouds of dust obscure the roads, and all is dull weary and languid. And this she will say is her spiritual state. Oh, we understand her well ; it is the state of barrenness, of insensibility, in which she finds herself ; the state of spiritual nakedness and destitution, in which we ourselves perceive no trace of the new life, and of the gracious presence of the Lord ; in which a difference between ourselves and the unregenerate is scarce discernible ; in which we feel no love, no necessity of prayer, and we begin to waver, and to doubt whether we are in a state of grace, or no. This is the noon in which we find the Shulamite.

II.—Shulamite in her distress applies to the Lord ; to him she will make known her grief. In this she does wisely. There is no helper besides Him ; and even though we may be unable to pray, we should prostrate ourselves in silence before him, as if we would say, Behold our misery ! It is vain to look elsewhere, this is the only well from which water can be obtained in time of drought. ' Thou,' she sighs, ' whom my soul

loveth!' Thou! What a singular address! Why
does she not add his name? Ah, in her present state
of mind she knows not what to call him. There are
times, in which we know not how to address the Lord,
except with a simple, Thou! Thou! and that is all.
Thus we sometimes experience sudden abstractions of
mind, like in the third heaven; moments of unequalled
mental vision and communion with Jesus; when suddenly he, who is the fairest amongst the children of
men, displays himself to our view in all his beauty, as
though we saw him face to face; and all the bliss, that
is eternal at his right hand, is imbibed into the soul, as
with one draught. The entire greatness of his love, is
unveiled to our view; the happiness of being recon-
ciled by his blood, is felt in all its magnitude, and the
delight of the heart exceeds all bounds. Then, indeed,
one would gladly speak, and call him by name; but
what name is sufficiently expressive to describe Him
whom we behold and taste. His most glorious titles
appear to us inadequate, and too mean for such a Lord.
Absorbed in admiration and excess of bliss, a simple
' O Thou!' is all we are able to utter. But there are
other states of feeling in which we know not by what
title to address him. By what name shall we call upon
him, when, as convicted sinners, we lie prostrate in the
dust before his throne of grace, and cannot venture
even to lift up our eyes. Shall we call him our Lord?
Ah, we are rebels, and not servants. Shall we address
him as Savior? How can we presume; what claims
have we on his mercy? Or as our Mediator and Intercessor? Alas, for creatures so deeply fallen as we are,
he will never intercede! All the sweet and endearing

titles by which his children are permitted to address him, falter upon our tongues; and Thou! Thou! is all that our trembling lips can utter. And when in his mysterious dealings he has again deprived us of all that he had once vouchsafed to us—has withdrawn himself from our view, and surrounded himself with clouds and darkness, so that we no longer taste his grace, or enjoy his love, as was the case with Shulamite,—how shall we then call upon him? By what name address him? As a friend? We no longer recognize him as such. As a Bridegroom? Ah, the days of our espousals are past. As a Prince of peace? Where is his peace! As our guide? Alas, we wander forsaken. At such times we are tempted to ask with Manoah, 'What is thy name?' And, Wonderful! is the only title by which we can address him! Sometimes even we appear to have lost all trace of him as a 'Wonderful God;' it seems as though he guided us no longer, or concerns himself no more about us. Then a sighing of 'O Thou!' is our only resource. Thus it was with our Shulamite. But the remainder of her address must cause us astonishment; 'Thou,' she says, 'whom my soul loveth.' How strange! We thought her love was at an end. Yes, that she herself also most firmly believes. But does she not say, 'Thou whom my soul loveth?' The words have indeed escaped her, but I believe she is not insensible of it. Ah! how frequently is this the lamentation of benighted and tempted souls. Their complaint is incessant, that there is no more love in their heart, no desire after the Lord, and yet, in contradiction to themselves, they continually exclaim, if not in words, yet most loudly by their actions: 'Thou whom my soul loveth!' Singular people! who do nothing else than run about from morning till night inquiring and seeking after Jesus, like sheep lost in the desert, bleating after their shepherd. How delighted would you be to find him again; and should any one advise you to abandon the search, "not for mines of gold, or royal diadems," would be your answer; " no, rather give up all than give up Christ." And yet, you say, you have no love to him after whom you long: no, not the smallest!! How strange, how singular! thus to run after one in whom you have no interest; thus to lament his absence with so much affliction. O ye favored children! This afflicted look, this oppressed mien, this painful lamentation, " I have lost the Lord"—this seeking and longing—what is it but an expressive, 'Thou, Thou, whom my soul loveth.' What is it, however its reflection may be concealed from yourselves, but a look of the purest love, which, be assured, still exists and works unseen in the deep recesses of the soul; which, in the children of God, can never be extinguished; which survives the bitterest temptations, the greatest spiritual desertions, and proclaims, under every change of circumstance, its existence and life, by manifold, though not unfrequently by very faint, manifestations. Yes, the lambs of Jesus always love him; and even when the lamentation escapes them, that they love him not, the tone in which the complaint is uttered, imparts to it an entirely different meaning; and a sensitive ear distinctly perceives in it the tender greeting, 'Thou whom my soul loveth.'

III.—Having listened to the salutation of the afflicted Bride, let us now hear what it is she really desires, and what the nature of the inquiry she has addressed to the Lord. 'Tell me,' she says, 'O Thou whom my soul loveth, where thou feedest, where thou makest thy flock to rest at noon; for why should I be as one that turneth aside by the flocks of thy companions?' His companions are the ministers of his word, the preachers and prophets whom he has called; and it is a great honor, which Shulamite confers on them, when she calls them the companions of Christ! Elsewhere, we are termed messengers in Christ's stead, and his fellow laborers. To what dignity are we here raised! Our hearts might well be oppressed, and force us to exclaim, "Lord God! send another, I am not fit to preach." The flocks of these companions, are those who have believed through their word, their spiritual children. Amongst these Shulamite had wandered; but she had no desire to do so longer; what had it availed her? Nothing; no sermon, however beautiful, no devotional exercises, no exhortations of the brethren, had been able to make her depressed and withered heart again to blossom, or to re-assure her sinking soul. 'Ah,' she says, ' suffer me no longer to wander in vain among the flocks of thy companions; but come to me thyself!' But the words may likewise be rendered thus, ' That I may no longer be amongst the flocks of thy companions, as one veiled'—that is, as a widow. "Ah," she will say, "while thy other children boast of the sweetness of thy presence, of the consolations they receive from thee, and of the frequency of thy visits; must I cast down my eyes in melancholy and silence; and be a barren tree amongst the fruitful, or as a sick

lamb amongst the vigorous of the flock ?   No one de-
rives benefit from me; I am to the brethren as one
dead; I have lost my beloved; my friend has forsaken
me; he cheers me no longer; I am solitary and disconsolate; and shall I not wear the veil of mourning ?
Such is the state in which Shulamite describes herself
to be, and she prays the Lord to relieve her from it.

'Tell me,' she says, 'where thou feedest, where thou
makest thy flock to rest at noon.'   Yes, that is what
she most desires to know.   In the first place, where he
is in circumstances like those in which she then found
herself, where he really feedeth ?   But what is it you.
wish so much to know, beloved Shulamite ?   We do
not understand your words.   Do you inquire where he
would then find food for himself?   Oh, he would find
abundance in your heart, although you do not think so.
This anxiety about him, this seeking and longing, this
inquiry and running after your lost friend, he is well
pleased to see; that is to him food, a delight, a sweet
repast; even in the barren desert he can find food. But
probably you wish to know what food he has provided
for such poor miserable sheep as you have now become ?
Secret food, hidden pastures.   He sustains them by an
unseen energy, with a concealed faith, of which they
are not sensible; and with a hope whose sweetness
they have not tasted; but yet it is near them.   He likewise sometimes feeds such afflicted lambs who know
not whether they belong to the Shepherd or not, upon
the field of their own early experience; he conducts
them back in spirit to the period when they certainly
experienced the kiss of his love, and when he made his
covenant with them.   With David they then remember

their song in the night; and the recollection, in some
degree, revives their courage. Or he points them, in
his word, to the promises which assure them that the
bruised reed shall not be broken, or the smoking flax be
quenched. In short, there is never any want of food
and spiritual nourishment for Christ's sheep; no, not
even when they appear to wade in the sandy desert,
where no vegetation regales the eye, where not a blade
of grass presents itself to their longing appetites. ' Tell
me,' the Shulamite asks again, ' where thou resteth at
noon?' That he rests—that she knows, that she feels.
The sound of his footsteps she no longer hears, neither
can she perceive any trace of his presence or his influence, either within or around her. Ah, beloved soul,
if thou didst but know it, he rests quite near to thee, in
thy bark, in thy chamber; yes, even in thy heart;—
though indeed thou perceivest him not. Now she has
no rest till she has again found him, till she again possesses him, and can say, ' My beloved is mine, and I am
his: he feedeth among the lilies.' Without Him, oh!
where can she be at peace, with all her sinfulness, her
misery, her weakness and infirmity? No, she must
have him again! She wanders from place to place;
now she seeks him in the solitude of her closet, if per-
adventure she may find him there; now she looks for
him amongst the assembled brethren, and asks, Is he
here? Then she searches for him in books and spiritual songs, if by any means she may find him. All kinds
of advisers come to her; " Oh!" they say, " be not so
vehement; wait with patience, till the Lord shows himself again." But she indignantly rejects such counsel.
The matter is too urgent. She must seek him. Or, it

23

is said, " Enjoy the beauties of nature, cheer yourself in
pleasant society." " Ah," she replies, " I covet no
rest, till I can enjoy it in the arms of Jesus." Her dejection increases, and she knows no other resource than
to call upon him, ' Tell me, thou whom my soul loveth,
where thou feedest, where thou makest thy flocks to
rest at noon ?'

IV.—Thus she inquires, thus she laments. At length
she obtains an answer. The Bridegroom replies to her
with another question ; and he asks, ' Dost thou not
know, O thou fairest among women ?' In what a delightful sense those words may be understood ! A child
in its distress flies to its mother for consolation ; she
listens to its complaints, and laughs away its tears. In
this sense must we understand the reply of Christ. Shulamite stands mourning and distressed before him ; she
thinks herself black, and that she no longer belongs to
the fold. The Lord laughs at her complaint, and seems
to say, " Yes, thou hast really cause to be dejected
about thy soul !" " Shulamite," hast thou then forgotten ? Dost thou really not know, O thou fairest among
women ? Thou who art arrayed with the glory of the Sun,
who hast been made partaker of my nature, who art adorned with my righteousness, the righteousness of God ; wilt
thou hang down thy head as a bulrush ? O thou fairest
among women ! be sensible of thy glory ; for know I
have invested thee with my own ; and in truth no angel is so beautiful as thou art. This is the meaning of
the words employed by Jesus. How often might they
be repeated ! How often do we meet with souls like
Shulamite, whose very appearance says, '. Do not look

upon me, O ye daughters of Jerusalem, I am altogether too black.' They will perceive nothing of the Divine nature in themselves; they deem themselves at a great distance, and rather number all others among the children of God, than themselves. Yet in all they say and do the seal of the Lamb that they bear upon them is visible: their sighs, their patience, their hunger and thirst, their love, all make it convincingly evident that they are the children of God, and are clothed with the righteousness of Christ, or that none are. And still they persist in believing that all with them is a delusion; and though we address them in the words of Christ, 'O thou fairest among women, dost thou really not know thyself?' What does it avail that we speak? They usually do not believe us.

V.—But yet Shulamite is again to be comforted, and to obtain peace. To this end the Lord gives her, in the first instance, the good advice to go forth. To go forth! And from whence? To go forth from herself. Undoubtedly much of our spiritual dejection arises chiefly from our thoughts being too constantly turned within ourselves, busied in the contemplation of our own frailty and misery. We ought, indeed, to watch over our hearts, and daily and hourly to be mindful of our wretchedness, misery, and sin; but we ought likewise to look out of ourselves. Many are as completely absorbed in the thoughts of their own misery, as if there were nothing else to be considered; as if no cross had been erected, and no blood had flowed from it, to wash away sin. They view their depravity, as if unatoned for on Golgotha, as if there had been no Son of God to pay all our

debts to the uttermost farthing; as if through Christ
no paternal heart had been opened in heaven; and as
if there were no such thing as free grace to justify the
sinner, requiring nothing, but bestowing all. What
can possibly arise from so partial a consideration of our
state but dejection and anguish. Go forth, thou afflicted soul, from the gloomy melancholy corner of thy
poor heart. Go forth to the pleasure garden of Gethsemane; visit Gabbatha, and the accursed tree of Golgotha: view the wedding garment, the glory that is
there prepared, and which Eternal Love presents to
every longing sinner, let his inward state be ever so
wretched. Such sights and contemplations, in spite of
the dreary state of thy soul, will revive thy courage.
Go forth also from thy great pretensions. Thy desires
are too vast; thou requirest greater things than have been
promised to the children of God in this world. Thou
wouldst taste and see; but this is the time of faith,
away, away, with such pretensions. Dost thou desire
the sweets and pleasures of heaven? Rejoice, O sinner,
if thou hast grace; and let grace suffice thee. Thou
wouldst wish the Lord to lead thee in the way which
thou thyself prescribest. Go forth from these wishes!
Offer them as a sacrifice. Go forth from thy own will,
and enter quietly and confidingly into the will of God!
Let him do with thee what he pleaseth; or wilt thou be
his counseller? Let Him provide for thee, and thou
wilt do well. All this the Lord requires, when he
commands ' to go forth.'

Let us now inquire what further counsel the Lord
gives her! ' Go forth,' he says, by the footsteps of the
flock.' The tendency of this advice likewise is to re-

store peace to the dejected Shulamite. In the first place, it contains a serious reproof, similar to that which was given to Peter; when not altogether satisfied with the career marked out for him by the Lord, he pointed to John, to whom so rough a course was not assigned, and presumed to ask, ' And what shall this man do ?' To which the Lord replied, ' What is that to thee ? follow thou me.' He says the same to Shulamite, in the words, ' Go forth by the footsteps of the flock. Observe the sheep; they do not wander where they please, but they quietly and silently follow their shepherd. Do thou likewise, my beloved Shulamite. Consider what happens when one of the lambs goes a little astray from the fold, how the Shepherd employs every means to restore it. Somewhat similar is the way that I deal with my sheep.' This is what the Bridegroom will in the first place intimate to her. But at the same time he will point out the way in which she may again obtain consolation. ' Yes,' he will say, ' I perceive clearly that thou no longer knowest thyself, O thou fairest among women. Thou art a child of God; but thou believest it not, and art a stranger to thyself. Thou art born again; but thou art no longer sensible of it. Thou art clothed with my righteousness, and hast every reason to be joyful; but thou canst not believe it. And why not ? Because thou feelest thyself barren, and thy spiritual life is not in a flourishing state. But that is no ground for despair. Go forth by the footsteps of the flock.' And Shulamite would certainly have done so. But what are we to understand that she has done ? She has observed other children of God, has considered the ways of the saints; and what has she there discov-

ered ?   That she is no solitary bird upon the housetop ;
and that her experience has nothing peculiar, or unusual.   Where did she find the footsteps of the saints ?
Alas ! not always on verdant and luxuriant pastures,
but most frequently on rugged paths and obscure cross-
roads, in barren deserts and dreary wastes.   The most
favored servants of God she has heard complain ; ' Ah !
my tongue cleaveth to the roof of my mouth ; my
strength is dried up like a potsherd !'   The most holy
she has seen prostrate in the dust, groaning and complaining.

And yet, miserable as they were, the Lord was with
them ; they were still the people after God's own heart,
the apple of his eye, his peculiar care.   But in due
time they had again their hours of refreshment ; and
showers of rain descended upon the parched and withered meadows ; and at length, after all the difficulties
upon earth, their footsteps still shone above the clouds,
among the stars of heaven ; they took their place in
the midst of Paradise, and appeared among the holy
angels, before the throne of glory.   Such was the discovery made by the beloved Shulamite.   O how encouraging and consoling was it to her, to find that all
who had reached Canaan had traversed the same path
on which she then was.   She could then again believe
that the Lord was with her ; that he guided and sustained her, and that her path also would terminate in
glory.   Thus she thought she had her Bridegroom
again ; she would again believe that He still holds her
by His right hand, though in darkness ; and her going
forth by the footsteps of the flock had been blessed and
consoling to her.

O ye that are dejected and disconsolate, who, like Shulamite, are languishing in the heat of mid-day, follow her example. Turn your gaze and your reflections away from your own hearts, and from your own misery. Go forth to the ocean of mercy and love which flows on Golgotha; the sight will produce an immediate change, and inspire you with other and more agreeable meditations. Then go forth by the footsteps of the flock, and learn that you tread the same path that the most distinguished saints have trod before you. This will support you; it will revive your courage and renew your hope. Then feed your kids and your young lambs beside the shepherds' tents. The Bride is here compared to a shepherdess with a flock of hungry lambs. Her heart hungers, her spirit hungers, her understanding hungers, to comprehend the darkness that surrounds her; her soul to be assured of the presence of the Lord; her weak faith hungers after strength, her glimmering hope after food, and her expiring love to be revived. O all ye weary souls, go ye likewise forth; and feed the kids beside the shepherds' tents. The shepherds are the men of God, who have spoken by the Holy Ghost, the ancient Fathers and Prophets, the Evangelists and Apostles; and where they speak, instruct and console; in their revelations, in their sermons, in their histories, and in their epistles; there behold their tents, and the most luxuriant pastures. There learn that God is faithful; that he ever views his people with complacency; and that, even when they have left their first love, he recollects with delight the love of their espousals, and their first surrender of themselves to him. There learn that the entire foundation of your hope is not to be found within but without yourselves. That will strengthen your heart and enable you to wait patiently till it please him again to pour down upon you his quickening grace. Rouse, then, thy afflicted senses! Know thyself again, O Shulamite, thou fairest among women, adorned with purple and jewels. Wait but a little, and thy feet, after all thy doubts and fears, will also tread the golden streets of the heavenly Jerusalem, in the land of rest, and of an eternal sabbath. O sweet termination of all complaints and sorrows! The Spirit and the Bride say, Come! And let him who heareth say, Come. And the Bridegroom saith, 'I come quickly. Yes, even so come, Lord Jesus!' Amen.

SERMON VI.

SOLOMON'S SONG II. 12.

And the voice of the turtle is heard in our land.

CHRIST, the heavenly Bridegroom, invites his Bride to go forth to the hills, and to the mountains, to rejoice with him in the verdure and bloom of a lovely spring. If is not the spring of nature that she is invited to enjoy. It is the influence of grace, the spring of spiritual life, which the plastic breath of the Holy Ghost, the comforter, has caused to put forth and blossom in the soul of sinners. ' Rise up my love, my fair one, he saith, and come away. For, lo, the winter is past; the rain is over and gone; the flowers appear on the earth; the spring is come; and the voice of the turtle is heard in our land.' Let us dwell for a short time on the last few words of our text,—and,

 I. Take a nearer view of the turtle.
 II. Listen to its voice in the land.

 I.—The Bridegroom speaks of a dove, whose voice is heard in the land on the verdure of spring. We have already seen, that by the dove, in some places of our song, the Shulamite, herself is intended; but that is not the case in the passage before us. Some commentators have supposed that the Lord here describes the dawn of the period of the New Covenant; and the turtle dove they imagine to be the voice of the preacher in the desert, the herald John. But under what similitude could this man, clothed in camel's hair, be less appropriately represented than under that of a dove? We are of opinion, that by the dove the Holy Ghost, the comforter, can alone be understood. As the Son of God condescended to choose the lamb for his symbol, the Spirit, in like manner, selected the dove. To whom does not the wonderful scene at Jordan at once occur? And the Spirit of the Lord belongs essentially to that spring of grace; for it is produced by this bird of heaven. That the spirit in the text is denominated the turtle-dove, is of little importance. The Lord compares the life of grace to the blossoming spring of nature, and to this simile the turtle dove was more appropriate than the domestic pigeon.

In order to discover the full meaning of this significant symbol, it will be necessary to take history as our guide. Three times the sacred volume presents to us this image; and each time the circumstances, the epochs, and the designs are similar. In the first place, Moses informs us, that the Spirit of God moved (literally rendered, brooded) upon the void and formless earth. The Spirit, in as far as it assisted in the formation of the earth, and in preparing it as a theatre of peace and joy, is here likewise compared to a bird (beyond a doubt the dove) with her wings expanded, as if brooding on her eggs. Some hundred years later the dove appears to us again, and it is remarkable, under decidedly similar circumstances and at a similar epocha. Again, her wings are expanded over a waste and void; again she moves over the face of the waters, but they are the thundering waters of the deluge—those devastating floods of wrath, in which, according to the Scriptures, the first world was destroyed. Over the vast watery grave of the former world she flies with the green olive-leaf in her mouth, the lovely harbinger of joy, hastening to convey to Noah the intelligence he so much longed to receive. And what does her appearance with the green leaf in her mouth announce? It announces the termination of the Divine judgment, the coming of a new creation; it proclaims the commencement of a time of grace; of a reign of peace, which, under, a new covenant, rich in promises, shall spring up for sinful man. For the third time the dove is seen on the banks of Jordan, resting on the head of our Savior, when, in the great act of baptism, he solemnly and formally took upon himself our guilt, and silently acknowledged it as his own; and now, tell me, my friends, if this third appearance is not of similar import with the first and second. Once again she moves over the waters, but they are those of John's baptism, in whose waves our Surety had just made, in the name of our souls, the great confession of sin; and in our stead had solemnly declared himself worthy of death, and of the Divine wrath. Once again she appears above a waste and void, above the desolation of humanity, but whose ruin now rests on our substitute. Once again she appears at the commencement of a new creation of that which the Spirit purchased by the blood of the lamb, will produce upon the earth; and again she is the harbinger of peace, joy, and mercy. We hail thy appearance, O sacred dove, upon yonder silent desert, and as a beautiful messenger of peace, over the baptismal waters of Jordan, that proclaim aloud our sinfulness, and our worthiness of condemnation, and death.   We might well have expected the eagle to flit across the heavens, with the cry of Woe! woe! and announcing eternal destruction to the world and its inhabitants; when behold, instead of the eagle, the dove appears above the waste and void—grace! grace! is the burden of her song, and peace and joy her welcome salutation!   We bless and receive her with shouts of joy!   O ye, who mourn and quake, why are ye cast down?   The lion on the top of Sinai, and of Ebal, has ceased to roar; the olive branch becomes green in our banners, and on the horizon of the new covenant days the dove is seen to hover.

Do we ask on what ground the Holy Ghost has chosen the Dove for its symbol?   So many points of resemblance present themselves to our view, that, for the sake of brevity, we must restrict our reflections to those which are most striking and important.   The dove, this tender, faithful bird, has been at all times, and amongst all people, an emblem of constant love; and in this respect, the Comforter may, with great propriety, be compared to it.   How astonishing is the love of the Eternal Father, who tore from his bosom his only Son, the child of his heart, to sacrifice him in the flaming fire of his wrath, and to expose him to the rage of hell, in order to snatch from the abyss of eternal torment a race obnoxious to death, and meriting destruction.   Deep and unfathomable is the love of our Redeemer, who left a throne of majesty, to ascend the accursed tree, there to pour out his precious blood for the

servants of Belial and of sin; to redeem, with this inestimable ransom, us wretches, against our will (for we
desired Him not), from the power of Satan and of hell.
No less great, wonderful, and unsearchable is the love of
the Spirit, who has voluntarily undertaken to destroy
the dragon's brood, to cleanse the dwellings of impurity, and the dens of rapine and of murder; and who, in
the execution of his office, visits scenes of the most disgusting depravity and lewdness. What chambers of
pollution are our hearts! Like the cities of the plains,
how full of corruption and uncleanness; but if the
Spirit once enters these Sodoms and Gomorrahs, he
departs not again till they are thoroughly purified.
How joyfully he causes the light of heaven to shine
into these habitations of darkness, and stores them with
the treasures of truth and wisdom contained in the
Scriptures, and from that fullness which is in Christ
Jesus. How unchanging and untiring is this love:
those who once become its objects can never be sever-
ed from its influence: ' I will send you another Comforter, said the Savior, that he may abide with you for
ever.' But, alas, how often do his people stray from
Him, and lose themselves again in the world; yet he
never forsakes them. How could he? he pursues them
into the vortex of dissipation, and leaves them no peace
in their sins. He chastises, warns, invites them; he
causes lucid intervals to break in upon them in the
midst of their revels: and never ceases to call after
them, Turn ye! turn ye! till they hear his voice, and
return dejected and afflicted to the fold from whence
they had wandered. Let none suppose that he will receive them with the bitterness of reproach, or over-

whelm them with the thunders of his wrath. Quite
the contrary. He seeks, by every means, to wipe away
the tears of his afflicted children, to inspire them with
confidence in the faithfulness of Jehovah; and repeat-
edly says to them, Weep not, there are gifts also, even
for the backsliding—nay, and perhaps bestows upon
them unusual consolations; if therefore the dove be in
truth the significant emblem of faithful love, it is the appropriate symbol of the Comforter. Of all birds, the
dove is the cleanest and most delicate. In filthy places
she will not abide. Thus it is with the Comforter.
Many of you are ready to exclaim, but our hearts—are
they not filthy? Indeed there is no deficiency of impurity there. But, let it be remembered, the dove is not
at rest within them. Is she not incessantly engaged in
detaching and expelling, in sweeping and garnishing?
Her habitation must be cleansed, and she would never
have entered it, but for the certain prospect of eventually rendering it completely pure and free from taint. If
there be a spirit within you that can be at ease in the
midst of impurity, and that can endure iniquity, be assured this spirit is not the dove. Where the dove re-
sides, there is a constant conflict in the soul against the
seed of the serpent—a holy and zealous desire to root up
every thorn, and to consume it with fire. This dove, saith
St. Paul, lusteth against the flesh, and the flesh against
the dove, and there is a constant warfare. Where the
Spirit dwells, the heart becomes the arena of strife; for
this Divine warrior rests not till he has bruised the head
of the last serpent within us, and destroyed the last
cockatrice egg. How sensitive is this heavenly dove!
Of the dove it is said, that the feather of a falcon, or

hawk, is sufficient to make her flutter and tremble. Thus it is with the Spirit in our hearts : if but the slightest impure thought arises within us, he is at once in emotion. Horror seizes him, and he casts the abomination from him with disgust and indignation. Are you sensible of the existence of such an uncompromising enemy to impurity within you?—then rejoice, for the dove is there.

The dove is gentle, and it is in this respect likewise a striking image of the Spirit of grace. In the form of a dove the Spirit descended upon Jesus. It was said of. him, ' He shall not cry, nor lift up, nor cause his voice to be heard in the street. A bruised reed shall he not break, and the smoking flax shall he not quench : he shall bring forth judgment unto truth.' When the village of Samaria had refused to receive the Lord, and the two sons of thunder angrily exclaimed, ' Lord, wilt thou that we command fire to come down from heaven, and consume them, even as Elias did !' Jesus turned and rebuked them, and said, ' Ye know not what manner of spirit ye are of.' The Spirit of Christ is like a gentle dove. It judgeth not, thinketh no evil; when reviled, it revileth not again, and is not so ready to call down fire from heaven. Where it enters, it introduces the dispositions of the dove. How could it be otherwise? It makes us feel that we are miserable sinners, and convinces us that free grace alone can save us. This humbles, silences, and renders us indulgent and mild. Then we willingly cease from censuring others ; we behold not the mote in our brother's eye, on account of the beam in our own eye. It is unhappily true, that the children of God do not unfrequently give way to

anger, jealousy, and a censorious spirit, and all traces
of the dove are obscured. But on such occasions it is
not the dove that stirs within us, but the Leviathan of
the old man, that has again caused his voice to be heard ;
it is not Jacob, but Esau with his rough skin, that is indeed mortally wounded within us, though he has not
yet ceased to breathe. It is the flesh, and not the Spirit. The Spirit is grieved ; it upbraids and chastens us,
and grants us no peace, till we are humbled and repentant. Thus it is evidently a dove—a spirit of peace and
love, mild and gentle.

Already inj the history of the creation, as we have
seen, the Holy Spirit is presented to us under the similitude of a bird—no doubt the dove. The Spirit of God,
it is said, brooded upon the face of the waters, as a bird
broods with extended wings upon its eggs. This figu-
rátive expression indicates that the Spirit also took part
in the creation ; that it formed the waste and void, and
gave shape and beauty to the earth. And spiritually,
the Spirit is incessantly executing the same work in the
human mind. While the heart is still as chaos, a world
ruined by Satan, waste and void, and shrouded in the
darkness and blindness of unbelief, the Spirit, impelled
by love, descends and overshadows it, as it overshadowed the Virgin. Now the command goes forth, ' Let
there be light !' and there is light. We look down into
the dark abyss of our desolate condition, and shudder
with horror. The light is separated from the darkness.
We perceive what we should be and what we are not.
We learn to jndge spiritually, and to discern good and
evil according to the rule of God's law. And God
calls the light day, and the darkness night. Thus be-

fore we are aware, the light of a new life has sprung up within us, which scatters and expels the darkness of the old ; and the evening and the morning are the first day. Under the wings of the plastic breath of the Comforter, this spiritual creation advances steadily towards perfection. The desolate soil thirsteth for grace, and is refreshed with the verdure of a new creation. The sacred flowers of faith and love spring up. A new world is called into existence. The morning stars extol the power of grace, and the inward spiritual man, renewed in the image of Christ, walks with delight in the blissful paradise of communion with his God. ' The Spirit moved on the face of the waters.' Thus it is still in the spiritual world. Many waters rise upon the believing soul ; but the Spirit breaks through them all, maintains the ascendency, and sustains the life it has imparted. The sensuality of our sinful nature may be accounted as one of these waters. How frequently do its waves swell tumultuously ; but the Spirit still moves above them. It resembles oil, which always floats upon the surface of water. Our sins of weakness may likewise be accounted a water. When we fall, the oil sinks ; yet it is but for a moment. Behold the tears of Mary Magdalen, and of Peter after his fall ! The oil rises to the surface ; the Spirit again moves upon the face of the waters ! The afflictions which befall us may likewise be numbered amongst the waters which rise upon the soul. When they break in upon us, we are alarmed ; we tremble and are dismayed. A raging flood overwhelms the soul, and the spirit is in the deep. But it is soon otherwise. Reflection comes, we bend the knee, and sigh, Lord help !' We throw ourselves

upon the tender mercy of the Eternal Father ; hope revives, and we ask our soul, ' Why art thou cast down ?'
We believe, submit, and are again comforted. The
waters are forced back, the Spirit soars above them.
Worldly thoughts, and the cares of time, may also be
accounted waters. How frequently do they overwhelm
the soul like a mighty torrent, and keep it groveling in
this lower sphere. But the dove soon ascends out of
these tempestuous billows ; and with a tranquil mind,
with an unconstrained and elevated spirit, we are enabled to rejoice in the midst of the tumult. Thus the
dove is never prevented from moving on the face of the
waters, and in every conflict is the last on the field.

When, however, the Scriptures speak of the Holy
Spirit as a dove, the allusion is especially to the dove
of Noah, that wished-for messenger bearing the symbol
of peace and of joy ; and it is his office of Comforter, of
which we are more particularly reminded by this delightful figure, than of any other of his works and
offices. When the Savior testifies of the Spirit, ' He
shall take of mine, and shew it unto you,' does he not
designate him as the dove which shall bear the olive
branch to the ark of the New Testament Church. The
Spirit is the appropriator, the sealer of that which the
Son has wrought out for us. What was outwardly prepared, he applies inwardly ; with the fruit of the cross
he nourishes the heart ; he causes the living waters of
the fountain opened to spring up within us, and be con-
veys the blood of the lamb, as a blood-sprinkling, into
the innermost soul. Oh what a delightful, welcome
vision, is this heavenly dove, when it appears unexpectedly with expanded wings above the swelling billows

of spiritual sorrow and conscious guilt, hastening with messages of mercy towards the trembling and afflicted soul. How blissful the calm after such a conflict, when the Spirit testifies with ours, that we are the children of God; and the pledge of our eternal redemption is more precious to us than crowns and sceptres. Now we sit under his shadow with great delight, and his fruit is sweet to our taste. Now all the promises of Scripture are ours. The Bible appears to us a richly laden tree, extending its branches towards us. On us the dying eye of Jesus rests, when from the cross he casts a last trembling look upon the earth; on us he thinks, when he exclaims, 'I lay down my life for my sheep;' and to us his blood-stained arms appear extended, while stretched upon the tree. The consolation of reconciliation distils like honey, and diffuses itself through our inmost being; the peace of God encompasses us; the overcharged heart expands like the ocean; the blessed dove has deposited the olive branch in the ark.

If we now reflect that the olive branch, whilst it is a symbol of victory and of triumph, is likewise a decoration of honor; and that Noah, to whom the dove brought the olive branch, was · a type of Christ; we shall again perceive in this figure a trait of the Holy Spirit, by which its existence in the converted soul is verified. This heavenly dove also knows a worthy head for every crown and garland; and the ultimate design of all its operations is to glorify the Lord Jesus. It deprives the creature of all honor, to confer it on the Lord, and on him exclusively; it indelibly impresses this sentiment on the believing heart: 'Not unto us, O Lord, not unto us, but unto thy name give glory, for

thy mercy, and for thy truth's sake;' and it imparts to
the mind, that holy frame, which makes it recoil from
the slightest wish to magnify itself, as from an infernal
spirit of rebellion.   The Savior himself says the same
of the Comforter : ' He shall testify of me.'

If then a spirit stir within you, whatever disguise it
may assume, which tempts you to magnify yourselves,
know that this spirit is not the dove.   The dove will
exalt the Savior only.

II.—Having thus glanced at the heavenly dove herself; let us now also listen to her voice: for her notes
are wonderful and enchanting.   ' The voice of the turtle,' says the Bridegroom to his Shulamite, ' is heard in
our land;' and we say, God be praised.   What discord-
ant notes would have resounded through the world, if
no spirit but that of man had ever prevailed in it. There
has never been a time, in which this heavenly dove has
been perfectly silent upon earth.   Here or there, in
gentle strains at least, she has ever caused her voice to
be heard.   That which at the time of the flood, spake
by the mouth of Noah so warningly and so cheeringly
to the hearts of sinners; that which, in the patriarchal
world, proclaimed such glad tidings, and announced a
day at which Abraham rejoiced; and that which spake
by Moses of a prophet, whom the Lord would raise up,
like unto him; that which on the hill of Bethlehem inspired the sweet strains of the royal bard; that which,
by the voice of the prophets, pronounced such wonderful sayings, and revealed such sacred mysteries; tell
me what was it ?   What else, my brethren, but the
dove; what else but the dove of that Spirit which

searches even the deep things of God, and which re-sounds through all the promises. In the Bible, that tree of life, she sits upon every branch, and her voice may be heard in an endless variety of tone and modula-tion; and those who have an ear for its melodies, know how affectingly and thrillingly she sometimes sings, how consoling and quickening her strains; so that the heart is penetrated, and almost dissolves in blissful emotion.

The turtle dove is heard in our land; not in the Scriptures only, but also in the land of our hearts: and here likewise her strains are harmonious, though varied. True it is, that other birds also coo therein, but the notes of the dove are easily distinguished. Dost thou hear, for instance, a spirit commend to thee any thing but Christ and his blood as the rock of thy salvation and the ground of thy hope; does it speak to thee of thy good qualities, of the powers that slumber within thee; close thy door against it. It is not the dove, but the raven. Does it cry, 'Peace, peace! there is no dan-ger!' close thine ear; there is an infernal spirit near thee. Does it say, ' Hasten from Sodom, and save thy soul!' give ear to it, it is the dove. Does it tell thee, ' Thy sins are too great for thee, there is no mercy !' then arm thyself; it is the lion's roar. Does it cry, ' And if they be red like crimson, the blood of the Lamb will make them white as wool!' it is the dove. Does it say, ' First become worthy, reform thyself, then come to Jesus !' give it to the winds; it is an erring spirit. Does it say, ' Come as thou art, come boldly, for the Savior receives sinners,' listen to its voice; let it not be said to thee twice; for the turtle dove is heard in the land.

The voice of the sacred dove speaks to our hearts,
and reverberates from thence in confessions, in exhortations, in prayer and praise; and thus again its voice is
heard in the land.   But is it always the voice of the
dove that is thus heard?   It is true, the raven voice of
the old man sometimes imitates so successfully the voice
of the dove, that it requires a fine and practised ear, to
detect the raven's voice in such melodious sounds.
Even mental conflicts and states of feeling occur, in
which the Holy Spirit has not the slightsst share, and
which must be entirely ascribed to nature, and not to
grace; and yet they so strongly resemble the operations
of the Spirit, that the clearest sight is often deceived,
and the nicest discernment frequently baffled.   Here
the well-known event in the history of Jephtha, the hero
of Gilead, occurs to me, who, after he had defeated and
scattered the Ephraimites, took possession of the passages of Jordan, resolved that none of the fugitives
should return alive to their native land.   Aware, perhaps, of their conqueror's intention, but obliged to
cross the river, or perish in the desert, they approach
the ford, and deny that they are Ephraimites.   They
are put to the test, all of them are required to pronounce the word Shiboleth! but they said Siboleth:
' for they could not frame to pronounce it right;' and
all were put to the sword.   What a serious and important truth does this scene present to us.   Before him
who holds the ford, beyond which lies the Canaan of
God, all depends upon an apparent trifle.   On the existence or non-existence of a something within us, irrespective of all other considerations, will it depend,
whether we shall be permitted to pass over, or whether

the sword of his indignation shall descend upon us. The spiritual resemblance between the man who is rejected, and the one who is accepted, may be as great as that between Shiboleth and Siboleth. Who can detect any material difference? But God is a keen discerner. To him the difference in the characters of the two men may be as decisive, as was to Jephtha that between Shiboleth and Siboleth, which marked the friendly Gileadite from the rebellious Ephraimite: Behold here two men. Both smite upon their breast, both weep, both call themselves the chief of sinners, and both are sinners. We see their tears, we hear their confessions. Both are afflicted, both complain. To us no difference is visible; we deem them both repentant sinners; and had we the crown of righteousness to bestow, we should invest them with the same decorations. Both appear at the passage of Jordan, both stand before the Judge: and behold! one only is crowned, and the other is lost. Gracious God! Why should this be? The one said Shiboleth, the other Siboleth. We observed it not; but the Lord is a nice discerner. Only *Si* instead of *Shi*, but the difference is sufficient to cause an eternal separation. The one smote upon his breast from fear, the other from love. Hell made the one to weep, the cross the other.. The complaint of the one was : Oh that I should have incurred such guilt! the complaint of the other was : Ah, that I should have caused thee, Lord Jesus, so much suffering! The one lamented the consequences of sin; the other, the transgressions themselves. Sin had not extorted a tear from the one, had it not rendered him miserable, for he thought but of his comfort; the other

would have abhorred sin, though it had exercised no
influence over his peace; for he sought the honor of
his God.   In short, when the characters of the two
were-developed, it was apparent that selfishness produced repentance in the one, and that the tears of the
other were those of love.   In the one was concealed a
repentant Cain; in the other, a weeping Magdalene.
In the one nature predominated; in the other, grace.
A difference less perceptible than that in Shiboleth
and Siboleth, yet immeasurably great, and lasting as
eternity!   Two men sit by the way side.   Both cry,
' Jesus, thou Son of David, have mercy on me!'   Neither of them are hypocrites, but both mean what they
say.   We pronounce both blessed; but will the Judge
confirm our sentence?   At the passage of Jordan it
will be decided.   Though their acts have been the
same, a mighty wind may there separate them for
ever; raising the one on high, while it precipitates the
other into the abyss.   And why should it be so?   To
us it seemed, that both had said Shiboleth.   Alas! the
one had only said Si; we did not observe it.   That was
his ruin.   The one cried to the Savior like Bartimeus,
and the thief on the cross; the other, like the devils;
' Lord do not command us to go down into the deep.'
The one thought within himself: ' Ah, if I had but
Jesus, what need I care for heaven!'   The other, ' Ah,
if I had but heaven, what need I care for Jesus!'*   The
one sighed for the love of Christ: the other for his
saving hand.   The cry of the one marked the fervor o
the lover; that of the other, the despair of the helpless

* This is according to Luther's translation of Ps. lxxiii. 25.—ED.

anxious for salvation, but indifferent by whom it is effected : the devil would be as welcome as Jesus, provided he could as effectually save from perdition.. To our dull senses this was not perceptible. But he who sits upon the throne heard at once that it was not the Shiboleth of the Gileadite. His ear listens for the voice of the dove. Nothing but Spirit and truth can stand before him.

We cannot say, therefore, that true heartfelt Christianity consists in tears, in penitence, or in an earnest longing after the bliss of heaven. We cannot say it consists in prayers, in Christian deportment, or in evangelical knowledge. Neither does it consist in love for the Gospel, in the emotions it awakens within us, or in zeal for the spread of Divine truth. Nor in an open confession of Christ, and the ability to testify and speak of him with eloquence, edification, and instruction. Brethren all this may only constitute a Siboleth ; and woe be to us, if at the passage of Jordan it should so appear. It may all proceed from the natural man, and be the mere workings of a selfish nature. But nothing will stand the Divine scrutiny, that is not the work and produce of the Spirit, and the essence of which is not the love of Christ.

That it is sometimes impossible for the nicest discernment to distinguish between seemingly devout sentiments, whether they are the effusions of the Spirit, or the mere promptings of the natural man, we have already seen. But there are cases, in which a difference may be perceived, like that between Shiboleth and Siboleth, by which we recognize at once a Gileadite or an Ephraimite. In sermons, hymns, books, and prayers,

though equally correct and true, devout and evangelical, there is a certain something which we feel but cannot describe, by which we are enabled to say, " Here is
the dove, and here some other bird; this is the spirit,
and this nature; this is genuine, and this spurious; this
is life, but this a portrait."

The dove speaks through the children of God; but
not always in the same accents.   Sometimes its strains
are sorrowful, interrupted by sighs and tears: ' Lord
Jesus, have mercy on me!'   At others languishing, and
expressive of the most ardent longings: ' Ah, when
shall I depart hence, that I may behold thy glory?'
Now they are those of dejection and complaint: ' O
wretched man that I am! who shall deliver me from
the body of this death?'   Then they breathe the raptures of nuptial joy: ' My beloved is mine, and I am
his; he feedeth among the lilies!'   They are sometimes eloquent and persuasive: ' Come and hear, all ye
that fear God, and I will declare what he hath done for
my soul!'   Then again they are short and ejaculatory;
a single ' Ah!' or Oh!' is all that we can hear—but
they are tones that reverberate through the choirs of
heaven.   Sometimes it ascends in sighs and groans:
' Put not thy servant away in anger : thou hast been my
help.'   Again its voice is heard through deep conflict
and distress ; in gentle accents it is true, but distinct
and full of consolation.   The powers of darkness may
sometimes succeed in bewildering a redeemed soul, by
confounding all its evidences ; by subverting its faith in
the Rock of its hope, and in the sacred volume; till, in
its perplexity, it is tempted to renounce all belief in a
God or Savior, in a heaven or hell.   What can here be

perceived of the note of the dove? Nothing, we are ready to reply. Here the raven's croak is heard. But let us listen attentively. It is true that in doubters, as such, the voice of the dove is not heard. But it may be recognized in the accents of complaint in which the tempted and benighted soul gives utterance to its doubts; in the sighs and groans with which it laments its unbelief; in the longing, wrestling supplications which the heart pours forth to the Lord, that He would again cause his light to shine. Thus, amongst the saints of God, it causes its voice to be heard in an endless variety of ways, and diversity of modulation: but it is every where the same dove.

The turtle dove is heard in the land! God be praised, a period has already dawned, in which these words have a delightful application to the land in which we dwell. The drooping and expiring church of Christ begins to revive, and put forth blossoms; the frosty night of winter has begun to yield to the genial breath of spring, promising a more glorious future; and the turtle, so long banished and forgotten, has re-appeared in the land. How many congregations, that once heard nothing but the raven-like croakings of the most comfortless unbelief, are now refreshed by the voice of the dove. What testimonies to the truth, what prayers and praises, have of late again been heard in the church; and the presence of the dove has been most manifest and refreshing. But the brightness that shines in our day, is but the opening splendor of an incomparably more glorious period that is rapidly approaching. Magnificent promises hang suspended over the church, like clouds pregnant with blessings. Blessed assurances,

like sweet messengers of joy, stand at her portals.   O
Shulamite, wait and be comforted!   Let not the tem-
pests and horrors which here and there may rage, excite thy fears.   It is but the struggle between spring and
winter, between life and death.   Death will be vanquished; and when thou least expectest, it will again be said
to thee, but in a fuller and more exalted sense, 'Rise
up, my love, my fair one, and come away: for, lo, the
winter is past, the rain is over and gone.   The flowers
appear on the earth; the time of the singing of birds is
come ; and the voice of the turtle is heard in our land !'
O blessed period! may the Lord hasten it.   Amen.

Lightning Source UK Ltd.
Milton Keynes UK
UKHW01f1259200718
326032UK00011B/469/P